What If I Married the Wrong Person?

What If I Married the Wrong Person?

DR. RICHARD MATTESON
JANIS LONG HARRIS

BETHANY HOUSE PUBLISHERS
MINNEAPOLIS, MINNESOTA 55438

Published by Bethany House Publishers
A Ministry of Bethany Fellowship, Inc.
11300 Hampshire Avenue South
Minneapolis, Minnesota 55438

Printed in the United States of America.

Library of Congress Cataloging-in-Publication Data

Matteson, Richard.
    What if I married the wrong person? / Richard Matteson and Janis Long Harris.
    p. cm.
    Includes bibliographical references.
    ISBN 1–55661–664–3
    1. Marriage—Religious aspects—Christianity. 2. Divorce—Religious aspects—
Christianity. I. Harris, Janis Long, 1951–   . II. Title.
BT706.M37   1996
248.8'44—dc20   96–45772
                                                  CIP

Acknowledgments:
Dr. Richard Matteson

This book is the brainchild of Janis Long Harris. When Janis first approached me with her idea and asked me to write along with her, I admit I didn't appreciate the significance of the title. *What If I Married the Wrong Person?* sounded like a title that could only herald a how-to book on getting a divorce.

But as I thought about it, I realized that behind the question is the issue unsettling most people in troubled marriages—or in even mildly uncomfortable ones. In fact, "Did I marry the wrong person?" is a question that almost every married person asks at one time or another. For that matter, it is a question most people ask before they wed. No one wants to marry the wrong person. Once married, as painful doubts begin to emerge, many people just don't know how to respond. With the dawning of this realization, I knew Janis was presenting me with a very important challenge. I have appreciated the opportunity to work with her. Her skills as a writer have been indispensable to this project. Though for ease of reading, the book is written in my voice, her insights as an active Christian layperson have been important as well.

In working with couples who are struggling to enrich, renew, or salvage their marriage, I have often been able to team up with their pastor. There have been times when the involvement of a pastor has been what made my efforts successful. Pastors who are faithful in their calling to preach the Gospel and to develop a vibrant and loving congregational life are the best colleagues a psychotherapist can have. In the long run their contribution to the lives of couples is far more important than mine. I hope that the approach I take in these pages indicates my sensitivity to the issues of spiritual significance that pastors work so hard to address. In many ways they are the unsung heroes in our culture. Therapists receive more than ample attention and accolades from government, media, and the public. Pastors are rarely noticed and receive far too little recognition and appreciation for what they do for people.

Among these pastors is Dr. F. Dean Lueking, pastor of Grace Lutheran Church of River Forest, Illinois. Our monthly lunches for the past fifteen years have helped me to think through the points of intersection between psychology and theology, between psychotherapy and pastoral care. Our friendship and colleagueship have proven to me that psychotheraphy is a team effort and that the best member of my team is a good pastor.

I hope that this book reveals to marital therapists that I am very much indebted to many people who are doing serious research in psychology and its application to marriage and family problems. Those who have influenced me most are Aaron Beck, M.D., and Neil Jacobson, Phd. Beck has been a pioneer in the development of cognitive therapy and has applied it creatively to marital therapy. Jacobson has successfully applied social learning theory in the treatment of troubled couples. No clinician today should presume to work with couples without a thorough knowledge of the work of these men.

I feel deeply indebted to my patients of the past twenty-five years. I know it has become a cliche to say it, but I am sincere in stating that I have learned more from them than they have from me. I am very honored that they have entrusted themselves to my guidance when they have been in the depths of despair. Our sessions are always sacred times for me. I pray that when we are in those sessions we are embraced by God in a special way—that we are never alone in our search for healing.

Needless to say, all the stories included in these pages are their stories; that is, each story is a composite of many. This, of course, is because I have pledged to them my confidentiality.

In the finaly analysis, this book would not have been possible were it not from my wife, Janet. She is my "right person." She has taught me all I know about the meaning of love between a man and a woman. And, in her genius for family building, she has surrounded me with loving children and an enlivening homelife. What more could a man want?

Acknowledgments:
Janis Long Harris

A few years ago, the editors at *Marriage Partnership* asked me to write an article addressing what they believed was a very common question: "What if I married the wrong person?" My first reaction was that it was a dubious assignment. What possible good could come from raising that issue? What if readers asked themselves the question and decided the answer was "yes"? Surely *Marriage Partnership*, a magazine wholeheartedly dedicated to strengthening and preserving marriages, didn't want to reinforce any underlying sense of doubt a reader might have about his or her marriage.

But as I began interviewing men and women in both strong and difficult marriages, I became convinced the editors were on to something. The more people I talked with, the more clear it was that many, perhaps most, married people doubt their choice of a mate somewhere along the line. That reality raised questions in *my* mind: Why do so many people wonder if they married the wrong person? Is there only one Right Person for any of us to marry? Does God expect two "wrong people" to stay together in a miserable relationship? Is it possible for two "wrong people" to become right for each other?

Questions like these are too big for a single magazine article, so I wrote two! After the *Marriage Partnership* article was published, *Today's Christian Woman* magazine asked me to write a piece on the same subject, but with more personal reflections on my own marriage. In the process of completing that second article, I began to suspect the questions I was raising really warranted an entire book. I had become convinced that most people marry someone who is "wrong" for them to some degree and that the key to a strong marriage isn't so much whom you marry—although that's obviously very important—but what kind of relationship you create. I became fascinated with couples I knew who had come to the brink of divorce, each spouse certain that the other had serious, unchangeable character flaws, but who had been able to repair their broken relationship after learning to view each other in a new light.

The kind of mental transformations I observed in these couples reminded me of similar transformations in a very different setting. Several years ago, I met a young Englishman who told me about his work with inmates incarcerated in British prisons. By teaching them the discipline of contemplative prayer, this young man helped hardened criminals overcome their tendencies to violent behavior. As I listened to my acquaintance talk about his work, it occurred to me that what he had done was teach these men—who had learned very early in life to respond to any perceived slight or insult with a punch or shove or torrent of abusive words—how to establish new habits of the mind.

Convinced that establishing new habits of the mind was also a key to transforming marriages, I asked Dr. Richard Matteson to work with me on this book. I sought out Dick because he is a psychologist who uses the principles of cognitive therapy in his marriage counseling, as well as being an ordained minister who believes in the power of the classic spiritual disciplines. Working with Dick over a period of many months, I was delighted to find that his strong philosophical commitment to marriage had borne fruit in a wealth of practical strategies for revolutionizing relationships.

In addition to Dick's experience and wisdom, this book benefited greatly from the comments and suggestions of several people, in particular Kathy Stockman and Debbie Birkey. I am very grateful for the patience and insight of our editor, Kevin Johnson. And I am indebted to my husband, Paul Harris, who was a tremendous support throughout the process of writing the book—and who claims never to have asked the question posed by the title!

How to use *What If I Married the Wrong Person?*

What If I Married the Wrong Person? is not just a book. It's an entire program for creating hope and renewal in your marriage. The assignments at the end of each chapter are designed to help you apply the book's concepts to your own life. Each piece of the materials is intended to heighten your awareness of the facts, feelings, thoughts, and actions that have given shape to your marriage. Making good use of these resources can help you gain a clearer picture of why you may be asking, "Did I marry the wrong person?"

We feel it is best to read the entire book to get an overview of its concepts and strategies. Then return to chapter 1. Work through each exercise, journaling assignment, and spiritual discipline. Do the same with each chapter. If you find that only certain assignments are relevant to you, concentrate on those. But if at all possible, do all the journaling assignments and spiritual disciplines.

Who should use this book?

Although the book was written primarily for people who are seriously wondering whether they may have married the wrong person, it will also help those who are simply experiencing a few wrinkles in their marriage, or the happily married who would like to enrich their relationship. Single adults may find the book helpful in raising issues they might face in a marriage. Singles can work through the program with a present or former relationship in mind.

How long should it take to complete the assignments?

You will probably complete most of the exercises in about ten minutes. The journaling assignments should take no more than ten more minutes, while the spiritual disciplines will likely take five minutes or less. Think in terms of a thirteen-week program, devoting one week to each chapter's assignments. Try to complete each chapter's exercises on one day early in the week. Journaling should be done daily, as should the spiritual disciplines. If you are highly motivated, you could probably complete the entire program in thirteen days, but doing so wouldn't give you enough time to really think through the issues and apply all the concepts to your life.

Is there any reason why a therapist might want to use this program?

Definitely. Marital therapy today is much more structured than in the past. A therapist might choose to have a couple work on the exercises during a therapy session, assign a journaling activity for the week and then close the session with a spiritual discipline (perhaps assigning it for use during the week as well). The following session would then begin with a review of the journal work, continuing the exercises and processing of both. The therapist can use the program to help identify important areas of conflict, sticking points, and opportunities for growth. Of course, it would be helpful as well if both partners read the book.

Can groups use this program? If so, why and how?

Yes, definitely. Some of the different kinds of groups that might want to use it include:

Single adult groups. Singles can gain insights that may prevent marital mistakes by coming together to discuss the concepts and issues presented in *What If I Married the Wrong Person?* Each meeting should be devoted to one chapter. Before the meeting, each participant should read the relevant chapter and work through the appropriate journaling assignments and spiritual disciplines. At the meeting itself, a facilitator should provide a chapter summary and then invite each participant to do the exercises. After the exercises, participants can break up into smaller groups for in-depth discussion of insights they have gained from the exercises and from the previous week's journaling assignment. Groups of six or more should break into threes, since people seem to feel safer to share more openly in this configuration. Following the small group discussion time, a representative from each group is asked to summarize that group's insights for the larger group.

Individuals in troubled marriages. Concepts from the book and exercises can equip people in even very difficult relationships to turn their marriages around. The same meeting pattern as above can be used in this setting, but with strict confidentiality guidelines added to prevent misuse of negative information.

Couples in basically good marriages. Even good marriages have wrinkles to be ironed out. This program can be a challenge to new growth. A group like this should be led by a competent therapist or other professional with established credentials for working with couples. It takes an experienced therapist to recognize when a couple needs follow-up and provide it on the spot. This kind of group can be structured according to the previous pattern, but instead of breaking into threes for discussion, married couples should discuss results from the exercises and journaling assignments between husband and wife. While they are together, they may want to share the spiritual disciplines. At the end of the meeting, an opportunity can be provided for couples to volunteer to share any insights. It should be made clear that such sharing is not required, however.

Troubled couples. Groups of couples in troubled marriages should only be led by competent therapists. Otherwise, the risk is too great that the participants will delve into issues they can't handle when they leave the meeting for home. That risk aside, a group like this offers couples in difficult marriages a valuable opportunity to learn from each other. The meeting format should be the same as with couples in basically strong marriages. It's especially important for this group to set guidelines for confidentiality.

Divorced persons. Groups for divorced individuals should follow the same basic patterns as those for other singles. The specific purpose of this type of group is to help participants understand what went wrong in their marriages so they can avoid similar problems in a future relationship. Confidentiality guidelines apply here, too.

Pastors and other nonprofessional therapists. By working with this program in groups, with or without their spouses, pastors can better understand the issues facing parishioners who seek help for troubled marriages. They can also use the exercises in the book as assignments for couples with whom they are working, or use the book as a basic curriculum, enhanced with their own wisdom and experience in counseling groups.

Men's or women's groups. The format for single-gender groups is the same as for singles groups. Again, stress confidentiality.

Contents

One

Confronting Your Disappointment

It's a cold feeling in the pit of your stomach. One day, perhaps after a fight or after one more disappointment, you look at your spouse and think, *I've made a terrible, terrible mistake. I married the wrong person.*

For anyone who places a high value on the vows of marriage, or who has children who would be deeply hurt by a divorce, that's a terrifying conclusion.

Still, it's a feeling that most people—even people with deep convictions about the sanctity of marriage—have had at one time or another. For some, it's a fleeting sensation brought on by passing fantasies of what it would have been like if they had married that high school sweetheart. But for others, the doubts are serious. Scary. Persistent.

When these doubts come, and don't go away, it's usually because the feelings you once had have diminished—or died altogether. Feelings of closeness, tenderness, and sexual attraction are a distant memory, replaced by feelings of resentment, alienation, anger, perhaps even disgust.

For most people, the doubts begin with tiny hints, fleeting thoughts. *I wonder what my life would have been like if I had married my old boyfriend? I bet he wouldn't take me for granted like my husband does!* Sometimes the good feelings are simply neutralized, replaced only by numbness. Sometimes they are malignantly transformed, like healthy cells transmogrified into cancer cells, from feelings of love into feelings of contempt, distrust, and despair.

As doubt grows, so does the evidence that you made the wrong choice of a mate: Your spouse has unchangeable character flaws. Someone else makes you feel better than he/she does. You can't stop fighting. Your values are incompatible. You have different views about child-rearing. You're ill-suited sexually. There's no more passion. Your family backgrounds are too disparate. You're at different places spiritually. Your careers are pulling you apart. There's no more respect or trust between you. You can't communicate. You're always angry. You're bored. You're numb. You're constantly on the defensive.

Doubt can quickly turn into panic. *Time is passing—will my entire life be wasted because I made the wrong choice?* Panic is often accompanied by depression. The future looks hopeless. Nothing fits. Nothing makes sense. Nothing can be counted on anymore.

If you're reading this book, there's a good chance that this scenario sounds familiar. You may be at a place in your life where you've concluded that despite your good intentions, despite all of your hopes and dreams, despite what seemed like the right choice at the time, you married the wrong person.

THREE CHOICES

If this is your situation, you have three choices of how to proceed: You can get divorced. You can force yourself to stay in the marriage despite the pain. Or you can consider the possibility that, instead of marrying the wrong person, you *created* the wrong marriage, and you can take steps to forge a new marriage to the same person.

For some people, divorce is the obvious solution. *If I married the wrong person,* they reason, *it only makes sense to get out of the marriage and try to find the right person.* Others, especially people of deep faith, may be extremely reluctant to get a divorce. Those who were raised to believe that divorce is wrong may have a lot of guilt feelings, but having come to a point where marriage feels unbearable, they opt to relieve the pain. Whatever a person's background, the reasoning often runs along these lines: *Surely God wouldn't be so unfair as to hold me to a wrong choice for the rest of my life. Surely divorce, tragic as it is, must be the lesser of two evils. Surely my spouse and I will both be better off if we're free to find more compatible partners. Surely our children will be better off if they don't have to live with battling parents.*

This logic has resulted in several decades' worth of staggeringly high divorce statistics. Yet it is contradicted by what is increasingly being recognized as the result of many, if not most, divorces: mental, emotional, and financial devastation for the former partners, and especially for their children.

People who leave a marriage in hopes of finding greater happiness in another relationship are fighting the odds: The failure rate of second marriages is even higher than that of first marriages. On the surface, this doesn't make much sense. After all, doesn't practice make perfect? If you made mistakes in your first marriage, can't you learn from them, grow and do better the next time?

It's possible—but less likely than you might think. The scars accumulated in a failed marriage are so deep and painful that they often make subsequent relationships extremely difficult. They erode trust. They heighten sensitivity to what might otherwise be minor issues. And the fact is, there are more issues in second marriages, not less.

Take the challenge of blended families, for example. What a seemingly benign, almost inviting, expression the term "blended families" is. What a wonderful thing to bring together two families to provide a much richer experience for everyone involved. What fun to have kids from two sets of parents live together as siblings. How interesting. How enriching. Think of the potential for sharing the strengths of unique personalities and differing household patterns! But almost anyone who's taken on the challenge of blending families knows the reality: It's easier to love your own children than someone else's. It's easier to put up with the frustrations of parenting when you're dealing with your own kids. It's hard to face the rejection of a child who resists your authority, your love, your very existence in his real parent's life. It hurts to try to love a child who has never given up hope that her real parents will get back together.

Then again, you might never have to face the challenges of blending families because there might not be a "next time." People who divorce in the hope of finding the elusive Right One are often shocked at how much harder it is to meet potential dating candidates, much less marriage candidates, the second time around.

Think about it. When you were dating the first time, you probably had a lot of single friends and spent time in places where there were a lot of single people—school, church, singles groups. But now, it's likely that most of your friends are married. Singles groups tend to be made up of younger people, or people who are bitter and scarred from their own failed relationships. There are dating services, health clubs, and matchmaking friends, but, statistically, the odds do not favor meeting that perfect person with whom you can achieve a successful remarriage.

For these and a host of other reasons, many people take *the second route:* They choose to grit their teeth and gut out an unhappy marriage.

Despite the fact that it has become very common, divorce still carries a heavy stigma, especially in conservative religious circles. Many evangelical Christians find that they are disqualified from church leadership after divorce. Many divorced Catholics who remarry are also relegated to lesser spiritual status, having been cut off from communion. These are daunting consequences for someone whose main sustenance in the midst of personal despair has been his or her participation in a community of faith. Some people would rather experience the loneliness of an empty marriage than the loneliness of being cast into a spiritual leper colony.

Similarly, some parents, when faced with an apparent choice between personal happiness (or relief from unhappiness) and happiness for their kids, will choose the latter without hesitation.

The problem with these seemingly idealistic choices is that they rarely achieve their intended results. It's difficult to experience the benefits of a rich spiritual life when you feel you're living a lie. It's nearly impossible to take comfort in marital martyrdom—staying unhappily married for the sake of the kids—when you see them suffering the devastating effects of continuing family tensions. Divorce is awful for children, but living with miserable parents is almost as bad.

The third choice, forging a new marriage to the same partner, is a difficult one because it requires an element of hope. If you've come to the conclusion that you married the wrong person, hope is precisely what you don't have.

Which brings us to the purpose of this book: to generate hope where none exists right now. Impossible as it may seem, there's a high probability that your marriage, no matter how disappointing, can be transformed into a strong and joyful union.

Sadly, some marriages *have* to end because of continuing abuse, infidelity, or the kind of deeply ingrained dysfunction that used to be called sin. But my years of clinical practice and a growing body of research have convinced me that most marriages, even marriages that shouldn't have happened in the first place, can and should be saved. Not just preserved, in all their disappointment and misery, but revolutionized. Partners who appear to be completely ill-suited, totally wrong for each other, can learn how to live together as lovers.

I have always believed that my role as a marital counselor is to keep marriages together. But twenty years ago I was far more easily persuaded than I am now that a given marriage was too far gone to be saved. Over the years, I've become a fierce advocate of preserving marriages, for two basic reasons.

First, I now have a much better understanding of why Jesus took such a hard line on divorce. That's because I now have a more realistic picture of its devastating effects. A high percentage of the people I see in my counseling practice have come to me for help in coping with problems—depression, anxiety, feelings of inadequacy, stress—that are direct results of divorce, either their own or their parents'. And a number of major research studies in recent years have revealed just how truly damaging divorce is, especially to children. The damage to children is so great that I've come to view divorce as a form of child abuse.

Second, while I've become much more pessimistic about the outcome of divorce, I've become much more optimistic about the long-term prospects for even very troubled marriages. I've seen couples step back from the brink of what seemed to be the certain breakup of their marriages—and forge remarkably strong and loving relationships. I've seen similar transformations in couples who had rejected the divorce option but who had lived together for years in a hostile, contemptuous hell on earth.

What each husband and wife did was abandon the old marriage and create a new one, to each other. You can do the same. It takes work—and knowledge of some basic principles—but it can be done.

If you find yourself wondering whether you married the wrong person, you owe it to yourself to take those doubts seriously, to examine the basis for those feelings, and to take some kind of action. This book is designed to help you through the process of putting your doubts into perspective, achieving an understanding of how you got to the point of questioning your choice of a mate, and deciding what to do next. I don't pretend to be unbiased in my opinions and advice: I am unabashedly advocating that you do everything in your power to save your marriage. And I hope to convince you that it *is* in your power to do so.

It's possible that you're among the few people for whom divorce or separation is the only answer. It may be that your relationship with your spouse will always be, to some degree, disappointing. But no matter how impossible your situation seems, I hope that, at least for the duration of this book, you'll temporarily suspend your sense of hopelessness and open yourself to viewing your spouse, yourself, and your marriage in a new light. I ask that you commit yourself to devoting the next few weeks of your life to creating a new marriage to your current partner—by becoming a new person in your relationship.

My commitment in return is to offer you some new ways of thinking about and living in your marriage, drawing on an approach I use in my private practice and in workshops. While no book or counselor can ever offer a guarantee, my experience gives me good reason to hope that you will be able to use the tools offered in these pages to accomplish what you haven't been able to do in the past: build a relationship that satisfies many of your deepest needs and longings.

The help offered here is based on our belief that life is a spiritual journey—and marriage is part of that journey. To make progress in your marriage, you'll need to make progress in your spiritual pilgrimage. So, along with some practical exercises aimed at healing and renewing your relationship with your spouse, I'll be suggesting some simple spiritual disciplines as a way of drawing closer to God. Working on a painful marriage can be difficult and exhausting, so you will need the strength and comfort that only God can offer.

One of the activities I will be suggesting is journaling. Journaling allows you to put your life on a piece of paper so you can look at it dispassionately. If you are feeling trapped and overwhelmed by the events that surround you and the relationships that absorb you, journaling can help you step away, evaluate, decide, and act.

Many people who journal report that it makes them feel less dominated by emotions and events, less likely to feel overwhelmed and confused. Journaling allows them to see their lives more clearly so they can sort things out and gain control over their feelings. The book's latter chapters will provide you some practical tips on how to journal.

At the end of each chapter you'll find specific prayer and Scripture reading assignments. It may be hard for you to motivate yourself to carry out these assignments initially because they don't seem "practical," and if your marriage is painful enough you're probably desperate for a quick fix. What you may not know is that many of the latest techniques in marriage counseling are based on teaching people to think about their partners in a new way, how to almost literally "transform their minds." The spiritual disciplines of prayer, contemplation, and Scripture reading are some of the most powerful ways to do that.

Besides being desperate for quick solutions, you may be depressed. And as people slide into depression and despair they often give up the very activities that could help them. This is especially true in a marriage crisis, which can be both emotionally and spiritually draining. If you are feeling so spiritually drained that you find it difficult to pray, you might try writing a prayer and then using it when you can't be more spontaneous. Or you could use prayers written by others, including those suggested in this book. If you use a pre-written prayer, think of it as being offered with your own prayers, as if you were in a prayer group.

If you suspect you've married the wrong person, you're probably feeling a sense of hopelessness about the future. The message of hope that fills the pages of the Bible can give you much-needed nourishment for the struggle—and it *will* be a struggle—that lies ahead. The ancient monastic orders structured their lives to include prayer, liturgies, preaching, and singing three times a day. That's not practical for most of us, but we can develop a habit of taking time out for brief interludes of contemplation. I like to carry with me a New Testament that includes a well-marked section of Psalms and Proverbs. It's a handy resource I can pull from my pocket for my own moments of contemplation.

This books offers help and hope for anyone who feels trapped in a disappointing relationship, but it is especially targeted to people of faith who take their marriage promise very seriously. When you view marriage as a covenant made before God, being faithful to your promise becomes extremely important. All your actions and decisions have a special weight because of the impact they have, not only on your relationship to your spouse, but also on your relationship to a God who values covenants. People of faith have to take the marriage vow seriously because God takes it seriously.

The problem is this: Sometimes even people who believe in a "forever marriage" end up getting divorced—or retreating into the emotional equivalent of divorce—because they can no longer stand the pain. After years of stuffing their feelings, or trying to keep the peace at any price, or finding themselves in another "death spiral" of conflict and alienation, they say, "I can't take it anymore."

If you feel like you can't take it anymore—if you have become convinced that you blew your choice of a life partner—don't give up yet. Maybe you did marry the wrong person, or at least the not-quite-right person. Maybe you made a less-than-wise choice of a mate. But consider this: Our world is difficult. And there are so many influences working against your chances of having a happy and fulfilling relationship that even if you had married a *perfect* person, you might not be much better off than you are now.

The good news is that you can do something about the problems that are causing you so much unhappiness. How? Turn to the next chapter and find out.

At the end of each chapter of this book, you will find some exercises, journaling assignments, and spiritual disciplines to help you understand how you and your spouse may have become "wrong people" for each other—and to help you restore the kind of relationship that will make you feel like you're right for each other again. However, I suggest that you read through the entire book before you plunge into the exercises. By waiting to do the assignments, you'll gain a better understanding of their purpose and consequently will get more out of them. Plus, you may find that some exercises are more relevant to your situation than others, so you can devote more time to those and perhaps even skip others. I strongly suggest that you do all the journaling and spiritual assignments, though, because they have value no matter what your situation.

The *exercises* and *journaling assignments* are designed to heighten your awareness of the events, feelings, and thoughts that have shaped your marriage as it exists today. They should help you better discern facts from impressions, become more aware of healthy and unhealthy patterns in your relationship—and make more rational decisions about the future. The *spiritual disciplines* at the end of each chapter are offered because you will need not only increased *understanding* but also increased *strength* for the work ahead. Because the journey you will be taking in the next weeks and months is, among other things, a journey of faith, you will need to draw on every spiritual resource available to you. As the story of Adam and Eve illustrates, we flawed human beings find it easier to be alienated— from God and from other people—than to be close. At a time when you may be tempted to distance yourself from God, I want to encourage you to nurture your relationship with Him instead. Not all problems in life (or in marriage) are caused by lack of spirituality, of course, but if you are working on your relationship to God you will have greater capacity to solve problems. It will be the key to overcoming both the spiritual and psychological sources of alienation in your marriage.

The exercises and spiritual disciplines are part of a single quest, something akin to what Proverbs 2:3–5 suggests: "If you call out for insight and cry aloud for understanding, and if you look for it as for silver and search for it as for hidden treasure, then you will understand the fear of the Lord and find the knowledge of God."

EXERCISE

This exercise is designed to help you pinpoint some of the sources of frustration and discouragement in your marriage. Listed below are some areas of potential conflict. Look at each category and write down a few notes about any problems you and your partner are having related to that area. That's the easy part of the assignment! The next part is harder: Try to think of a strength that you, your spouse, or the two of you together could bring to bear on this problem. This is important. While it's helpful to identify specific problems, focusing on them can blind you to strengths—especially in your mate. So give it an honest try.

Area of potential conflict	Problems	Strengths
Interpersonal relationships		
Extended family relationships		
Finances		
Work/career		
Roles		
Parenting		
Values		
Faith life		

JOURNALING

For the next few weeks, keep a structured journal of your interactions with your spouse (see example below). The structured approach is designed to help you stay focused. Later, if you wish, you can adopt a more unstructured form of journaling. But if you opt for the unstructured approach, be sure to keep in mind the issues discussed in each chapter.

Start your journaling by recording the interactions and events in your marriage. Answer these questions:

- What interactions took place between my spouse and me today?
- What, if anything, was going on around us that affected how we acted toward each other?

Example: Monday morning: John and I snapped at each other during breakfast. I don't remember what was said but it wasn't pleasant. He had gotten to bed later than usual. His mother's one-hour phone call kept him up until 11:30.

Monday afternoon: We didn't talk to each other on the phone this afternoon like we usually do.

Monday evening: John and I had little to say to each other during dinner. John watched TV afterward. I took Cindy shopping for shoes.

You obviously won't be able to describe all the interactions you have with your spouse, so select the ones that seem most significant to you. Although the example describes negative interactions, some of the incidents you record may be positive.

Most people do their journaling late in the evening, but you can journal whenever is most convenient for you.

After about a week of journaling, start to look for patterns in the way you and your partner relate to each other. In the example, John was touchy on Monday morning after having a long conversation with his mother the night before. Through her journaling, a wife might discover a pattern in her husband's grouchiness.

As you journal over a period of time, you may be surprised at the patterns that appear. Your interactions with your spouse may be more negative than you realized. There may be more positive things going on than you realized. Whatever it is that you see, you'll probably find that you gain new perspective on what's happening in your relationship.

Later on, I'll ask you to expand your journaling. But for now, try to restrict your journal entries to recording the actual events and interactions between you and your mate.

SPIRITUAL DISCIPLINES

A Spiritual Checkup

The following "spiritual checkup" is designed to help you assess whether or not you are taking sufficient advantage of the spiritual resources and disciplines that are available to strengthen and equip you for the struggle to redeem your marriage. Not all these resources are helpful or appropriate for every person. But by reviewing the list and comparing the ones you think are important with those you are actually practicing, you may get some ideas for how you can enhance your spiritual vitality, invigorate your relationship to Christ and His people, and gain strength for your marriage pilgrimage.

Review the following list (there is some overlap). Check the ones you think are important. Then check those you are actually practicing. Reflect on whether any of those you aren't practicing could help you achieve greater spiritual vitality to help you in your difficult relationships, including your relationship with your mate.

	Important	Doing	Will Do
Personal disciplines			
Prayer			
Bible study			
Devotional readings			
Contemplation/meditation			
Reading Christian books			
Using Christian symbols			
Listening to Christian music			
Singing and studying hymns			
Attending retreats			
Other _____			
Participating in the community of faith			
Attending church			
Bible study group			
Prayer group			
Sharing group			
Integrating faith with life study group			
Theology study group			
Christian parents group			
Couples group			
Women's group/Men's group			
Sunday school/ adult education			
Retreats			
Service to the community of faith			
Teaching			
Preaching			
Singing			
Visiting the sick			

Donating money   _____ _____ _____
Donating time   _____ _____ _____
Other _____   _____ _____ _____

Outreach
Helping the poor   _____ _____ _____
Counseling   _____ _____ _____
Visiting the less fortunate   _____ _____ _____
Evangelism   _____ _____ _____
Other _____   _____ _____ _____

Contemplation

One of the spiritual disciplines that is most neglected in modern times is contemplation (sometimes referred to as meditation). This practice of reflecting on God's character and words—and the implications they have for our lives—has the power to infuse us with the strength we need to live in fellowship with God and the people around us.

I once spent a week in a Protestant monastic community in Taize, France. The pattern of disciplined prayer and contemplation I experienced there made a powerful impression on me. But since I don't live in a monastic community, it's difficult for me to recreate my Taize experience. My life doesn't readily organize around several twenty-minute periods of contemplation each day. But I can and do make sure I take time each day to turn to a Psalm or a hymn. I read it slowly and thoughtfully, allowing its truth to empower me.

I suggest that you include a similar pattern of contemplation in your life. You might start by meditating on the words of one of the great hymns of the church, *Great Is Thy Faithfulness*:

Great is Thy faithfulness, O God my Father! There is no shadow of turning with Thee; Thou changest not, Thy compassions, they fail not; as Thou hast been, Thou forever wilt be.

Great is Thy faithfulness! Great is Thy faithfulness! Morning by morning new mercies I see; all I have needed Thy hand hath provided—great is Thy faithfulness, Lord unto me!

Pardon for sin and a peace that endureth, Thine own dear presence
to cheer and to guide; strength for today and bright hope for tomor-
row—blessings all mine, with ten thousand beside!*

Two

Why You Chose Your Mate

I can see the disillusionment on Denise's face as she sits in my office. "I'm really wondering about my marriage," she is saying. "Ed and I like and respect each other, but our relationship seems terribly empty. I often don't miss him when he's gone. Sometimes I'm more lonely when he's home than when he's away. Sometimes I wish he weren't around—ever.

"I guess Ed's presence is just a reminder of something I'd hoped for in life but I guess I'll never have, a relationship that makes me feel secure, affirmed, and supported. I don't get any of those feelings with Ed. Even when he tries to convey good things, it doesn't matter to me anymore. The hurt from all the negative stuff just never goes away.

"I don't understand how I ever got into this situation," she continues, breaking into tears. "Obviously, we weren't right for each other to begin with."

Listening to Denise talk about the hurt she feels over the way her husband treats her, I can easily imagine Ed to be an emotionally lifeless man, a heartless person incapable of loving. But years of counseling have taught me to reserve judgment. I rarely hear a story from a hurting wife when there's no hurting husband and vice versa.

As I suspected, Ed was feeling pain in ways that Denise could never have guessed. Ed had fallen in love with Denise on their first date. She was the most beautiful woman he had ever spoken to, much less dated, and she was at least his equal in talent and intelligence. If his friends hadn't dared him, he never would have had the nerve to ask her out in the first place. Even after they started dating regularly, he couldn't imagine ever marrying her. He didn't feel he could ever measure up to what she deserved. Eventually, he worked up the courage to propose to her. When Denise accepted, he felt a mixture of elation and panic: elation because he was going to be married to this beauty, panic because he felt unworthy of her and anxious that he might lose her.

Ed's emotional pattern of elation and panic continued through their marriage. When he was elated, he was very good to Denise. He couldn't be with her enough, couldn't do enough for her. When he felt anxious, he withdrew. Sometimes he said and did things deliberately to hurt his wife, telling himself he was testing her love.

Ed feels profoundly guilty and depressed. He is convinced it was a mistake—even a sin—for someone like him to marry a woman like Denise. He has come to the conclusion that their marriage vows were a sham.

Denise is disillusioned because the dream she once had for her marriage is shattered, not by abuse or infidelity or any other dramatic behavior, but by the weight of thousands of small incidents. Her sadness is compounded because she sees her vows as a promise made to God as well as to Ed—as a testimony to a world where commitment no longer seems to have real meaning. She really believed that her promise would never fail, just as God's promises never fail. But the emptiness she feels now seems to contradict the validity of her promise. Was their marriage wrong from the beginning? Did she make her vows to the wrong person?

Ed and Denise's story is told over and over again in an infinite variety of ways by desperate couples who finally seek counseling in a last attempt to save their marriages. Before these couples can get help, they need to understand what brought them together in the first place. Before you can get help, you need to understand what brought you together with your spouse.

If you're having serious doubts about your choice of a mate, you've probably asked yourself many times how you could have made what appears to have been such a huge mistake: *Why didn't I see he was totally*

*controlled by his parents? Why didn't I realize she was hypercritical? I should
have known he was unreliable when he showed up late for most of our dates.
I should have realized she was overly materialistic when she insisted on a
huge diamond engagement ring. Whatever made me think I should spend the
rest of my life with this person?*

On the other hand, you may be at the point where you no longer care
how you got into this situation. You just want relief from the pain. You
fantasize about being free—free from your hostile or distant spouse, free
from anger and conflict, free from contempt and distrust, free from the
oppressiveness of your marriage.

Or you may be just sad and disappointed. You had such high hopes
for what married life was going to be like. Now that you had somebody
to love you, life would be full of passion, adventure, romance, tenderness.
You'd be the ideal married couple. You'd do things together—worship together, play together, raise beautiful children together, listen to each other's problems with great understanding, make love every day.

But the reality doesn't quite measure up.

So why did you choose to marry your spouse? What was it that convinced you that of all the people in the world, this particular person was
someone you wanted to live with the rest of your life—sharing not only
a bed, closet, bank account, and, potentially, parenting responsibilities—
but also hopes and dreams and fears?

For most people, at least those of us who grew up in the Western Hem-
isphere, the answer seems obvious: *I fell in love.* But that still doesn't answer the question, because "falling in love" is a highly complex, variable
process. That's fortunate. If the requirements for falling in love weren't
so individualized, we'd all want to marry the same person!

Each of us has a unique grid of thoughts and emotions, forged through
a combination of our inborn traits and personal histories, that filters how
we experience the world and other people. While we are all influenced by
the culture around us—most North Americans, for example, find a trim
physique more attractive than the extreme obesity that was once highly
prized in Hawaiian culture—we are also influenced by important people
and events in our own lives.

Our personal experiences—and perhaps even our genes—predispose
us to be drawn to people with certain physical characteristics, personali-

ties, values, family backgrounds, education levels, and aspirations.

This doesn't necessarily mean that if your mother was a petite blonde, you're destined to choose a short spouse who has fair coloring—or that if your father had a terrible temper, you're doomed to marry someone who yells a lot. Sometimes that's the case, but often the opposite is true: A woman will marry a man because he seems so even-tempered, in contrast to her volatile father. Or a man will marry a woman who seems warm and accepting, unlike his critical mother. Still, it's likely that the person you choose to marry fits some physical or emotional or relational template from your past—that he or she evokes in you a certain feeling of comfort and familiarity, of being "at home."

Despite the uniqueness of our thinking/feeling grids, there are some common patterns in the way we humans pick our mates. Most of us want to marry someone who is sexually attractive to us, whom we feel comfortable with, who has common interests, who shares our core values, who has a personality that appeals to us, and who has compatible dreams. Someone we can be proud of. Someone whose esteem we value.

While it seems there is a uniform standard of physical attractiveness in our culture—how often do you see an overweight, or even a full-figured model in a magazine advertisement, or an acne-scarred romantic lead in a movie?—individual people have surprisingly different ideas about what constitutes beauty. For example, Janis tells of a friend who has been considerably overweight most of her life and never dated until she got out of college. Then she met an artist who fell in love with her in part because she reminded him of a Renaissance painting. To him, she was beautiful, just like the full-figured women in a Rubens masterpiece.

Whatever your own standards of beauty, it's likely that one of the most powerful factors in your choice of a mate was physical attraction. There's nothing wrong with that! God created us so that we would be drawn to the opposite sex. There is a danger, of course, in allowing physical attraction alone to dominate your choice of a mate. But it would be foolish to ignore the importance of mutual sexual attraction in marriage. The chemistry between a man and a woman who find each other sexually appealing helps to smooth the way through many of life's rough spots.

Shared values, especially shared spirituality, is another important component in the choice of a mate. It's unusual for two people to get married if they disagree violently about what's important in life—if only because in pursuing our deep values we tend to run into other people who share those values. If you had a deep spiritual commitment as a single person, for example, you may have acted on that commitment by attending church, joining a university Christian fellowship group, or volunteering for a service organization. In pursuing your spiritual values you associated with like-minded people, some of whom were probably attractive members of the opposite sex. Many people meet their spouses this way. Whether or not that was the case for you, you probably chose to marry someone whose values, including spiritual values, seemed to be in sync with your own.

Shared interests is another reason people get together. Like deeply held values, shared interests—in politics, sports, music, art, professional pursuits, or a host of other activities—are often what bring couples together in the first place. If you love to play tennis but are tone deaf, you're much more likely to meet your future spouse on the tennis court than at the opera. And while physical attraction is often the initial spark for a romantic relationship, shared interests are often what hold it together. Think back to your dating days: You might have gone out with someone once or twice just because he or she was good-looking, but if you had nothing in common, you probably got bored pretty quickly. Most likely, you chose your spouse in part because you both seemed to enjoy doing some of the same things.

It's also likely you married your spouse partly because he or she made you feel comfortable. Usually, we are attracted to and feel comfortable with people who share or at least seem accepting of our social group, ethnic tradition, spiritual values, friends, family, educational background—all the many components that make us who we are. If a prospective spouse doesn't fit in with our friends or family, we feel uneasy. And with good reason: Marriage is more than a union of two people. It's a corporate merger. Just as in the business world, if there's a clash in the cultures of the corporations being merged, it spells trouble ahead.

Similarly, if one person feels superior or inferior to the other, the relationship is in trouble. It's likely that when you chose your spouse you made a conscious or unconscious assessment that he or she brought about the same amount of "value" to the social marketplace that you did. The story of Beauty and the Beast is just a fairy tale: if you ranked yourself on the "beast" end of the social scale, it's highly unlikely that you set your sights on a "beauty" or vice versa.

You were undoubtedly attracted to your mate because he or she made you feel good about yourself, at least at some point in your relationship. As one woman said about what she had seen in her ex-boyfriend, "I loved the way he loved me. He made me feel great about myself." She didn't point out his sterling character qualities, or his looks, or his achievements—what she valued most was the way he made her feel about *herself*. Most of us want somebody in our lives who makes us feel important, someone who will take care of us and nurture us. Usually, we want that person to be our spouse. (Unfortunately, choosing somebody because he/she makes us feel good is often a compensation for feeling bad. So when the initial good feelings wear off, we often feel deceived.)

When we get married, we commit to merging our future with someone else's. So most of us choose to marry someone who has compatible dreams. Witness the hours engaged couples tend to spend talking about how many children they're going to have, what kind of house they're going to buy, what careers they're going to pursue, what vacations they're going to take.

These are often items on our conscious agenda as we pursue a life partner. But there are also unconscious agendas. Whether we realize it or not, many of us are attracted to people who fill unmet needs left over from a previous stage of life. Perhaps you didn't receive enough attention and affection from your parents—or as much affirmation and acceptance as you wanted from your peers—during childhood and adolescence. You probably chose your spouse because it seemed that he or she would be able to make up for whatever was missing in your earlier experiences.

Even if we don't like to admit it, the simple fact of availability is another huge factor in the choice of a spouse. You may have had an enormous crush on someone who fit all your selection criteria—physically attractive, similar values and interests, pleasing personality, compatible dreams—but who didn't return your interest. Unless something changed, you didn't marry that person. There may have been someone who lived several states away who would have been a near-perfect match for you, if only you had met—but you didn't. Even if you had met, the logistical difficulties of carrying on a long-distance courtship may have been too great an obstacle to overcome. I know one man who worked on the boats that travel the Great Lakes shipping lanes. During his travels Sean met and fell in love with a woman who lived in Quebec. Marie loved Sean as much as he loved her, but because his home was in Chicago, they found it difficult to keep in touch. So despite Sean's feelings for Marie, he ended up marrying a woman from his home port. As this story shows, availability, whether because of geography or some other reason, is a big factor in our choice of a mate.

Why did you choose your spouse? Because you fell in love, of course. But the feeling of "falling in love" is more than a mystical chemical process, it's a complex combination of many factors. Of course, every relationship is different and not all the factors I've mentioned have to be present for a couple to feel "in love," but it's likely that you picked your mate for at least two of these reasons: Because he or she was physically attractive to you. Because you shared many of the same values and interests. Because he or she made you feel comfortable—and good about yourself. And because you had compatible dreams.

Although none of these factors is sufficient in isolation, in combination these are all good reasons for choosing a life partner.

So why do you feel like you may have married the wrong person? Check out chapter 3.

EXERCISE

There are two parts to this exercise—which is designed to help you remember why you chose your mate and why there may be good reasons to keep trying to improve your marriage. The first part of the exercise involves simply responding to a checklist of some of the common factors that enter into the choice of a mate. Circle these according to how important you think they were in your decision to marry your spouse.

Physical attraction

Very Important   Important   Somewhat Important   Unimportant

Shared values

Very Important   Important   Somewhat Important   Unimportant

Comfortable

Very Important   Important   Somewhat Important   Unimportant

Feeling of being equals

Very Important   Important   Somewhat Important   Unimportant

Made me feel good about myself

Very Important   Important   Somewhat Important   Unimportant

Compatible dreams

Very Important   Important   Somewhat Important   Unimportant

Unconscious needs

Very Important   Important   Somewhat Important   Unimportant

Availability

Very Important   Important   Somewhat Important   Unimportant

Other _____

Very Important   Important   Somewhat Important   Unimportant

Are any of these factors, or changes in these factors, contributing to disappointment in your marriage? If so, why have they become issues? How are these issues affecting your relationship with your spouse?

List some qualities that attracted you to your mate:

If you had any misgivings about your spouse or the marriage before your wedding, list them below:

Has your spouse changed since your marriage? If so, describe how:

How do you think you have changed since your marriage:

If there have been any crises in your lives (death in the family, job loss, financial crisis, major illness, chronic illness, trouble with the law, etc.) since your marriage, list them below and describe what impact they have had on your marriage:

Describe the way you view your spouse now. Make an effort to list both positive and negatives characteristics.

(1) Positive characteristics

(2) Negative characteristics

What ongoing conflicts have you had in your marriage?

What effect have the changes you perceive in your spouse had on the conflicts in your marriage?

What effect have the changes in *you* had on the conflicts in your marriage?

Have the crises you described earlier affected the way you perceive your spouse now—or contributed to ongoing conflicts? If so, how?

JOURNALING

After two weeks of journaling, review your journal entries. Then take a sheet of paper and list any patterns you see in the way you and your spouse relate to each other. For example, using the illustration of John and Ellen from the previous chapter, Ellen might write down the following patterns:

- John and I bicker a lot.
- When we bicker, we tend to avoid each other the rest of the day.
- When we bicker, I tend to use any excuse to get out of the house, like taking our daughter out shopping.
- John and I never talk about why our bickering occurs or what to do about it.
- John seems to get into a funk every time he has a long talk with his mother.

It's important to be a careful observer of the patterns in your relationship because it is usually patterns, not isolated incidents, that either solidify or erode a marriage.

Do any of the patterns you've observed in your journal point to any positive or negative traits in your spouse? What are they? What positive or negative patterns did you see in yourself?

Did any of your observations point to qualities that originally attracted you to your spouse? If so, which ones?

After reviewing your patterns from the first two weeks, add another element to your journaling. Make two columns on your journal pages. Label one column INTERACTIONS. Label the second column FEEL-INGS/SENSATIONS. Under the INTERACTIONS column, continue recording the incidents that occur in your marriage as you were doing previously. Under the second column, record your feelings and physical sensations during the incidents. The two questions you will be answering in this column are:

• What am I feeling emotionally?
• What am I experiencing physically?

Example:

Interactions	Feelings/sensations
John and I snapped at each other during breakfast. I don't remember what was said but it wasn't pleasant. He had gotten to bed later than usual. His mother's one-hour phone call kept him up till 11:30.	Angry, frustrated

We didn't talk to each other on the phone like we usually do in the afternoon.	Angry, sad, lonely, headache
John and I had little to say to each other at dinner. He watched TV afterward. I took Cindy shopping for shoes.	Sad, frustrated, lonely, very tired

What's the purpose of recording your feelings and sensations? By monitoring your feelings and reactions, you can get a better handle on what's triggering them. You will probably find that some of your spouse's attitudes and behaviors have taken on symbolic importance. As a result, they create powerful negative emotions in you. Your feelings may be so strong that you actually experience physical reactions. Knowing what triggers these reactions can help you evaluate them and better assess the significance of your partner's behavior.

The journaling exercises suggested throughout the book are aimed at three goals: (1) Helping you become more *aware* of what is going on in your marriage, (2) helping you *evaluate* what is going on in your marriage, and (3) helping you *build* on your new awareness to create a more hope-filled and satisfying marriage.

Contemplation

Continue to meditate on the words of the hymn, *Great Is Thy Faithfulness*. Allow the words to serve as a reminder that you are not alone in your journey.

If you are not already doing so, add the discipline of confession to your times of contemplation. Confession, admitting wrongdoing, is important because it gives us a way to deal with the overwhelming effects of sin on every aspect of our lives. Sin mars our relationship to God and to all the people around us, but confession brings cleansing and renewal.

Meditate on these words from 1 John 1:8–10:

"If we claim to be without sin, we deceive ourselves and the truth is not in us. If we confess our sins, he is faithful and just and will forgive us our sins and purify us from all unrighteousness. If we claim we have not sinned, we make him out to be a liar and his word has no place in our lives."

Take time each day to examine how your own sin is interfering with your relationship to God and to your spouse. Confess your sin to God and ask for cleansing.

Prayer

As a help in establishing the discipline of confession, consider beginning your time of contemplation by saying the Jesus Prayer, an ancient petition to God that has been used by devout Christians throughout the centuries. You may be uncomfortable with this at first, because contemporary Christians aren't as used to this kind of spiritual exercise as some of the great people of faith who lived in earlier eras. But give it a try anyway. Before beginning the prayer, meditate silently on how you may have contributed to pain in the lives of others: your spouse, children, extended family, friends. As each incident comes into your mind, picture Jesus as a witness to it. Then pray:

JESUS CHRIST, SON OF GOD, HAVE MERCY ON ME, A SINNER.

Meditate on your priorities. Then ask yourself, what do these words of Jesus mean? "If anyone would come after me, he must deny himself and take up his cross and follow me" (Matthew 16:24). Have your priorities affected your marriage? Jesus is your witness. Are there any sacrifices He calls you to make that would affect your priorities? Pray:

JESUS CHRIST, SON OF GOD, HAVE MERCY ON ME, A SINNER.

Meditate again on these words from 1 John: "If we confess our sins, he is faithful and just and will forgive us our sins and purify us from all unrighteousness." Imagine that Jesus is speaking these words of forgiveness directly to you. Pray:

JESUS CHRIST, SON OF GOD, HAVE MERCY ON ME, A SINNER.

Reflect on a past situation where you have sought out and received forgiveness from a friend or relative. Try to recall the sense of cleansing and healing you felt at the time. Try to recapture that same feeling after each time of contemplation, confession, and prayer. Remember, though, that God's forgiveness is real whether you feel anything or not.

Three

Why You May Be Doubting Your Choice

Just five years into her marriage, Andrea felt tremendously sad and hopeless about her relationship with Steve. She couldn't imagine leaving him—she didn't believe in divorce and would never do anything to hurt her children. In fact, she didn't want to do anything to hurt Steve. But she couldn't see herself ever being happy with him again. Their marriage, which had started out with such joy and hope, now seemed like a huge mistake.

Andrea had married Steve as much for his devotion to his family as for his intelligence and good looks. She was sure that, married to Steve, she'd be able to have a "real" family. As a child growing up with an alcoholic father, Andrea had often fantasized about a "real" family. To her, a real family was one where the parents loved each other and showed it. Where the parents and children did things together, like taking vacations or having celebrations that included everybody. Where the father showed his love by helping the children with homework or attending their school activities. A real family was very different from the one she grew up in.

In Andrea's eyes, Steve had a real family. Everything that was missing in Andrea's family was abundantly present in his. Steve, along with his older married sister and her family and his younger brother and his fiancée, gathered at their parents' house every week for Sunday dinner—a friendly, busy, boisterous occasion. They never missed getting together for holidays. Andrea was especially impressed by how Steve's relatives were so totally available to each other. No issue was beyond discussion. No need was out of bounds for family assistance. Steve's sister confided in her mother. Steve ran errands for his mom and helped his dad around the house. He replaced the roof on his parents' garage, even installed a half bath in the basement. His siblings were equally helpful. The family seemed to work together beautifully, and Andrea had fit right in. She had especially loved being included in the hustle and bustle of "Sundays at Mom's."

After they got married, Andrea and Steve continued spending their Sundays at his parents' house. At first this was fine, but because they both had heavy work schedules, and Sunday was the only day they could spend alone together, they occasionally would forego the Sunday afternoon visits to do something else. When that happened, Steve's mom would always let it be known that she was disappointed. And Steve would feel guilty.

Soon, the expectation that Andrea and Steve should make the weekly pilgrimage to his parents became a source of bitter contention between them. Andrea resented the expectation that she and Steve give up the only time they had to be alone together. Steve stubbornly resisted any change in his family tradition.

After their first child was born, the tensions increased dramatically. At a time when Andrea thought she and Steve should begin starting some family traditions of their own, she felt even more pressure to spend Sundays—not to mention all holidays—with his family. Steve was unsympathetic with her concerns. As the stress between them heightened, Andrea and Steve started snapping at each other over minor irritations.

The more upset Andrea became over how they spent Sundays and holidays, the more she noticed a behavior pattern on Steve's part that increasingly infuriated her: He was more available to his family than he was to her. Steve would work on his parents' car before he'd get around to hers. His sister's dripping faucet got his attention before the broken garage door opener at home. His brother's front porch was rebuilt before he installed the new door lock on their family room.

Over time, Andrea began to lose respect for Steve. She felt as though he were a little boy seeking his parents' attention and approval. As far as she was concerned, he was a mama's boy who had never disengaged from his family long enough to become his own person. He had never grown up.

Andrea's increasingly contemptuous view of Steve began to affect every aspect of their life together, not the least of which was their sexual relationship. It was hard for Andrea to respond to Steve's romantic overtures when she thought of him as a needy little boy. It was hard for her to respond to him positively, period. Because of her convictions against divorce, she told herself that she would just have to live with the situation. Sometimes, when other areas of her life were going well, that seemed okay. But other times, Andrea was overwhelmed with the prospect of spending the rest of her life with someone she no longer loved or even respected.

THE DEATH SPIRAL

Andrea and Steve's story is very, very common. Two people enter a marriage for what they believe are good reasons. They have high expectations and good intentions. They are convinced they are meant to be together. But over a period of time—a few months or many years—they lose sight of all the positive traits they once saw in each other, and instead they see mainly negatives. A "death spiral" begins: As each spouse becomes more and more aware of the other's negative traits, they begin attributing these traits to unchangeable character flaws. Irritation evolves into blame and contempt. One spouse becomes constantly defensive. Sometimes both do. The future, and certainly the prospect of ever redeeming the marriage, begins to look hopeless.

At this point, the point of despair, some couples end their marriages. Even people with strong convictions against divorce, who never thought they would even consider it, reach a point where they can think of nothing but escaping the pain. Other couples settle into a pattern of constant arguing without ever solving the issues. Still others hunker down into an uneasy, armed truce—or simply live separately in the same house.

Why does this happen? And why does it happen so often?

AWAKENING TO REALITY

It really shouldn't be surprising that so many married people look across the breakfast table one morning, stare at a spouse and think, *You're not the person I thought I married.* Dating, the process which leads to marriage for most couples, doesn't really lend itself to developing a realistic view of another person. Most of us are on our best behavior during courtship. We go through elaborate preparations. We make a concerted effort to be charming, attractive, witty and attentive. We try to minimize or hide our flaws. And since we're only with the object of our attentions for limited periods of time, it's possible to maintain the illusion of near-perfection over a period of months, and in some cases, years.

The energy, effort, and expense people go through to make an impression while dating can put them at a disadvantage later on. It's almost impossible to continue that level of effort, which accounts for the sudden shock of many post-marriage morning sightings. Whatever a person does to look great at bedtime fails to flatter the reality upon awakening.

Then there's the infatuation factor. For most of us, the experience of falling in love brings with it clouded vision, twisted logic, and denial of reality. The powerful physical and emotional pleasure we feel in the presence of our love object completely overwhelms us, short-circuiting our rationality. We become addicted to the rush of feelings that surge through us at the mere thought of our beloved. Trying to study, concentrate on work, balance a checkbook, or pay attention to the speedometer becomes an exercise in futility in the face of "love."

The feeling of being in love is so delightful, and so addictive, that lovers have a marked tendency to ignore any warning signs suggesting they might not be right for each other. And the amount of time people spend together while dating doesn't make it easy to detect the warning signs. Two to four hours per date is typical, and it's almost always spent having fun. Unlike marriage, dating is not about work, or taking care of kids, or planning a budget, or working out household duties, or deciding whether to spend the holidays with my family or yours. No wonder so many people are disillusioned when they wake up to the realities of marriage.

Even if you thought you got married with your eyes wide open, there was probably something you didn't see or understand about your spouse-to-be during courtship. Then, too, you may have consciously chosen to overlook certain things prior to marriage. Many of us do that. It feels so good to be in love we don't want to spoil the experience. Or we just reach a time in our lives when we want to stop dating and start living. We want to leave the searching and competing behind. We want to end the loneliness. We want to share dreams and build a life with another person. So we look past a few things.

COURTSHIP MISTAKES

Although just about everybody engages in selective sight to some degree before marriage, people of deep faith are especially vulnerable to the tendency to adjust reality. Here are some common mistakes many devout Christians make during courtship and early marriage that can result in a lot of pain later on:

Placing too much faith on a shared spiritual commitment.

There's no question that having similar beliefs and a shared level of spiritual commitment are important ingredients for a successful marriage. But they aren't *all* that matters. Too often, Christians allow a sense of spiritual kinship to overshadow traits that might otherwise evoke doubt about a potential mate.

Judy and Aaron met at a Christian fellowship group in college. It seemed natural for them to start dating. They were so spiritually compatible, and both of them considered spiritual compatibility to be the most important ingredient in choosing a marriage partner. So they got married. From the start, they saw their marriage as a response to a calling. Aaron felt called to the ministry. Judy saw her vocation as Christian education. It seemed to be a perfect combination. They agreed that Judy would work full-time while Aaron went to seminary and then, after they'd had a chance to start a family, Judy would attend graduate school to pursue her ministry. Their life unfolded essentially as planned until they had their first child. Since Aaron was still in seminary, adding a baby to the family caused some financial stresses. Some small but perceptible fissures began to appear in their relationship. Judy began to resent Aaron's lack of attention to her and their child. She saw him devoting himself to his studies and his part-time job as an associate pastor at the expense of his family. His professors thought Aaron was wonderful. The people in their church thought he was wonderful. When they would tell her how lucky she was to be married to such a dedicated, godly man, she would respond with a weak smile.

During the final months of Aaron's seminary career, Judy became pregnant with their second child. It was a difficult pregnancy, but no matter how awful she felt Aaron seemed incapable of sympathizing, much less responding in helpful ways. When she was too nauseated and exhausted to keep going, she desperately wanted his physical presence, his emotional support, and his help in caring for their toddler. But most of the time, Aaron was too distracted to notice what Judy needed. When he did notice, he was impatient with her.

Despite Aaron's lack of support for her, Judy uncomplainingly supported him throughout the demanding process of being interviewed for and placed in a congregation. She choked back her resentment at the enthusiasm with which potential churches received her husband. His reputation as an outstanding seminarian and student pastor combined with his good looks and dynamic preaching made him a rising star in the denomination. Judy began to suspect that the attention Aaron received from his achievements was what was most important to him—that she and their child were at best peripheral. She looked to the future and saw her life bounded by the four walls of a parsonage.

Still, Judy continued to dutifully support Aaron in his quest for a pastoral assignment. Her only request was that he choose one of the several offered to him that would bring them closer to her parents. Since she saw no immediate hope of a closer relationship with her husband, she wanted to alleviate some of her loneliness by spending time with her folks. Aaron didn't respond one way or another, so Judy pinned her hopes on the prospect of living within visiting distance of her mom and dad. Her hopes were dashed. Without consulting her, Aaron chose an assignment that was too far away for Judy to spend any regular time with her parents. She was crushed. She began to have frequent bouts of uncontrollable weeping throughout the day. She carefully hid these episodes from Aaron, though. His impatience with her was more than she could bear.

Three months after Aaron started his new job, Judy delivered their second child. Aaron was at a pastor's conference when she left for the hospital. He arrived to be with Judy shortly after the baby was born, and then returned to the conference within a few hours. Judy's loneliness deepened even further.

Her mom came to help for several days after the birth, but when she left, Judy's life took on a predictable pattern. She took care of the kids and occasionally attended church functions, but other than that had little social contact. Aaron was busy with church work. The congregation loved him, with good reason: He was devoted to his work, rarely taking a day off. As for family life, he came home for meals but little else.

Judy's sadness had turned to anger, but the angrier she got the more guilty she felt. After all, what right did she have to feel neglected when Aaron was doing the Lord's work? She prayed for deliverance from her hostility and resentment.

By the time their third child was born, Judy had lowered her expectations of marriage and was adjusting to her loneliness. She was able to hang on because she now had a plan: As soon as her children were old enough, she was going to go back to school and complete the training she needed to become a Christian education director. She had hope again because she could define an end to her sense of isolation and insignificance.

Then two things happened that broke Judy's spirit completely: She got pregnant again. And Aaron announced that he was going to get a Ph.D. The combination of these events sent Judy into a depression so deep she had to be hospitalized. Aaron's response? Instead of realizing how his neglect had contributed to her depression, he lectured Judy on her need for more faith. He told her that her illness was her own fault, an obvious sign that she wasn't completely surrendered to God. He urged her to check out of the hospital, quit taking antidepressant medication, and get on with life. Judy's depression became total despair. Both she and Aaron eventually concluded there was no hope for their marriage.

What happened to this couple? They started out their marriage with a commitment to being partners in service to God. They both believed they were called to ministry. They both devoted time to prayer, Bible study, and service. They both believed in forever marriage centered around a relationship with Jesus Christ.

Ironically, despite their obvious differences Judy and Aaron also shared one key—and mistaken—assumption: That a shared spiritual commitment is the only really important ingredient in a marriage.

Trusting that God will change a spouse-to-be (or seeing a person's potential and marrying for what might happen).

God can and does work miracles, but people who count on God's help to make their love object fit their specifications are setting themselves up for disappointment. God is likely to be less pushy than we are when it comes to changing a spouse or spouse-to-be against his or her will. He gives humans free will. If someone doesn't want to change, He rarely forces the issue.

Joan learned this lesson the hard way. She was shattered when her husband, Jerry, walked out after eight years of marriage. It couldn't have happened at a worse time. Their daughter had just been diagnosed with severe diabetes, and her prognosis was not good. She had to be hospitalized several times, and the doctors were having difficulty getting her disease under control. Unable to handle their daughter's illness, Jerry opted out of the marriage.

In retrospect, Joan says there were plenty of warning signs that she should have heeded early in her relationship with Jerry. For starters, he was an agnostic and she was a Christian. Jerry's lack of interest in spirituality bothered Joan, but she felt sure she could convert him, given enough time. Then there were Jerry's two previous marriages. He had left his first wife and their son because he thought his in-laws were too intrusive. He divorced his second wife because she balked at the idea of leaving her family and friends to move across the country in pursuit of one of Jerry's many get-rich-quick schemes. Joan knew about Jerry's marital history before she married him, but she explained it away—or rather he explained it away and she let herself be persuaded.

Joan's friends tried to talk her out of marrying Jerry, not because of his previous marriages, but because of the way he behaved toward her in their presence. He interrupted her when she was talking, ridiculed her ideas and interests, and generally treated her—and all women for that matter—with contempt. But Joan was so exhilarated at having been "chosen" by a man as handsome and seemingly dynamic as Jerry that she downplayed her friends' warnings and her own doubts. She felt sure that if she tried hard enough she could make the marriage work. And she did work hard, all the way up to the time that Jerry left.

For most people, marital reality dawns much more gradually than it did for Joan. Typically, the delight that two people feel in the early days of living together gives way to the decidedly unromantic, less-than-mysterious dailiness of life. It is usually the erosive impact of a slowly accumulating list of minor grievances, irritating little habits, and idiosyncrasies, not a dramatic betrayal, that penetrates married people's illusions and wakes them up to reality.

If you've woken up to a reality about your spouse that you think you can change—with God's help—consider this: God's view of your spouse may be different from yours. The changes you want may not be the changes He wants. Contrary to the expectations of some Christians, God isn't a coconspirator in the "let's change my spouse" game.

Believing that God will provide the strength to deal with a spouse's problems.

Yes, it's true that with God's help people can endure a lot. Many Christians of the past and even around the world today have endured torture and death. It's also true that God uses marriage as a refining process for each of us. But the purpose of marriage isn't to put two people to the test by placing them in a relationship that causes constant turmoil and frustration. Marriage should be a partnership in which both parties reach levels of growth and fulfillment they couldn't achieve alone. Life is full of pain, but married people should face it together, not continually inflict it on each other.

Unfortunately, even when two people make a genuine effort to be open about their respective flaws before marriage, even when they try to plan for how they might deal with potential problems, they may have unrealistic ideas about what they should expect from God, and what they should expect from themselves. Take Frank and Donna, for example.

It's rare for an engaged couple to come to a psychologist for premarital counseling—they usually wait until after they're married and have serious problems—but Frank and Donna were an exception. They came to see me shortly after they were engaged because of Frank's recurrent problems with severe depression. Although his depression could be controlled with antidepressant medication, Frank refused to take it. He was convinced that if he just had enough faith, God would cure him of his emotional problems. Since neither his internist nor I was able to convince Frank to take medication, I did what I could to point out to Donna the realities of living with someone who is chronically depressed. But she felt sure she could cure her fiancé with the strength of her love. So, against my advice, they got married.

Three months later, Donna was back in my office, miserable over what seemed to be an intolerable situation. Even though Donna knew Frank suffered from depression before their marriage, she had no idea what that meant until she lived with him. In the midst of his depressive episodes, he would stay in bed ten to twelve hours a day. He didn't go to work, didn't talk, didn't do anything. Sex was out of the question. Donna, who had been passionately in love with her husband, became depressed and distraught herself. The future loomed before her as a frightening void.

How did this couple go wrong? After all, Frank had been entirely open about his emotional problems, and they had even sought out premarital counseling. Unfortunately, both Frank and Donna overestimated their individual capacities for dealing with a serious difficulty. This is a common mistake, especially for couples who share a deep faith. Because they were both devout Christians, Frank and Donna believed that through prayer and Bible study, he would eventually be able to triumph over his depression and, in the meantime, she would be able to control her reactions to it. Later, when he was unable to overcome his depression, they both began to question God's reliability and power at a time when they needed Him most. Having confused the reality of their faith with the wisdom of marrying each other, they came to the conclusion that faith—that God—had failed them.

Like Donna, Marty knew about her husband's problems before they got married but overestimated her ability to cope with them. Marty met Tim at a church singles' group. She was attracted to him right away because he was exceptionally good-looking and because he seemed to be so sensitive and understanding. Plus, unlike other men she had dated, Tim attended church eagerly and talked openly and unashamedly about his faith.

A real achiever herself, Marty felt somewhat protective toward Tim because he had been through some extremely rough times and was obviously having trouble getting himself together. During a group sharing time at a church meeting, he had opened up about his past problems with drugs and brushes with the law. He said it was all behind him now, though. God had turned his life around. What Tim didn't mention—but Marty's friends warned her about—was his history of violence. He had beaten up several of his previous girlfriends. Marty was a little shaken by that, but she ascribed his violent tendencies to the drugs he had been taking. Marty's friends told her Tim wasn't totally out of the drug scene, but she was convinced that with her help he could overcome his problems.

So, after a brief courtship, Marty and Tim got married. Two months later, Marty fled their apartment for a friend's house in fear for her life. Shortly after the wedding, Tim had begun flying into emotional rages. His violent outbursts intensified as Marty began to question him about aspects of his life he had previously kept hidden from her. She discovered he had credit card debts of over $18,000. She became convinced he was still using and possibly dealing drugs, because he continued to hang out with his old drug crowd and often couldn't or wouldn't account for long periods of time when she had no idea where he was. She learned that he was about to be fired from his job because of erratic attendance.

These situations—Marty's and Donna's—are extreme, but they point to a scenario that occurs on a less dramatic level in many relationships. Even people who go into marriage thinking they are being totally realistic, who have recognized the flaws and weaknesses in their potential partner, underestimate the degree to which those flaws are going to cause problems. Or they overestimate their ability to deal with them.

Assuming that it is a Christian's responsibility to look for the best in other people.

The reason this assumption is so dangerous is that it's partly right. We shouldn't dwell on the faults and frailties of others. This is especially true in marriage. After all, everyone has flaws and dwelling on them just makes the "dweller" and the "dwellee" miserable. *Prior* to marriage, however, it's important to be realistic about a potential partner's weaknesses—as well as our own. Some flaws can work together and others can't. Some are tolerable. Others aren't. Some are tolerable if they don't have to be endured over a long period of time. Singles who choose to focus on the good in a spouse-to-be while ignoring significant problems, thinking it's their Christian responsibility to do so, fail to understand the Christian principle of discernment.

While these are examples of common forms of selective sight, especially among people of faith, there are other reasons why marriage partners so frequently have a sense of suddenly seeing the truth about their spouse—and not liking what they see.

THE SEEDS OF DISAPPOINTMENT

Once a man and woman marry and start living together, they're suddenly seeing each other at all times of the day and night, not just when they're spiffed up for a date. They're together when they're feeling good and when they're feeling bad, when life is interesting and when it's boring. Little flaws and weaknesses and annoying personality traits start to surface. One or both partners begin to suspect that the other person isn't who he/she appeared to be. The disaffected spouse begins to turn off sexually. A sense of distance, sometimes even disgust, sets in. That's what happened with Brenda and Jack.

When Brenda first started dating Jack, she was so swept off her feet by his muscular physique and movie star good looks that she never even noticed how often his breath had a stale, foul odor. Her senses were so numbed by love that she remained oblivious to his lack of personal hygiene—he rarely brushed his teeth more than once or twice a week—until several months into their marriage. Then she really noticed. And she realized his dental hygiene wasn't the only issue. He showered erratically. He rarely changed his underwear. In short, he was a slob. Brenda was so turned off she began to think she couldn't bear to live with Jack if he didn't change.

As Brenda's image of her husband dissolved from that of a macho hunk into a picture of a dirty, careless little boy, she began to avoid sex. She wouldn't even kiss him except when she felt she had no choice. Since Brenda never even hinted at the reason for her sudden lack of interest in sexual intimacy—she was afraid of offending him—Jack was hurt and angry. He began picking fights, criticizing her housekeeping and personal appearance. He even accused her of being involved with someone else. Eventually, he became involved in an affair with another woman. He knew it was wrong, but justified it on the grounds that Brenda refused to sleep with him.

By the time Brenda and Jack finally came to marriage counseling, so many issues had accumulated that neither of them could remember what started their problems—until Jack bitterly reminded Brenda that, not only would she not have sexual relations with him, she wouldn't even kiss him. Then it all tumbled out. When Brenda tearfully related her disgust at Jack's personal hygiene, he was first offended, then furious. Why hadn't she said anything to him before? He had never brushed his teeth more than once a week, even when they were dating. If his breath was so bad, why had she married him?

Although the initial problem that triggered this couple's marital crisis was almost ridiculously simple to solve—by Jack brushing his teeth more often and taking more showers—the avalanche of subsequent issues had made them so bitter toward each other that they were never able to muster the will to repair their relationship. Instead, they opted to end their marriage. Almost immediately after the divorce, Jack adopted a new approach to hygiene. Had Brenda been more aware of reality from the beginning, or at least given Jack some gentle hints about his breath problem when she first became aware of it—before so much damage had been done to their relationship—they both would have been spared a lot of heartache.

Even as I tell this story it sounds so absurd it's hard to believe it happened, but I have counseled couples with almost identical stories a number of times in my practice. What's important to understand, though, is that Jack and Brenda's disillusionment grew out of small issues that took on huge proportions over time—something that happens in almost all troubled marriages.

TOO MUCH OF A GOOD THING

Some people come to the conclusion that they married the wrong person not because they discover some previously hidden negative characteristic or because they overestimated their ability to deal with a recognized problem but rather because a trait they once saw as a strength has started to look like a weakness.

Remember Andrea and Steve, the couple who fought about how much time he spent with his relatives? Andrea was initially drawn to Steve because of his devotion to his family. But after living with Steve for a couple of years, she began to see the downside of his unusually strong bond with his parents and siblings. Steve's love and commitment to his family of origin seemed to outweigh his love and commitment to his wife. What had once seemed like a strength began to look like a weakness. An essentially good quality had gotten out of balance.

Philip and Lori are another example of how what once seemed like a positive trait can begin to feel like a negative one. They were an ideal couple in the eyes of their parents and friends—two people who were totally devoted to each other. They met in high school, dated throughout college, and got married shortly after graduation. From the beginning, Philip was entranced and flattered by Lori's attentiveness to him. She was the most beautiful girl who had ever shown any interest in him and, amazingly, she appeared to love nothing more than spending time in his presence. In fact, Lori didn't seem to care about socializing with other people at all. During their courtship, they rarely went out on dates. Instead, they went to church, took long walks, watched television—activities that didn't require much effort, planning, or money, and allowed them to be together without interacting much with other people.

What Philip failed to notice at first was that, as their relationship developed, he was beginning to neglect his other friends and withdraw from involvements that had been important to him in the past. Before he and Lori began dating seriously, he had been active in his church and local politics and occasionally did volunteer work for a nearby food pantry. He loved drama and occasionally performed bit parts in college plays and community theater productions. All this changed once he and Lori got engaged. They spent almost all their free time together.

But shortly after their marriage, Philip gradually started picking up some of the activities he had set aside to be with Lori. She objected immediately. Having assumed they would spend even more time together as a married couple, she interpreted Philip's outside involvements as rejection. Soon his evenings and occasional weekends away from home resulted in serious conflict. The tensions were only exacerbated after their first child was born and Lori quit her job to become a full-time mother. With few friends or outside interests of her own, she felt isolated and eventually became depressed. She began to make more and more demands of Philip, which came across to him as nagging and whining. Suffocated by her neediness, Philip became increasingly turned off by Lori. The flattering attentiveness of the beautiful woman he had married had begun to feel like an ever-tightening noose around his neck. The quality that had attracted Philip to Lori in the first place had created tremendous tensions in their marriage.

That's how Connie felt about her husband Josh's involvement in their congregation. She and Josh met at church, where they were both active in the choir and where Josh taught Sunday school and served on several committees. From the very beginning, Connie was impressed by the depth of Josh's biblical knowledge and the strength of his commitment to living out his spiritual values. If ever there were a man who had his priorities straight, it was Josh. The way he spent his time was strong evidence that he put God and the church first in his life. Connie felt unusually blessed to have fallen in love with such a wonderful, godly man. About a year after their marriage, however, she began to feel less enthralled with Josh's priorities. She had assumed that because Josh's spiritual interests so closely paralleled her own, they would be drawn even more closely together in marriage. Instead, Josh's church involvements seemed to be keeping them apart. He had church meetings almost every night of the week, and what little free time he had left over he spent reading the Bible and theology books.

At first Connie was reluctant to complain. She had friends whose husbands neglected them for golf, football, or their buddies. One friend's husband was having an affair. How dare she feel dissatisfaction—much less express it—with a husband whose primary passion appeared to be directed toward God? Connie loved Josh in large part because of his spiritual devotion, but now that devotion appeared to be driving them apart. She remembered laughing one time when she heard someone described as "so heavenly minded he was of no earthly good." As she thought about her relationship with Josh, the description no longer seemed so funny.

What do Andrea, Philip, and Connie have in common? Each was initially drawn to his or her spouse because of a characteristic that seemed to be a great strength, but which eventually came to feel like a weakness. In each case, the trait in question was intensely attractive during courtship, but too much of a good thing in marriage. The spouse who had seemed to be "the right one" began to look like "the wrong one."

WHAT'S THE REALITY IN YOUR RELATIONSHIP?

Whether you anticipated them or not, once your spouse's flaws began to surface in your marriage, it's likely that they began to overshadow any good qualities he or she may have. So while it may seem that you finally woke up to reality, it's quite possible that you are once again viewing your spouse from a skewed perspective. Only this time your image of your mate is clouded by disappointment and resentment instead of infatuation.

Part of the journey back from disappointment in marriage is learning how to view your spouse with new, more genuinely realistic, eyes. You'll find help for that process in the pages ahead.

EXERCISE

Take a few minutes to reflect on any experiences you've had over the years that have awakened you to the reality of who it is you married. Try to think of incidents that have endeared you to your spouse as well as those that have disturbed you. In the chart below, jot down some notes about these experiences. Summarize the reality you discovered, your feelings at the time, how you reacted (how you thought about your spouse and how you behaved toward your spouse), and how the incident may have changed your relationship.

Year 1

Reality:

Your Feeling:

Your Reaction:

Change in Relationship:

Year 2

Reality:

Your Feeling:

Your Reaction:

Change in Relationship:

Years 3–4

Reality:

Your Feeling:

Your Reaction:

Change in Relationship:

Years 5–7

Reality:

Your Feeling:

Your Reaction:

Change in Relationship:

Years 8–10

Reality:

Your Feeling:

Your Reaction:

Change in Relationship:

Years _____

Reality:

Your Feeling:

Your Reaction:

Change in Relationship:

Years _____

Reality:

Your Feeling:

Your Reaction:

Change in Relationship:

Years _____
Reality:

Your Feeling:

Your Reaction:

Change in Relationship:

JOURNALING

1. Add a third column to your journal with the heading THOUGHTS/
OBSERVATIONS. Use it to record any thoughts and observations you may
have in response to any chapter material, exercises, journaling assignments, or spiritual disciplines. Start by reflecting on what you've discovered about the interaction patterns you've identified so far.

2. After you've gotten comfortable with structured journaling, move on
to some more open-ended journaling: (a) Elaborate on some of the experiences you summarized in your chart; (b) Reflect in writing on how
your evolving awareness of the reality about your spouse—both good and
bad—is affecting your marriage today; (c) Be especially attentive to incidents that have made you aware of positive traits in your partner. Try
to list at least ten of your spouse's positive characteristics. Chronicle your
thoughts in response to these questions:

   (1) Why don't your spouse's positive traits mean as much to you as
       they used to?

(2) What could you do to become more aware and affirming of these traits?

SPIRITUAL DISCIPLINES

1. Continue to make regular time for contemplation of Scripture and other spiritual resources, such as inspirational hymns and worship songs and the Jesus Prayer.

2. As you pray about your marriage, either spontaneously or using written prayers, keep in mind that you are working on a relationship not only with your spouse but with a personal God who enters into and understands your experiences. Before speaking the words of your prayer—the ones suggested below or those from your own heart—offer to God a wordless prayer. Pray through a mental picture of bringing your spouse to meet Jesus. Imagine what the surroundings would look like, what the temperature would be, the color of the sky. Imagine how Jesus would greet your mate. What words would He say? What tone of voice would He use? Would He say anything to you? Would He give you any advice?

Try using this prayer or one like it:

Lord, this is the person I married: (Describe the way you view your spouse). I committed myself to _____ before you and in the presence of your people. These are the hopes and dreams that I had in making that commitment: (Tell God what you wanted your marriage to be like.) The reality of my marriage isn't living up to my dreams. I am deeply disappointed. With my dreams broken and my hopes dashed, how can I love _____ ? I pray for your guidance. Amen.

Four

So What Did You Expect?

Expectations, as innocent as they might seen, often cause major problems. Couples rarely go into a marriage with negative expectations. But many, if not most, have unrealistic expectations. Inevitably, this leads to disappointments that can have serious consequences. However, even if you get married with perfectly reasonable expectations, expectations you thoroughly discussed and agreed on with your spouse-to-be, there's STILL a good chance you'll be disappointed—because people and circumstances change!

Not surprisingly, expectations—both realistic and unrealistic—are a source of unhappiness in a great many marriages. A husband or wife whose expectations aren't being met may think about a spouse, *You betrayed and deceived me!* In reality, though, it was most likely the expectations themselves that did the betraying and deceiving.

Some men go into marriage with an unrealistic belief that they're still going to be able to run off to the gym several nights a week to play basketball with the guys. Some women go into marriage with the unrealistic supposition that their husband will outearn Rupert Murdoch—and still have hours left over every day to shower her with attention. When their expectations aren't met, they conclude that they must have married the wrong person.

Some people expect that they're always going to have the same intense feelings about their spouse that they had during courtship. They mistakenly believe that if two people are right for each other, they'll always feel "in love."

A woman came into my office one day announcing that she wanted to divorce her husband, but she wanted to do it in a way that would guarantee that both he and their two daughters would remain psychologically intact. The first thing I did was tell her about the devastating impact of divorce on children. Then I explained that it might be possible not only to spare her children the pain of divorce, but to actually make her marriage work well. "If you want your marriage to work," I said, "you have to work on your marriage." She was aghast at the very idea. "No!" she sputtered. "If two people are in love and right for each other there should be no work involved. Love should flow freely and naturally! It should be spontaneous! If the marriage is right, it shouldn't require work!" Obviously, this woman didn't want to hear, couldn't hear, what I had to tell her. She stopped coming to see me, saying I was a "hellfire and brimstone" psychologist. Unfortunately, too many people share this woman's unrealistic expectation—that if a marriage is "right," feelings of love should continue at the same passionate level. And that passion will flow without any work. When their feelings diminish or even wither and die, they assume they must have married the wrong person.

Other people draw the same conclusion from different but similarly unmet and unrealistic expectations. For example, couples bring surprising expectations about sex to marriage. They foresee unlimited time and a roughly equal need for sex. They underestimate the degree to which children will affect their sex life, giving them less time, less energy, less freedom, and less privacy for lovemaking. They underestimate the dampening effect of the dailiness of life on sexual ardor: There is nothing very romantic or sexy about getting up in the morning and confronting each other's puffy eyes, disheveled hair, and sour breath. They rarely expect that, like most aspects of marriage, they'll actually have to WORK at sex. *Of all things!*

Unrealistic ideals about in-laws and other extended family members is another factor that waylays couples. It makes no sense to think that just because you get along with your spouse, you'll get along equally well with your spouse's parents, sisters, brothers, and cousins. Surprisingly, even with the abundance of in-law jokes, that is precisely what many people expect. I have had a number of male clients who expected that their wives would become soul mates with their mothers. Even though these men never called or wrote home during college and rarely kept in touch afterward, once married they expected their wives to instantly establish and maintain a relationship with their—the husband's—parents. Some of my male clients have even expected their wives to pal around with their sisters. That would be wonderful if it happened. But to expect it is unrealistic. And what really causes problems is when an expectation like this breeds "either/or" thinking: *Either you like my sister or our marriage is a failure.*

Some couples have an unrealistic expectation about the degree to which they will share each other's interests. Shared interests *are* an important variable in marital satisfaction, but it's not necessary for a husband and wife to share *all* interests. Take football, for example. Based on what I hear in my counseling office, football—or, rather, widely differing levels of interest in watching football on TV—is one of the most divisive issues in American marriages. (Golf runs a close second.)

In our house, my wife is the football fan, not me. I rarely watch football. When our beloved Chicago Bears played in the Super Bowl, I watched about ten minutes of the game. My wife watched the whole game—plus the pre-game coverage, post-game coverage, anything there was to watch. Afterward, anytime anything appeared on television about the Super Bowl victory, she watched it. Or so it seemed to me. I got sick of it. If Janet were as avid a baseball fan as she is a football fan, we would probably have to take up residence in separate states!

Now sailing is a different story. I love to sail. I love to read about sailing, talk about sailing, dream about sailing, you name it. Unfortunately, Janet has no interest in the sport. She's only been out in our boat with me twice. The first time there was no wind. The second time we lost our outboard motor—and came close to losing our boat—in an encounter with some high waves and a sandbar. That was the last time Janet went sailing. But she's still a good sport about the time I spend on it, and I'm *trying* to be a good sport about her interest in football. The point in all this: If we expected to share each other's interests equally, we'd be in trouble.

Perhaps the most unrealistic yet most common expectation people bring to marriage is that their spouse will meet all of their needs. This is especially true when it comes to social needs. People who led boring lives prior to marriage expect to suddenly live exciting lives after marriage. Men and women who couldn't think of anything more interesting to do than to watch TV every night of single life think that their spouse will take responsibility for entertaining them after they're married. But what really happens is this: Two people with boring lives get married, experience the short-lived thrill of living with another person, and then settle into everyday patterns that are just as boring as the ones they had on their own. They can't believe it. They begin to wonder, *Is it possible to be bored with life and be married to the right person? I thought being married would make me happy.* They begin to mentally accuse each other: *What's the matter with you? Something is missing. If you were only more exciting, more interesting, more SOMETHING, my life would be better.* I hear the "something is missing" phrase so often in my office that it's the first phrase I expect to hear from a troubled couple. The other common complaint is, "We've grown apart." I have an almost knee-jerk internal response to these statements: "What's missing is effort and imagination. And you've grown apart because you haven't grown together."

Often, the real problems with these couples is that they have simply merged their boring lives. Their expectation that getting married would cure their boredom was unrealistic.

So all you have to do is make sure your expectations are realistic and everything will be fine, right? Wrong. The expectations that two people bring into a marriage can be entirely reasonable, but different. Sometimes, spouses get into trouble *even though they had discussed their expectations prior to marriage and thought they agreed!*

THE PROBLEM WITH FULFILLED EXPECTATIONS

When I got engaged to Janet, we agreed that we wanted to have a traditional marriage. I would be the main breadwinner and Janet would be the primary nurturer of the four children we hoped to have. I would work outside the home and she would work in the home. We agreed that Janet would work part-time to help with expenses, if necessary, but we both were willing to sacrifice some possessions in order to allow Janet to be available to our children on a full-time or close-to-full-time basis.

As it turned out, our family life unfolded pretty much as we had planned. We got the four children we were hoping for (although a little more rapidly in succession than we had pictured). We both fulfilled the roles we had agreed on. But from time to time, we both felt some disappointment over our assigned responsibilities. There was a period, for example, when I felt insecure about my job, oppressed by financial demands, and worried about my capacity to make money. Although Janet was already working one night a week as a nurse, taking care of our home, and being available to the kids twenty-four hours a day, I started pressuring her to work more.

This was not what she had bargained for. I was not being the person she wanted. So Janet justifiably resisted, reminding me that our children needed her time, that maintaining order in our household was a lot of work, and that I required as much maintenance as the kids. I had to admit she was right. We had agreed on our roles and responsibilities early on, and now I was trying to change the rules.

Janet and I had lived out our expectations, but somehow the *results* weren't what I expected! They never are in marriage, at least not completely. Marriage partners have to be careful about reopening the terms of an original agreement. Sometimes, of course, it's necessary. But our original understanding has a powerful hold on us, and trying to change it unilaterally can be very destructive. Pushing changes that are unacceptable to the other person is unfair.

The bottom line on expectations, both realistic and unrealistic, is this: They tend to lead to "either/or" thinking. *Either my life works out the way I pictured or I'm going to be miserable.* The problem is this: Life never works out exactly the way we expected, no matter who we married. Even when our expectations are met, the results aren't what we pictured. If you can't be happy unless all your expectations are met, you won't be happy in marriage—to anyone. (More about either/or thinking in a later chapter.)

You Don't Make Me Feel Good About Myself Anymore

The degree to which the two people involved make each other feel good about themselves is one of the most important measures of a relationship. Most people choose a marriage partner at least partially on how that person boosts their own self-esteem. Think about it. How could you not love someone who thinks you're good-looking, charming, competent, and smart—and loves your company! Conversely, one of the deadliest consequences of unmet marital expectations is criticism that ravages self-esteem. If the person who once adored you suddenly begins pointing out your weaknesses, not only noticing your little failings and mistakes but also drawing permanent, negative conclusions about you because of them, it's likely your self-esteem will be seriously damaged—demolished, in fact, if the criticism is continuous, because in marriage criticism is interpreted as rejection. Nothing is more hurtful to self-esteem than rejection by someone you love.

Often, a change in the balance of power in a marriage is what erodes the self-esteem of one of the spouses. In marriage, power is often connected to who has more money, looks, popularity, talent, intelligence— sometimes even who controls intimacy within the life of the family. The partner with little or no perceived power often feels inferior and starts struggling with a serious loss of self-esteem. Some people consciously try to change the balance of power in their marriage relationship, but often it happens quite unexpectedly.

Polly and Clay didn't have any significant problems in their twenty-year marriage until Polly made some changes that gave her more power in the relationship. For the first two decades of their marriage, Clay was the wage earner. For Clay, that meant he controlled most of the important decisions in their life together. Polly accepted this situation for years, but as soon as the youngest of their four boys graduated from high school, she went back to school to learn some computer skills. She enrolled with great trepidation but gained tremendous confidence after earning straight A's her first semester. At first, Clay was only mildly disapproving of Polly's new venture. But as she gained self-confidence, his disapproval mounted, especially when she no longer had time to make the lunches he took to work or shop for his clothes or run errands for his business. The last straw for Clay was when Polly took a part-time job. Empowered by her own income, new skills, and a world of work that valued her contribution, Polly was transformed into a confident, independent woman her husband no longer recognized. Suddenly, the balance of power in their marriage changed. Clay didn't like it. He had gotten much of his self-esteem from his role as the breadwinner in the family. He had liked Polly's dependence on him—it had made him feel needed. Polly's job gave her more power in their marriage. And that power made Clay feel as if he had less power.

Ken and Abbey experienced a similar change in their marital balance of power, but over a different issue: weight. Ken, a 5'11" former football player, had nearly doubled his weight during his eleven-year marriage to Abbey. He had been a 180-pound star athlete when they met in college—Abbey felt lucky to have beaten out plenty of female competition for his attentions. But after their marriage, Ken started packing on the pounds. Abbey, who had felt so honored at having been "chosen" by Ken, became less and less concerned about pleasing him. As his weight increased, so did her power. Ken began to act like a little puppy dancing on his hind feet, trying to keep Abbey's attention and approval. Ken's income had grown proportionately with his weight, and Abbey began to spend money lavishly. Meanwhile, she treated her husband with contempt, criticizing him constantly for his ballooning size. Eventually, Ken began to resent his loss of power. Determined to lose weight, he started jogging and became a vegetarian. It took two years, but he finally got back down to 180 pounds, the same size he'd been as a college football star. Because he no longer felt socially inferior to Abbey, Ken wasn't as inclined to yield to her every wish. Abbey, suddenly feeling demoted from her role as a pampered princess, could no longer depend on Ken to bolster her self-esteem with his worshipful devotion. The dramatic change in the balance of power in their marriage eventually sent them into counseling.

These are just two examples of many instances in which a change in the balance of marital power affects the self-esteem of one of the partners. However it happens, the spouse who has lost power starts to feel inferior and almost always succumbs to resentment. He or she may begin to ask, *How can this be the "right person" if I feel so lousy about myself?*

Outside Influences Are Taking a Toll

Often, the seeds of discontent in a marriage come from outside the relationship. It's impossible, for example, to overestimate the influence that modern American culture has on marriages. Both men and women have a tendency to compare their spouses to the cultural ideal and find them wanting. Surrounded by media images of young, beautiful women with smooth skin and lithe bodies, a man comes home to a wife whose face is beginning to show some lines and whose body may be less than perfect. He feels cheated. A woman dreams of a man who is like the hero in a romantic novel—handsome, successful, commanding in his presence—and finds herself married to a husband who by comparison seems like an underachieving wimp.

In a culture that puts an enormous value on career, work issues can have an extremely corrosive effect on marriages. I have to admit that there have been times in my own marriage when I've been so involved in my work that I have neglected my family. I didn't realize it at the time, but in retrospect I see my failings. It was especially true when I was working as associate pastor of a 2,400-member congregation. My pattern was to work in the office in the morning, make calls at the hospital in the afternoon, come home for dinner, and then go out to meetings again in the evening. One day my wife said to me, "Dick, it's so sad how much you're missing." I said, "What do you mean?" Janet replied, "Well, it is such a neat experience to spend time with the kids before they go to bed, to give them their baths, tell them a story, sing a song, say their prayers with them." She wasn't scolding or nagging or badgering me. She was genuinely sad because I was missing an important—and enjoyable—time with our children. I took that in, and as soon as I could alter my schedule a bit, I did. I started taking time to help put the children to bed. I quickly realized my wife was right—it was a wonderful thing to read to them, sing with them, say prayers with them. Pointing that out was a real gift from my wife to me. Among other things, her comment rescued me from workaholism. And workaholism can destroy a marriage, not to mention a family.

The problem with a workaholic is that she or he is so focused on work that there is no time or energy left for personal relationships. A marriage needs time. Marriage partners need to spend time together to understand and support each other as they traverse life's unpredictable terrain—or one or both partners will start resenting the lack of emotional availability and begin closing down emotionally. And when that happens, someone will exit the relationship, either mentally or physically.

The process of closing down emotionally starts with that first stab of disappointment, that first dose of reality. It can be a sudden, overwhelming process, or it can evolve over years of accumulated hurts and small disappointments. But the result is the same: a conviction that you married the wrong person.

If you feel that you married the wrong person, perhaps you've fallen prey to some of the common mistakes and patterns discussed in the last two chapters. Before marriage, you may have engaged in selective sight. Going into marriage, you may have brought with you expectations that are causing problems now, either because they aren't being met or perhaps because they *are*. Once married, you may have allowed yourself to lose sight of all the positive traits you once saw in your spouse, and now you instead see mainly negatives. You may even be viewing your partner's strengths, or what once appeared to be strengths, as weaknesses.

These are all possible reasons for why you've come to see your spouse as such a flawed human being, for why you feel such a deep sense of disappointment in your marriage.

But there's another possible reason, one you might not have considered. That's the subject of the next chapter.

One of the challenges of marriage is distinguishing the difference between realistic and unrealistic expectations. Although having realistic expectations is no guarantee of marital satisfaction, it's an important starting point for creating a marriage that works. Following are some examples of realistic and unrealistic expectations in marriage.

It's realistic to expect that your spouse will (and for your spouse to expect that you will)

- be sexually faithful
- work with you to develop common goals
- respect your values, interests, opinions, and important family/friendship relationships
- try to understand and respond to your emotional needs
- join with you in working out mutually acceptable roles and responsibilities

- prioritize the marriage above his/her family of origin, friends, or immediate personal pleasure
- stand by you in times of change, illness, and crisis
- work at keeping romance alive
- work at identifying and pursuing a set of common interests and commitments
- join with you in working out inevitable disagreements by finding mutually satisfying solutions
- support your growth

It's unrealistic to expect that your spouse will

- meet all your emotional, social, and intellectual needs
- make life interesting for you
- like your family
- have the same degree of interest in sex that you do
- have a consistently intense level of feeling for you throughout the years
- have exactly the same spiritual needs and ways of meeting those needs as you do

EXERCISE

Although we all bring a set of expectations to marriage, we're often not fully aware of what they are. If our unconscious expectations are being met, we tend not to give them much thought—or our spouse much credit. If our unconscious expectations *aren't* being met, we often feel a sense of disappointment without knowing exactly why. To help clarify how the assumptions you brought to your marriage are affecting your relationship with your spouse, list the expectations you now realize you had at the time you were married. Then indicate the degree to which they were fulfilled. When you're done, check those expectations that you think were realistic according to the guidelines discussed in this chapter.

Expectations	Not at all	Somewhat	Mostly	Completely fulfilled
_____	_____	_____	_____	_____
_____	_____	_____	_____	_____

_____   _____   _____   _____
_____   _____   _____   _____
_____   _____   _____   _____
_____   _____   _____   _____
_____   _____   _____   _____
_____   _____   _____   _____
_____   _____   _____   _____

If possible, have your spouse complete this exercise, too, and then share your results. Talk to each other about how the expectations you both brought to your marriage are affecting your relationship today. Reflect on the degree to which either or both of you were aware of your respective expectations at the time you got married. Before starting your discussion, make it a ground rule that neither of you will blame the other for any failed expectations. If your relationship with your spouse is too conflicted to cooperate on this assignment, completing it yourself will still be helpful.

JOURNALING

Continue your journaling as before, but start to look at how expectations—both yours and your partner's—have affected your day-to-day relationship. (If you are keeping a structured journal, record your observations in column 3. Otherwise, just write your thoughts in a free-flowing way.)

- Where are expectations an issue for you?
- Do you think they might be an issue for your spouse?
- Do unfulfilled expectations cause frustrations, disillusionment, and resentment?
- Were these expectations known and expressed when you got married?

As you reflect on what you've written, look at how your early expectations may be affecting your marriage and your view of your spouse today. Think about the degree to which your expectations are/were realistic or unrealistic.

How have changing circumstances affected the degree to which your expectations could be realistically fulfilled?

What fulfilled expectations have you not been aware of BECAUSE they have been met?

What new expectations have evolved over the life of your marriage? How are those new expectations affecting your marriage today?

SPIRITUAL DISCIPLINES

Working through the issues of a painful marriage, struggling to find the truth, is such a difficult process that sometimes it feels as if the wounds will never heal. Acknowledge your woundedness, but open yourself to God's comfort and strength as you continue your journey.

Contemplation

Continue using the hymn, Scripture, and prayers from previous chapters for meditation and reflection. Then reflect on these words from Psalm 25:4–6, NKJV:

"Show me Your ways, O Lord . . . teach me Your paths."

Lord, I have dreams about the way my life should unfold, about the course I should travel. I have a vision for how those around me should respond to my dreams. But only in You is there a path that leads to life, for me and for all the people You have given me as companions for my journey—my spouse, my family, my friends, my neighbors.

"Lead me in Your truth and teach me, for You are the God of my salvation; on You I wait all the day."

It's so easy for my dreams to become illusions, unrealistic expectations of myself and others that I pursue with passion and conviction. Because of my illusions, my companions suffer—most painfully, the partner with whom I am joined. Dispel my illusions, Lord. Only You can rescue me, and those around me, from the untruths and half-truths to which I cling. I wait for Your deliverance.

"Remember, O Lord, Your tender mercies and Your lovingkindnesses, for they have been from of old."

I trust You, Lord. No other power can make me whole. No other love can uphold me as I seek a vision for what is true. Be with me as I work to live that vision for myself and the one to whom I am joined through a covenant made before You.

"Show me Your ways, O Lord; teach me Your paths."

Reflect on some way in which your spouse has failed to meet your expectations. Write it down. Then hold it before you as you contemplate these words from 1 John 4:7–11, NKJV:

"Beloved, let us love one another, for love is of God; and everyone who loves is born of God and knows God."

Picture the failed expectation and the person behind it.

"He who does not love does not know God, for God is love."

Picture the failed expectation again, along with the person behind it. Now, look within yourself. How do you respond to the person who has failed you?

"In this the love of God was manifested toward us, that God has sent His only begotten Son into the world, that we might live through Him."

Picture the failed expectation and the person behind it. Look within. Does God have anything to say to you about how you respond to the person who failed you?

"In this is love, not that we loved God, but that He loved us and sent His Son to be the propitiation for our sins."

Picture the failed expectation and the person behind it. Look within. Who is loved by God? For whom did God's Son die?

"Beloved, if God so loved us, we also ought to love one another."

Picture the failed expectation and the person behind it. Look within yourself. What is God calling you to do?

Prayer

Think of one of your spouse's characteristics that either fulfills or exceeds your expectations. Try to picture this trait through concrete experiences and then include these experiences in a prayer of thanksgiving. Example:

Lord, I'm grateful for the fact that _____ is a sensitive and committed parent. I delight in the way my spouse plays with the children and thank you for what this means for their happiness. Help me to recognize and focus on more of _____'s gifts and strengths. Amen.

Five

Did I Create a Monster?

I was just a kid when the horror film *Frankenstein* was first released. Boris Karlov was a perfect choice for the role of the monster. To us kids, he made Frankenstein even scarier than our school principal, Miss McLain. The fact that Frankenstein was the creation of another human being made him all the more frightening. What if other people got the idea to create a monster? The neighborhood could be crawling with Frankensteins! Think of it. Monsters crashing through our living room doors. Carrying us kids off to fog-enshrouded castles. Dumping us into dark dungeons where we would remain forever. We'd never see our moms and dads again. Never again play baseball or follow the adventures of our favorite radio heroes. It was enough to give us nightmares. Even Miss McLain was better than Frankenstein, the movie monster who seemed very real.

Thinking back, the Frankenstein monster who haunted my childhood dreams was much scarier than the one in the movie. I took the movie character and, in my mind, made him into a creature who was much more predatory, much more malevolent, than even Boris Karlov. And in my nightmares, the monster was always coming after ME!

As a therapist, I see countless people create monsters in their minds and in their marriages. When pain, disillusionment, and disappointment come into their lives, they search for a monster to blame. They fasten on a "monstrous" trait or behavior in someone close to them, label the person accordingly, and then treat them in ways that bring out the worst. The behavior and labels that follow perpetuate the pattern and guarantee that nothing changes.

When you feel like you married the wrong person, you need to face some difficult questions honestly: *Have I created a monster? Have I helped shape the person who now annoys or hurts or disappoints me? Am I blaming the wrong person for the marriage that has come to feel like a claustrophobic dungeon?*

In a stressful marriage, it's easy to become convinced that your partner is the main cause of all your troubles. It's not so easy to see how your own attitudes and behavior have contributed to the situation.

Janis tells the story of how her son MacKenzie once knocked over his milk at the dinner table and immediately declared, "I didn't do it!" Being three, he didn't grasp the fact that the rest of the family had witnessed the accident and knew precisely who it was that had knocked over the milk.

That incident reminds me of a similar episode with my three-year-old grandson, Andrew. One night, Andrew's mother, Debbie, put him to bed (for the third time) with firm instructions not to get up again. But within seconds of settling down in the living room, she and her husband heard suspicious noises coming from the second floor. A quick investigatory trip upstairs revealed that Andrew was indeed up to something. He was scurrying about, transporting from his toy box to his bed an armload of playthings. "Andrew, I told you to stay in bed!" his mother scolded. "But, Mommy, I didn't know I was going to get out of bed again," he protested in a variation on the old "devil-made-me-do-it" routine.

These instances of typical three-year-old behavior aren't all that different from how adults often try to deflect blame when something goes wrong. It's human nature to point a finger at someone else when problems come up.

That's why most of us are quick to fault our spouses when problems develop in our marriages. And like MacKenzie and Andrew, we really believe it's the other person who is at fault. Why? Because it's human nature to deflect blame? Yes, but also because it's so easy to see someone else's flaws—and so difficult to recognize our own.

In this chapter, I want to help you explore how you may be contributing to the problems and disappointments in your marriage. Take a deep breath and don't close this book! I'm not suggesting that you are a bad person. I'm not even surmising that you are the person most at fault in your relationship. But I would like to help you identify ways you may be thinking or behaving that accentuate your spouse's weaknesses or minimize your spouse's strengths. I'd even like you to consider the possibility that you may be the "wrong person" in your marriage!

I have often heard my clients say, "My husband/wife isn't the same person I married." It's probably true. But why is it true? What has changed about your spouse since you got married? One key difference in your spouse's life has been living with you.

People who live together inevitably influence each other, either positively or negatively. Ideally, marriage partners help each other become all God created them to be. Instead, what happens all too often is that one or both partners creates a mental caricature of their spouse, diminishing all the good things about a mate and magnifying all the bad things. Moreover, the more attention (either positive or negative) given a particular trait, the more pronounced it becomes. Bad traits eventually take on huge proportions.

If you think your spouse has become a different person since you got married, it's very possible that all the wonderful traits you saw during your courtship are being suppressed in reaction to your behavior. You may be bringing out the worst in your mate. You may have *turned* your spouse into the wrong person!

Let me illustrate with the story of Ed and Marie. When they first came to me for counseling, I initially thought there was no hope for their marriage. Since I am a strong advocate of keeping marriages together, I rarely start marital counseling with the assumption that a couple should part. But in this case, Marie walked in with a badly bruised eye—and Ed admitted he had hit her.

I have no tolerance for violence. When it enters a marriage, I'm inclined to think the relationship should end—at the least that the couple should separate. But so much is at stake in marriage I believe it's important to find out why the violence is occurring before taking radical action.

In Ed and Marie's case, it was Marie who initiated the physical aggression.

Ed was a businessman who traveled all over the world, gone for weeks and sometimes months at a time. Marie was an artist who worked at home for a small clientele. Because of the flexibility of her situation, Marie could have joined Ed on some of his trips, but he rarely asked her to come along. He said it would be too expensive and that while he was traveling he would be too busy to spend time with her anyway.

Marie was deeply hurt that Ed didn't ask her to travel with him. She was a lonely person who had difficulty making friends. When Ed was gone, she was isolated. She craved the closeness and acceptance she felt she had never had as a child and adolescent. She longed for physical and emotional intimacy. Whenever her husband was away, she dreamed about a romantic reunion, about the two of them spending hours together talking about his travels and her art. But instead of fulfilling Marie's romantic dreams, the first thing Ed did when he came home was to go through the mail and check that he had been paid what he was owed during his absence. Then he would turn on the television. He and Marie would eventually make love, but with little emotional connection. Exhausted from his travels, Ed had little energy for the conversation and romance Marie not only wanted, but demanded.

Marie interpreted Ed's behavior as lack of interest in her. She accused him of being insensitive and even, in a moment of great frustration, of being unfaithful. She started criticizing him from the time he came home from one trip until the time he left for another. Her anger and frustration built up to the point that she started following him around the house, demanding that he communicate with her. "Talk to me, talk to me!" she would shriek. But the more she badgered Ed, the more he withdrew. Unable to get a response, Marie got physical. She pushed, pulled, punched, and slapped at her husband, alternating verbal insults with tearful demands that he talk to her or make love to her.

One morning, Marie followed Ed into the bathroom as he was getting ready to shower and threw a shoe at him. In the process of dodging the shoe, he slipped and fell. As he was getting up, Marie hit him again. Pushed to the limit, Ed swung back—and gave her a black eye. That was the incident that brought them to my office.

Although their behavior had gotten so out of hand that I initially saw little hope in their relationship, what became clear as I counseled this couple was this: While their situation had grown extreme, these two people were much like many other couples who come to me for counseling. As is so often the case in marriage, they wanted to be loving and close, but they were bringing out the worst in each other.

Marie didn't understand that Ed needed her just as much as she needed him. His capacity for intimacy was no less than hers, but she didn't know how to bring it out in him. She didn't understand that when Ed came home from a trip, he was physically and emotionally drained. That even though he loved her, he didn't feel like talking immediately. That he needed reentry time. By badgering her husband, Marie was actually forcing him into the behavior she most resented.

For his part, Ed didn't understand how his behavior was triggering Marie's memories of past rejections. He couldn't fathom why she might feel jealous of the women he worked with or rejected by his lack of interest in conversation. He was completely confused by her demands for closeness and communication. In his confusion, he withdrew even more— causing Marie to become even more demanding and hysterical.

Fortunately, I was able to make some suggestions that turned this marriage around. I urged Marie to give Ed some decompression time when he came home from a trip. I suggested that she let him go through his routine of sorting the mail and watching TV when he got home, but to sit down with him—without demanding any conversation—while he was doing it. To hold his hand and simply be physically close. And then wait.

I asked Ed to call Marie at least twice a week during his trips. When he protested that it would be too expensive—most of his trips were overseas—I pointed out that phoning home would cost a lot less than long-term therapy or the fees of a divorce attorney.

As Marie learned to coax the responses she wanted from Ed instead of demanding them, and as Ed learned to be more intentional about communicating with Marie, their marriage not only survived but grew into a strong and loving relationship.

Your situation may not be as extreme as Ed and Marie's, but it's possible that you are actually causing or accentuating the behavior you most dislike in your spouse, just as they were doing. With that possibility in mind, consider some of the attitudes and behaviors that got Marie and Ed in trouble—and ask yourself if any of them apply to you.

Mind reading

Marie mentally added up a list of Ed's offenses—long trips, few phone calls, few letters, more attention to mail and TV than to her—and came up with an interpretation that fit her preconceptions: Ed obviously didn't miss her at all when he was gone, had no craving for her sexually or emotionally, and must be having an affair with another woman. She assumed she knew *why* he was acting the way he did—the hallmark of "mind reading."

Ed was also guilty of mind reading. He assumed Marie's behavior was proof she didn't care about the pressures he faced. He concluded that she didn't respect or support him in his efforts to be a good provider.

Emotional reasoning

Emotional reasoning—interpreting events and behavior according to one's feelings—was another factor in the near-disintegration of Ed and Marie's marriage. Like many lonely, isolated people, Marie craved intimacy and feared rejection. Then, when Ed's behavior triggered feelings of rejection, she assumed she was being rejected.

Ed did the same thing. The only child of a successful pediatrician, he had always felt like a failure because of his parents' obvious disappointment in his lack of interest in medicine. Ed's feelings of failure ran deep, despite his significant achievements in the business world and despite the fact that his income was higher than his father's. So it isn't surprising that his reaction to Marie's dissatisfaction with him was to assume she felt he was a failure—a failure in business because he traveled too much and a failure in their marriage because Marie wasn't happy. Because of his emotional reasoning, he couldn't hear or accept the messages Marie tried to give him early in their marriage, long before her frustration led to violent behavior.

Demands

Even before the violence started, Marie pushed her issues and complaints aggressively. She didn't *request* that Ed make changes, she insisted.

She gave no reasons for her demands, no clues that Ed's behavior was hurting her. She never even asked him why he acted the way he did. She just demanded that he change.

The problem with demands? They rarely work. Most people resent and resist them. Ed certainly did. Making demands rarely produces the desired result, yet many married people resort to demands and ultimatums when their frustration has built up to an intolerable level. The only prevention is discussing issues and problems before negative feelings get out of hand.

Myopia

To some degree, myopia, or shortsightedness, is part of the human condition. We all have trouble seeing beyond our own issues and concerns. Realistically, there's no way we can *fully* understand another person's point of view, even if it is articulated clearly and openly. But we can *attempt* to understand. Unfortunately, Marie and Ed didn't make that attempt. Marie never even considered that there might be more than one way to interpret Ed's behavior. And Ed never gave a thought to how his pattern of withdrawal was affecting his wife. They were trapped by their myopia.

Nagging

Chronic faultfinding is so common in marriage it has become the stuff of endless jokes, the nagging wife a cliché. Like making demands, nagging is a behavior that gets repeated and escalated—despite the fact that it never works. In Marie and Ed's case, Marie just wouldn't let her husband alone. She harped on everything he was doing wrong and everything he wasn't doing at all. But no matter how long or how loud she complained, Ed didn't hear her message. He withdrew to shut out the chatter. That's what usually happens: Either the nagger doesn't make the message clear, or the "naggee" isn't listening. In either case, the naggee eventually shuts out the message. At that point, the nagger becomes more desperate and escalates the harping. That's what happened with Ed and Marie. When Ed stopped listening, Marie just increased her verbal onslaught.

Tuning out

The opposite of listening is tuning out. Ed tuned out Marie's verbal pleas, while Marie tuned out Ed's nonverbal pleas. Even though the walls of their home reverberated with Marie's high-pitched shrieks, Marie couldn't get through to her husband. His mind was porous as a brick. When Marie lashed out at him in my office, he would turn white, his face like that of a pale, nervous little "see no evil, hear no evil" monkey with its hands flattened against its ears. What she didn't realize was that Ed had to tune out her clamorous demands. They were too painful and confusing for him to listen to. He was completely disarmed by the fact that he had never been spoken to in this way. He knew of only one way to respond: tune out. Marie was equally impervious to hearing any messages communicated in her husband's behavior. Their marriage could have been wholly different if Ed had tried to listen to what Marie was trying to say, and if Marie had tried to understand what was behind's Ed's withdrawal.

Verbal abuse

Verbal abuse tends to occur when an insecure person feels powerless and angry at the same time. When Marie got angry, she made liberal use of verbal put-downs. She was good at them! Knowing where Ed was vulnerable, she picked just what insults to hurl at him to lacerate his self-esteem. Ed wasn't a verbal person, so he was powerless against Marie's attacks. Instead of responding, he limped away to lick his wounded ego. And of course his withdrawal only further infuriated Marie.

Withdrawal

Withdrawal is a retreat from conflict. Ed thought his withdrawal was a good way to avoid pain. While it may have minimized his pain in the short run, it inflicted more hurt on Marie—and eventually on him. Instead of defusing her anger, Ed's withdrawal fanned the flames of Marie's frustration. It fueled her feelings of rejection and added data to her suspicion that he was eventually going to abandon her. Withdrawal is dangerous in marriage. It signals disrespect, causes confusion, and heightens negative feelings. What's more, it invites attack.

For some people, withdrawal is a way of fighting. When they know that their withdrawal hurts their spouse, they use it to deliberately inflict pain. That wasn't the case with Ed, but the hurt he inflicted on Marie was still very real.

Disconnecting

Ed was a master at intentionally turning off his feelings. He learned that when he disconnected by withdrawing and shutting down emotionally, Marie's attacks didn't hurt as much. But he was also shutting himself off from Marie's feelings. What Ed didn't understand was that each of us has to make ourselves vulnerable to being hurt in order to comprehend the hurt of another person. When we disconnect from a marriage partner, we create despair in that person—who may react by either giving up on the relationship or by venting explosive rage.

Physical abuse

When Marie realized she would never get through to Ed with words—even her angry, abusive words—she resorted to physical attacks. That's a common scenario. When verbal attacks fail to achieve their purpose, which they rarely do, the next step is often violence. Fortunately, most couples don't reach the physical abuse stage, although verbal abuse is a serious warning sign. But when any form of violence enters a marriage, it's critical to get outside help and to establish some distance. If physical abuse becomes a pattern, it probably means the marriage needs to be ended—or at least that the marriage partners need to separate (see chapter 12 for more about what to do about an abusive situation).

There is absolutely no excuse for physical violence in marriage, even though it sometimes frightens couples enough that they finally seek outside help. That's what happened with Ed and Marie. But they would have been far better off if they could have avoided the degree of distrust and alienation caused by Marie's angry assaults. Their reconciliation and recovery was much harder than it would have been if they had sought help before their marriage reached the stage of physical attacks.

Disprioritizing

All right, this isn't really a word, but it seems to describe what happens when people make their marriages anything less than a high priority. For a marriage to be successful, it has to be a top priority for both partners. In practice, that means a couple needs to spend as much time thinking about and planning how to nurture their relationship as they do on anything else—including child-rearing, work, and individual hobbies or recreation. It means that each partner lets the other know that he or she is more important than anything or anyone else in the world—in their lives. Ed was guilty of "disprioritizing" his wife. In his defense, the nature of his work made it hard for him to be intentional about nurturing his relationship with Marie, but he could have taken steps to assure her that he would rather lose his job than lose their marriage. For example, he could have taken her on a business trip occasionally. It would have been expensive, but not nearly so costly—in both money and human despair—as a shattered marriage.

Distancing

Distancing is a continual pattern of withdrawal and disconnecting. In extreme forms of distancing, one or both partners organize life in such a way that they rarely have to interact with each other, thereby avoiding confronting any painful issues. There is no touching, no personal talk. Over time, Ed's pattern of withdrawing from Marie turned into perpetual distancing. He deliberately avoided spending time with his wife out of fear that she would make demands on him. Of course, the more he distanced himself, the more demands she made.

Defensiveness

When the negative interactions in a marriage begin to overshadow the positive ones, one or both partners become defensive. Gun-shy, they anticipate that any innocent comment will spark a hostile, caustic, or critical response. Ed's usual reaction to Marie's criticism was withdrawal. When on a few occasions he did respond to her, it was defensively. He made excuses for his behavior. He refused to take responsibility for the way his actions made her feel. He discounted what she told him about her emotional needs. Ed and Marie became verbal boxing partners—one an expert at jabbing, the other an expert at blocking. Almost inevitably, their verbal sparring turned physical. Both forms of abuse, physical and verbal, hurt.

Think about these behavior patterns, patterns that almost destroyed Ed and Marie's marriage by bringing out the worst in both of them:

- Mind reading
- Emotional reasoning

- Demands
- Myopia
- Nagging
- Tuning out
- Verbal abuse
- Withdrawal
- Disconnecting
- Physical abuse
- Disprioritizing
- Distancing
- Defensiveness

Do some of these patterns describe you?

Of course, the negative patterns in Ed and Marie's marriage are examples of only a few of the ways people create monsters in their marriages. To test whether you may be turning your spouse into a Frankenstein of your own creation, consider the following questions:

Is your negative thinking obscuring your spouse's positive qualities?

One way you may be functioning as the "wrong person" in your marriage is by allowing your negative thoughts about your spouse to blind you to his or her positive characteristics. *Your spouse undoubtedly has real weaknesses.* Everyone has faults, some of them major.

In successful marriages, however, the partners have learned to accept each other's flaws (see chapter 12 for more on this) and support each other's strengths.

If Tony had known that, he might have been able to save his marriage.

By the time Tony and his wife, Mary, came to me for counseling, Tony was so hurt and angry that he could no longer see a single good quality in Mary.

Mary was, frankly, a spoiled brat. The apple of her father's eye, she had always gotten everything she ever wanted. When she graduated from high school, her dad gave her a car. When she graduated from college, he gave her an even nicer car. Although her parents weren't wealthy, she always had the best clothes, the most advantages.

After Mary and Tony got married, she expected the pattern of her childhood to continue. Accustomed to being indulged by her father, she indulged herself. She ate at fancy restaurants, bought designer clothes, went on expensive vacations, and lavished her friends with gifts.

Although both Mary and Tony worked, neither of them made a lot of money, so Mary financed her extravagant lifestyle with credit cards. When she got behind financially, her father would bail her out—just as he always had—and she would start spending again. The pattern came to an abrupt halt, however, when Mary came to her father for help after accumulating nearly $60,000 in credit card debt. By this time he was retired and under financial pressure himself. There was no way he could come up with an extra $60,000. For the first time in Mary's life, she had to face up to the consequences of her self-centeredness.

Without the cushion of her father's money, Mary and Tony had to file for bankruptcy. Tony felt angry and humiliated, even more than he had felt during all the years Mary's father came to her rescue when he could not. But it wasn't until two years after the bankruptcy that the marriage really exploded. Tony discovered that Mary had once again built up a significant debt, borrowing from friends and relatives without his knowledge. Now they were beginning to ask for their money back. Tony found out what was going on when friends started declining their social invitations because they were so upset that Mary hadn't paid anything toward what she owed, despite numerous promises.

Tony blew up. Years of stress and embarrassment over Mary's behavior had taken their toll. He demanded she change her ways immediately or he would leave.

Mary was deeply shaken. She knew her marriage and her friendships were in jeopardy and, for the first time, she truly made an effort to change. But by this time, Tony had completely closed down emotionally. No matter how hard Mary tried, he refused to acknowledge her efforts. He had become so negative in his view of her that all he could do was criticize. He had lost his ability to see any positive characteristics in his wife. This was sad, because despite her financial profligacy, Mary had many wonderful traits. She was warm, outgoing, and generous—generous to a fault. In fact, her generosity was a big factor in her money problems. She gave to other people without thinking of whether she could afford it. When she went out to lunch with a friend, for example, she insisted on picking up the tab. She enjoyed giving people gifts as much as she enjoyed indulging herself.

Mary was also generous with her affection. She was extremely nurturing with both Tony and their children, and supportive of him emotionally. Except for her out-of-control spending, Tony couldn't have asked for a better wife.

But by the time Tony and Mary came to me for counseling, Tony couldn't focus on anything but Mary's faults. Despite the obvious progress she was making and the fact that he had contributed to her excesses by ignoring them for so many years, Tony became increasingly derogatory toward Mary, distant from her emotionally, and at times verbally abusive in front of their children.

If Tony had been willing to do some work in counseling, he might have been able to recognize the role that he had played in supporting Mary's irresponsibility. He might have learned to acknowledge her many genuinely wonderful qualities, instead of dwelling on her weaknesses. He might have learned to support her efforts at change, instead of finding fault with her at every turn. But his hurt and anger had festered for too long. Despite all my efforts to foster reconciliation, he finally left Mary. She was devastated, as were their children. But Tony just couldn't turn back.

Tony and Mary's story is an example of how dangerous it is to allow yourself to focus exclusively on your spouse's faults. If you have come to a point in your marriage where you can only see your partner's negative qualities, it's time to take action! Brooding on your spouse's weaknesses will inevitably lead to alienation. And once alienation reaches a point where one or the other of you closes down emotionally, you will find it terribly hard to reconnect.

Are you too critical?

Criticism is dangerous in marriage. Only physical violence seems to produce as much stress in a relationship.

Criticism undermines self-esteem and distorts behavior. It often creates the monster it is intended to slay. When you disparage your spouse, he or she is likely to respond with hurt, anger, defensiveness—and, frequently, more of the kind of behavior you criticized.

Sally was a big woman who had always struggled with her weight. She had been self-conscious about her size ever since high school, when she had desperately wished she could be transformed into a petite, adorable cheerleader. She carried around painful memories of teenage boys telling her she'd make a good center on the football team. The fact that this was a gross exaggeration didn't matter. She felt like an Amazon woman.

Sally's husband, David, didn't expect her to look like the emaciated models that appear in fashion magazines, but he strongly preferred the way she looked at her "best" weight. Unfortunately, he was totally inept in the way he expressed his preference. He'd make remarks like, "You know, I think you need to get a larger size skirt." Or he would make a point of talking about other women who were "looking especially good lately." Some of these women had dimensions Sally could never achieve. David undoubtedly hoped his remarks would motivate Sally to lose weight. What they did was make her feel unattractive, unaccepted—and resentful. Although she talked constantly about needing to lose twenty pounds, she did nothing about it. In the meantime, their marriage suffered.

Sally reacted the way most people react when they are criticized—she tried to neutralize the impact of the criticism by attacking the source. Because she felt demeaned by David, she demeaned him back. She lashed out at him where he and many other men feel most vulnerable—in his provider role. She hinted as much about the shortcomings of his salary as he did her excess weight. It didn't take long for them to find themselves engaged in full-scale warfare.

Criticism is poison in marriage, especially when it's of the "let's hit him when he's down" (or "hit her when she's down") variety. Wally and Ginger are an unfortunate example.

Wally was totally disgusted by his wife's sudden inability to carry out her usual household and child care responsibilities. Ginger had always been a well-organized, competent person, but over a period of a few months she had turned into what Wally called "a wreck." She felt worthless, helpless, and hopeless. She cried frequently and was so paralyzed by fatigue that she couldn't force herself out of bed in the morning—all classic signs of clinical depression. But Wally didn't care what was causing Ginger's behavior, he just wanted her to get her act together. So he hammered her with criticism: What kind of mother couldn't get herself out of bed to get the kids ready for school? Why couldn't she pull together a decent lunch for their seven-year-old? Why was she ordering in fast food four times a week instead of cooking regular meals? Why couldn't she keep the house in any semblance of order anymore?

Wally, a consultant who traveled much of the time, finally resorted to hiring a housekeeper to take over many of the tasks Ginger no longer seemed capable of handling. They could easily afford the woman's salary, but Wally bitterly resented having to pay it. It was the principle of the thing. Ginger should be holding up "her end of the marriage." Not a single failing escaped his attention—and withering critique.

Ginger desperately wanted to be her old self again, but she had no control over her condition, the result of a recent illness and a long series of traumas. Wally's lack of understanding and constant criticism only made things worse.

The heavy load of Wally's criticism, added on top of the depression, was so great that Ginger eventually attempted suicide and had to be hospitalized. Only then was Wally able to see how harmful and unfair his carping had been. Ginger eventually recovered from her depression, but her memories of Wally's criticism at a time when she was most vulnerable made the recovery of their marriage a much longer and more arduous process.

Although Wally and Ginger's story is extreme, it points to an obvious conclusion: constant criticism can shatter self-esteem and destroy a marriage.

Have you become too defensive?

Remember how Ed and Marie brought out the worst in each other with their defensiveness? Defensiveness is epidemic in marriage. It is one of the main ways husbands and wives function as the "wrong person" in their relationship with their spouse.

When I am tired or don't feel good about myself, I get defensive. I don't want to see, hear, feel, or smell anything that suggests I'm as awful a person as I think I am at that particular moment. At times like these, the person I'm most defensive with is my wife. She's the person I love the most and consequently the one human being who can hurt me the most.

I want to look good in her eyes. So when I'm not looking good in my own eyes, I'm highly sensitized to words or even subtle glances that remotely suggest criticism. There are days when the least little criticism or suspicion of criticism jars me into defense mode.

Occasional defensiveness because you're having a bad day is understandable. But when defensiveness becomes a habit, your usual response in interactions with your spouse, you need to consider how your behavior affects your spouse. It's possible that some of the negative traits you see in your partner are actually caused by your defensiveness.

The primary message of defensiveness is "I'm innocent!" There are several problems here. As Shakespeare knew ("Methinks she doth protest too much"), insisting on your own innocence often is taken as proof of guilt. Or interpreted as an attack. A husband, for example, may reason like this: If my wife protests that *she* is innocent, she must be implying that *I* am guilty. Then too, defensive words tends to infuriate spouses who hear in them the message, "I'm accepting no blame, no matter what the facts are!"

All too often, what you intend as a defense, your spouse interprets as launching your forces "over the top," like the trench warfare of World War I. Naturally, your partner hunkers down, too, drawing on his or her own arsenal of defensive tactics and tools. What happens next is like an old war movie. Everyone is crouched out of the line of fire, occasionally peering over the top of the trench to watch for anything suggesting trouble. Every once in a while, a combatant tosses a grenade in hopes of catching the other side off guard, then ducks down to wait. The two sides never see each other.

Sometimes defensiveness in marriage is more like a discouraging barrier than an attack. When one partner feels the other is putting up an impenetrable barricade against any new information, frustration sets in. After all, if no new light can enter the scene, if no new insights can be gained, what hope is there for change?

Meredith was shocked when her normally calm and caring husband, Dick, started having what she described as "tantrums" about how to spend their Sunday afternoons. Dick wanted to make Sunday afternoons a time for family outings to the zoo, the aquarium, parks, the local swimming pool, and so forth. But Meredith wouldn't hear of it—she needed that time for her extensive church committee work. "Can't you take a few hours a week away from your volunteer work so we can build a life together with the children?" Dick pleaded. Before he could get out two more words, Meredith launched into her knee-jerk response—a litany of the church's needs that only she could meet. Besides, she said, Dick knew how much importance she placed on her church work when he married her. In Meredith's mind, the matter was already settled. She was not accepting any new information. She had put up her defenses against any possible change.

Meredith's defensiveness changed her husband, Dick, from a calm and caring husband into an angry and frustrated one. That's what defensiveness does in a marriage—preventing positive change, it causes undesirable change.

Have you stopped listening?

If you are seriously questioning whether you married the right person, you may be so overwhelmed by negative feelings that you are no longer able to listen to your spouse. Or perhaps the start of your marriage wasn't built on a pattern of careful listening. Either way, you may not be hearing the issues your partner is struggling with—and not realizing how those issues are affecting your spouse's behavior.

That's what happened to Kim and Todd, whose marriage was in serious trouble when they came to me for counseling. It's amazing that they even bothered to come in, because Todd in particular was ready to call it quits. His alienation—and Kim's confusion and hurt—began after the birth of their first child. They both agreed that Kim should continue her career, but when she went back to work after her maternity leave, she wanted to spend as much time as possible with the baby during her off hours. Kim and the baby developed a close relationship, and Todd felt like an outsider looking in. They both felt stressed by the demands of work and parenting.

Their stress multiplied when Kim gave birth to a second child and Todd changed jobs. His new position was extremely demanding, and he felt he deserved some appreciation and support from Kim. But she had no energy left over for him. She was totally drained by her own career and by taking care of the children. On the few occasions when she sensed Todd's desire for nurturing from her, she resented it. After all, he was no baby. And who was going to nurture her?

Todd became increasingly distant, alienated by Kim's lack of attention. He began lashing out at her over small incidents. Kim, frightened by his withering outbursts, retreated from him even more.

My task in working with Todd and Kim was to get them to start listening to each other. At a time when they most needed each other, they had stopped listening—and consequently stopped supporting each other.

Todd needed to listen and understand that for Kim the stresses of work, of being a mother, and of being attacked by her husband were more than she could bear. Kim needed to understand that Todd felt left out when she devoted her attention to the children. She needed to understand that he felt heavy pressure to make good in life because, even though Kim worked, he was the primary wage earner in the family. When Kim and Todd started listening to each other again, they made a huge breakthrough in their marriage.

If your spouse is starting to look like the wrong person, perhaps you've stopped listening. It may be that you've become emotionally deaf—you aren't picking up the messages your partner is trying to send you about the stresses in his or her life. Your spouse's behavior may be desperately shouting to you, but you can't hear.

Are you too needy?

I counsel with people all the time who want more time and loving attention from their partner. Because their spouse isn't "meeting their needs," they conclude they must have married the wrong person. I gently try to point out another possible conclusion: Their needs—or perceived needs—are so great that they couldn't possibly be met by anybody.

It's quite common for one spouse to be more emotionally needy than the other. Sometimes the "needier" spouse has realistic expectations and sometimes not.

How can you tell if you're too needy? Here are some warning signs. You're too needy if:

- You think you and your spouse should do everything together.
- You can't tolerate your spouse having separate interests.
- You have rigid and specific measures of whether or not your spouse is

meeting your needs (e.g., "If my spouse really loves me, he'll bring me flowers every week").

- You get upset when your spouse has to be away from you.
- You live in constant fear of losing your spouse's love.
- You are distressed when your partner has different opinions than you, feeling that different views automatically create distance between you.
- You worry about what you may have done wrong whenever your partner is in a bad mood.

Are you expecting your spouse to be a mind reader?

We humans have a tendency to go to extremes. For example, in marriage, we are often either overly critical—overly communicative—or totally *non*communicative about our needs and expectations.

While constant criticism is toxic to marriage, so is lack of communication. If you haven't talked to your spouse about the issues that concern you in your marriage, you shouldn't be surprised if nothing changes. Your partner isn't a mind reader. And as pointed out earlier in the chapter, spouses who attempt to mind read by assuming they know what their partner is thinking usually cause big problems in the marriage.

Often, troublesome issues in marriage don't get raised because one spouse—perhaps both—are afraid of conflict. It may be that you have good reason to fear conflict, because your spouse has overreacted to issues you've raised in the past. If that's the case, you need to reflect on how you typically approach your spouse with tough issues. Are you hostile and blaming? Do you go on the attack? If so, no wonder your spouse reacts with anger and defensiveness! Try raising the issues again, this time in a loving, nonconfrontational way. But be prepared for the possibility that your partner will react with hostility anyway. If you are deeply troubled by your spouse's behavior, it's better to voice your concerns and risk disturbing the peace than to let your negative feelings smolder. Silent, unrelieved resentment will destroy your marriage faster than temporary conflict.

If there is a Frankenstein in your marriage, it may be one of your own creation. While your spouse undoubtedly has some negative characteristics, it's possible that you have accentuated those traits into a grotesque caricature of a marital monster. You may have even developed some monsterlike qualities of your own. Like Ed and Marie, you may be guilty of mind reading, emotional reasoning, unreasonable demands, myopia, chronic faultfinding, tuning out, verbal abuse, withdrawal, disconnecting, disprioritizing, distancing, defensiveness, and perhaps even physical attacks. Your negative thinking may be obscuring your spouse's positive qualities. You may have become so defensive that you and your partner have become like combatants lobbing grenades from deeply dug trenches. Maybe you're too needy, or you've stopped listening, or you're expecting your partner to be a mind reader.

If any of these patterns sounds familiar, ask yourself this question: *Have I become a "wrong person" in my marriage?*

EXERCISES

Fill out the chart below to help you be more objective about your reactions and assess how they are helping or hurting your marriage. In Column 1, list some things that discourage you about your spouse or your marriage. In Column 2, describe how you react to these sources of discouragement. In Column 3, rate how effective your reactions are on a scale of 1 to 10 (1 being very hurtful to the marriage and 10 being very helpful to the marriage). In Column 4, next to ratings of 5 or less, list some better ways of reacting to the things that discourage you in your marriage.

Sources of dis-couragement	Your reaction	Rate your reaction	Better ways to react
_____	_____	_____	_____
_____	_____	_____	_____
_____	_____	_____	_____
_____	_____	_____	_____

JOURNALING

Continue your journaling as before. Review the list of patterns that are likely to bring out the worst in your spouse (see below) and make notes in the third column of your structured journal about any incidents in which these patterns have played a role.

- Try to honestly assess if you have a tendency to fall into any of these patterns. For each pattern that applies, think of a specific incident involving your spouse.
- For each incident, describe how your spouse reacted. Did your behavior bring out negative traits in him/her—or didn't it seem to matter?
- How might you have behaved differently. If you had, how might your spouse have behaved differently?

Patterns

Mind reading	Withdrawal
Emotional reasoning	Disconnecting
Demands	Physical abuse
Myopia	Disprioritizing
Nagging	Distancing
Tuning out	Defensiveness
Verbal abuse	

SPIRITUAL DISCIPLINES

Contemplation

Find a time and place where you can be silent and pray the words of Psalm 139. Ask God to help you see any ways you have contributed to the deterioration of your marriage. Reflect on the fact that the root problem in your marriage is the root problem of humankind: it is easier to be alienated than reconciled.

O Lord, you have searched me and you know me.
You know when I sit and when I rise;
   you perceive my thoughts from afar.
You discern my going out and my lying down;
   you are familiar with all my ways.
Before a word is on my tongue you know it completely, O Lord.
You hem me in—behind and before;
   you have laid your hand upon me.
Such knowledge is too wonderful for me,

>   too lofty for me to attain.
> Where can I go from your Spirit?
>   Where can I flee from your presence?
> If I go up to the heavens, you are there;
>   if I make my bed in the depths, you are there.
> If I rise on the wings of the dawn,
>   if I settle on the far side of the sea,
> even there your hand will guide me,
>   your right hand will hold me fast.
> If I say, "Surely the darkness will hide me
>   and the light become night around me,"
> even the darkness will not be dark to you;
>   the night will shine like the day,
>   for the darkness is as light to you.
> Search me, O God, and know my heart;
>   test me and know my anxious thoughts.
> See if there is any offensive way in me,
>   and lead me in the way everlasting.
>
>   Psalm 139:1–12, 23–24

Prayer

Lord, as you search me and know my thoughts, help ME to know my thoughts. So often I feel like I'm on "automatic pilot." I'm oblivious to the impact of the things I say or do. You know me better than I know myself. I need your strength and wisdom as I try to gain better control of myself and the way I live my marriage. It is awesome, yet comforting, to know how well You know me. Show me the ways in which I have contributed to alienation in my marriage. Give me the courage to admit to my failings and do something about them. Make me mindful of your presence in all my interactions with _____. Don't let me forget that Your hand is holding me. I treasure knowing that You will be my strength and my deliverer. Amen.

Six

Why Stay Married to the Wrong Person?

I hope that previous chapters have given you a better understanding of what you may be facing in your marriage—and some optimism that what has gone wrong can be fixed. But it's possible that the questions raised so far have made you even more pessimistic about your relationship to your spouse:

Why did I choose my spouse?

Because I didn't know any better.

Why does my spouse feel like the wrong person?

Because he or she IS the wrong person.

Am I a wrong person in my marriage?

Yes, of course. The fact that we don't get along proves that we're each the wrong one for each other, so why not cut our losses?

What did I expect?

A whole lot more than I got.

You're unhappy. When you get right down to it, does it matter *why* you chose your spouse? If you feel cheated and disappointed in your marriage, what difference does it make which one of you is the "wrong person?" What difference does it make what you expected going into marriage?

If you've tried and tried to get close to your spouse again, but nothing works, why keep frustrating yourself? Why not just reconcile yourself to a disappointing marriage and look to other areas of your life for satisfaction? Or why not just claim God's forgiveness for your wrong choices and get out of the marriage while you still have time to find someone else? Why bother to stay in such a difficult relationship when there may be someone out there for you who is a true soul mate?

Even Jesus acknowledged that some marriages are irretrievably broken. How can you know whether yours is one of them? Why—and when—should you stay married to the "wrong person?" And if you do stay in your difficult marriage, is there really any alternative to gutting it out? Are you doomed to marital martyrdom? The answers to these questions grow out of more questions.

Is there really "one right person" for you?

I've never had anyone come into my office asking whether there was One Right Person he or she was destined to marry—and perhaps missed. It may be that this question is more theological than psychological, or that people just phrase the question in a thousand different ways. Whether rooted in a concept that God has a perfect (and specific) plan for every detail of our lives or in a highly idealized view of romantic love, it's such a common, troubling question that *Marriage Partnership* magazine asked Janis to write an article on the subject. The following is adapted from a portion of her original article, which was also the source of the title and concept for this book.

I am married to a man who claims to believe in the "One Right Person" theory—that God specifically chose me for him and him for me. He doesn't have a tightly crafted theological framework for this belief. Circumstances (and probably his romantic nature) have just convinced him that we were meant to be together. For example, he likes to tell the story of our first date, when in his view I tried to "blow him out of the water as a dating candidate."

"I'll never forget it," he always says. "We were turning the corner onto Lincoln Avenue and Janis leans back against the door of my car, folds her arms and says, 'So, what do you think about libertarian theory?'

"Now, it just so happens," he chuckles, folding his arms behind his head, "that I took two courses on libertarian theory in college. . . ."

Was Paul's decision to study a minor political movement for a whole year in college part of a complicated divine blueprint? Was my brief flirtation with libertarianism as a young adult part of God's plan? Did God ordain that I should marry Paul and only Paul? Does God have one right person in mind for any of us to marry?

This last question is important not only because it affects how we go about looking for a mate, but also how we view our commitment once we're married.

THE SEARCH FOR THE "RIGHT ONE"

Most people of faith believe that God offers guidance for decisions—at least for ones as important as whom to marry. While Christians disagree on whether God has a specific will for each person down to the most minute details, most agree that He speaks to His children through broad principles in Scripture, through conscience, and often through an inner conviction of the heart. The problem is that the part about the "inner conviction of the heart" leaves a lot of room for interpretation—and misinterpretation.

One well-known author whose advice is often sought by young people says he frequently counsels singles who are, in his words, "obsessed with finding The Right One." One time, for example, he got a letter from a young woman who had seen a tennis star on TV and prayed that the Lord would confirm her impression that this athlete was the man for her by showing her a Nevada license plate. Lo and behold, several Nevada license plates appeared. She called this guidance. He calls it immaturity.

A friend of mine looks at the issue from the other side of the guidance equation. During her sophomore year in college, two young men announced to her separately that God had told him it was His will for her to marry him. Strangely, God hadn't said a thing to her about it. Or been too clear with either of them.

My brother Scott contends that God certainly has a will about whom we should marry, but speculates there may be more than one person who fits His will.

"If my wife asks me what I want for dinner," Scott says, "she's asking me my will. Usually there's a category of things that fit my will and a category of things that don't—a lot of things I'd like and a lot of things I wouldn't like. But that doesn't rule out the possibility that on a specific evening I might say, 'I really feel like having meat loaf.'

"I suspect that God's will is the same way. In a lot of instances there may be a kind of person He wants you to marry, but more than one person could fit the category. That doesn't rule out the possibility that for some individuals He could have a specific person picked out."

The danger in the search for The Right One—or in reflecting on whether you've married The Right One—is falling into the needle-in-a-haystack mentality. If your concept of God's will for marriage causes you to think it's possible to blink and miss the right person—you've probably got a wrong view. If your concept of God's will leads you to believe that because you're in a disappointing marriage, you must have married the wrong person—you may need to reconsider your concept.

When problems crop up in marriage, it's tempting to think, "Boy, if I'd only married someone else." But, as we've pointed out in earlier chapters, blaming your spouse for everything that's wrong in your relationship ignores how many problems are intrinsic to marriage and how many are intrinsic to you. And dwelling on the question of whether or not you married the right person ignores God's stake in the choice you already made.

Author Tim Stafford says a lot of people come to him for marriage counseling feeling they made a mistake. They tried to make a good choice, but now feel they didn't. It seems unfair to them that God would hold them to a wrong choice for the rest of their lives. Shouldn't they just cut their losses and move on? The answer to that question, says Stafford, lies in an understanding of the God who values covenants. "The whole Christian understanding of the marriage vow is that it's not just a human choice, but a choice that God takes a stake in and validates," he says.

"But," protests my friend Karen, "we're dealing with human frailties. This is not a perfect world where everybody plays by God's rules. Reality falls short of that." Karen had been married for seven years when her husband told her he wanted a divorce. "I very much believed in forever marriage and was very disappointed when my husband wasn't willing to stick with it," she says. "If he had been more willing to try and resolve our problems, I'd still be in the marriage."

Even so, Karen says, in situations like hers, "Maybe it's better to back away from a relationship you can't seem to make viable than to stay in it and keep beating yourself up."

Peter, a self-described "wrong person," thinks that's a cop-out. "Ellen and I are a risky combination," he says about his marriage to a woman whose strong will matches his own, "but even though we're the wrong people for each other on a human level, we have a pretty strong marriage.

"The most common thing I hear from my divorced friends is, 'I loved her when we got married, but I'm a different person now. I have to deal with the new person I've become.' I think that's baloney. I'm a different person than when I married Ellen, but I if I had just concluded that I married the wrong person, I probably would have opted out of our marriage. I could have chosen to either be with Ellen and change myself, or opt out and go look elsewhere. By sticking with it, I'm a better person now and I'm grateful."

Did God choose One Right Person for you to marry? The answer to that question probably can't be resolved any more definitively than the age-old theological question of predestination versus free will. In any case, here's the important point: *Once you're married,* the way you answer the question really shouldn't affect the choices you make. Jesus made God's intention clear: a husband and wife should stay together throughout their lives. Even when we marry someone who in retrospect seems like a wrong person, God can redeem our unwise choice. Peter and Ellen's stormy but strong marriage is powerful evidence.

Sadly, there are some marriages that are for all practical purposes irredeemable. In most of the unfixable marriages I have observed, though, the main problem was not so much that the partners had made a bad

choice—but that one or both of them didn't want to do the work of redeeming the relationship.

People of faith know that God is more ready to forgive us than we are
to forgive ourselves. This is a liberating truth. But it can be dangerous
when misunderstood. It's liberating to know we can make mistakes without losing God's love. But it's dangerous when we take God's love lightly.
The "enlightened" view of our times, even in some communities of faith,
is that you don't need to worry about your choices because God will
quickly and easily absolve you of all responsibility.

It's true that God's forgiveness is always available. But the consequences of our choices remain even after we've been forgiven.

Difficult marriage—or difficult stage of life?

It's important to consider whether your spouse, who seems like the
wrong person for you now, might seem more like the right person at a
later stage in your life. Most of us have differing needs and perspectives
at different times in our lives. Research is showing, for example, that marriages are most vulnerable when couples have small children, precisely the
time when they need to be the most strong. A little over half of married
couples report that their marital satisfaction diminished when their children arrived. Only 20 percent report that their marriage satisfaction improved after having children, while about 30 percent indicated their marriage remained the same. There are many reasons for the temporary dip
in satisfaction—including conflicts over role expectations, money, work,
social life—but the point is that each stage of life has different stresses and
satisfactions. So it's wise to consider whether your uncertainty about your
choice of a mate relates more to your stage of life than it does to your
partner. Remember, your responsibilities and opportunities will change as
your life together unfolds.

Are you sure you understand the consequences of your choices?

I can't begin to count the number of divorced people who have told
me that if they had known the consequences of their decision to leave a
troubled marriage, they would have tried a lot harder to save their relationship.

The effects of divorce are much more traumatic than is widely recognized, although researchers are beginning to document these effects, especially on children. Evidence is mounting to suggest that the impact of divorce on children is lifelong. As a therapist who often works with the children of divorce, these findings are not at all surprising to me. I see the crushing effects of divorce every day in my office.

I'll never forget the little sixth grader who sat in my office weeping for the full hour of her scheduled session, saying over and over again, "I thought families were forever." Her pain in response to her parents' announcement that they were getting divorced was so deep that I couldn't allow her to leave within the usual allotted time. When she had cried as much as she could, she finally left, limp with exhaustion, laden with grief that I know will have permanent effects.

I'll also never forget the story of Matthew, a kindergartner whose parents were going through an acrimonious divorce. They fought bitterly, and little Matthew witnessed many of their hate-filled battles. Even worse, both parents put him in the middle, competing for his loyalty and affection. They used him as a source of solace, individually pouring out their woes to the bewildered little boy. He became the parent, comforting and consoling two people he loved but who didn't love each other.

While his parents were confiding their troubles to him, Matthew had no one to whom he could confide his troubles. His teacher reported that Matthew had difficulty making friends. He was too rough, intrusive, and uncooperative. Most of his classmates avoided him. When he finally found one boy who seemed to like him, he clung to him, followed him around, and made impossible demands for exclusive friendship. Eventually, even this boy began to avoid him too. Matthew's desperate loneliness and fear became scripted into everything he did.

One morning Matthew's teacher looked around to see where he was. She had to keep him under close scrutiny because he often distracted the other children from their work. But this day he had disappeared. Panicked, she asked the rest of the children to help her find him. They looked everywhere. No Matthew. She was about to call his mother and the police to report that Matthew had run away from school, when one of the children discovered him. He was lying in a closet in a fetal position, rocking back and forth, moaning and muttering to himself, "I can't take it any-more. I can't take it anymore."

When Matthew's parents' marriage ended, his world ended with it. The center of his universe, his most precious relationships, were perma-nently altered. *The same is true for all children whose parents divorce.*

The love you have for your children is mediated in part by your re-lationship to your spouse. If you cease to love your mate, it takes away from the love you share with your child. It diminishes the amount of love in your child's life. When you attack your spouse with angry words, those words ricochet off your partner and injure your child. Children feel the pain felt by the parents they love.

Every relationship in a child's life—with mother, father, sisters and brothers, grandparents, aunts and uncles, cousins, friends—is affected by a divorce. Every developmental task in a child's life is made harder by divorce. Children of divorced or divorcing parents often take an academic nose-dive in school, because they've been drained of the resources they need to tackle difficult assignments. Research shows that children of di-vorce tend to be more erratic in their learning, more moody, more ag-gressive, less cooperative, more frequently in conflict with or wholly with-drawn from their peers.

Children of divorce often lose their ability to form close relationships. When the most important people in your life prove they can't be trusted to maintain your world, you learn that no one can be trusted. When you can't trust, you find it difficult to make friends. If you find it difficult to make friends, you have trouble developing the relationships that lead to marriage and family.

It's almost impossible to overestimate the degree to which divorce is harmful to children—for life. But what almost everyone underestimates is the effect of divorce on the adults involved. From the vantage point of a therapist, I see the process of divorce as a state of temporary insanity. Previously reasonable and caring people turn into demonlike caricatures of themselves. Having their world blown apart has the same effect on their personalities, their spirits, as fire has on skin and bones. And the scars can be just as deep and ugly. I see the bearers of those scars in my office every day.

One of the many painful consequences of divorce is the burden of having to start all over again. Most people have a vision of life that includes finding a person with whom to share a loving relationship, one that leads to a lasting marriage. But it takes time to find an acceptable candidate, especially one as interested as you are and willing to make a commitment. And once you find a candidate, it takes time to test whether that person is really someone with whom you want to spend your whole life. If you have children, you have to consider whether the new person in your life is acceptable to them—no small matter.

The older you are, the more unreal it feels to be back on this course. And the whole process is shadowed by the fact that second marriages have less chance of success than first marriages. About 60 percent of second marriages fail. For all these reasons, starting over can feel like a burden instead of a release.

Another harmful effect of divorce on adults is what it does to memories. Memories are important because they are reminders of the occasions and celebrations that tell you your life has been worth living—that your relationships have been worth forming, that your work has been worth doing. Your memories remind you of challenges you've met, victories you've achieved, and crises you've survived. Your memories tell you that you can accomplish things you never thought possible. The confidence you get from your memories fuels the energy and courage you need to take new risks at every new stage in life. Humans are only able to keep going in life when they can build on a history of worthwhile endeavors.

Divorce poisons memories and strips identities. When the memories that used to energize you, give you a sense of meaning in life, and fill you with good feelings about yourself suddenly overwhelm you with a sense of failure and rejection and guilt, the past becomes something to forget. Pictures and memorabilia that recall the past may need to be put away. Robbed of your memories, you may ask yourself, "Who am I without my past?"

Divorce also brings with it ongoing doubt and guilt.

Consider Beth. She left her husband Larry because he worked such long hours that they had precious little time together. When they did get time together, he was good to her. But those occasions were few and far between. Beth wanted a husband who was a friend, a confidant, a companion. Larry didn't fill the bill in any of those categories. Since he seemed to have so little interest in her company, Beth assumed he had no interest in her. She never told Larry how she felt because she figured he wouldn't listen. Instead, she left. What Beth never imagined was the impact the collapse of their marriage would have on her husband. He was devastated. He stopped working, so his business failed. He remained unemployed for three years.

Beth hadn't understood the reason Larry worked so hard. He wanted to make a good life for her, and to buy a home so they could have children. His work was his way of showing love. Without her, his work didn't matter anymore.

Could Larry have learned more sensitive ways of showing his love? Would he have scaled back on his work if Beth had opened up to him about her feelings? She'll never know. But thoughts of what might have been—and the knowledge of the pain she caused in Larry's life—continue to plague her. Guilt has become her constant companion.

Loneliness is another frequent derivative of divorce. Most people who divorce encounter serious loneliness on the other end. Having tasted closeness to another human being, they become painfully aware that it is gone. Even people who leave marriage for another person suffer from unexpected loneliness. Often, for a variety of reasons, they never end up marrying their new flame. Even if they do, they find loneliness in interrupted relationships with their children. At the times when they most need to feel close to their kids, they always seem to be at the other parent's house for "visitation."

Speaking of visitation—what an irony that a word people once used to associate with funerals and death is now used to describe post-divorce relationships between parents and children. The new meaning of visitation is still attached to death. It is the death of somebody's world.

The combined weight of poisoned memories, guilt, and loneliness often leads to depression. Depression is a modern plague easily spread by divorce. Divorce causes depression in everyone involved—children, partners, even extended family members. The parents of divorcing couples, for example, are often deeply depressed by the unchosen loss of relationships divorce brings to them. They are suddenly distanced from a son-in-law or daughter-in-law they may have come to love. They are distanced from other in-laws with whom they may have developed friendships. They are frequently distanced from their grandchildren. They are deeply troubled by the pain they see in their children and children's children.

There are similar effects throughout a family system. Brothers, sisters, cousins, nieces and nephews—the relationships between these extended family members are all affected by the loss of a whole chunk of the family.

Divorce isn't good for children. It isn't good for the adults involved. It isn't good for the extended families of the adults involved. And it isn't good for communities. Every divorce contributes to the fragmentation of the surrounding community. A ten-year study published under the title *The Search for Community* showed that children cared for by the community—with the cooperation of families, schools, and social service agencies—do far better than children whose community has broken down and have only professional social service agencies to depend upon. Children whose primary caregiver is a social service agency tend to live in communities where there is a high rate of family breakdown through divorce or high rates of birth to unwed mothers.

Intact families are the building blocks of society. Neighborhoods are built on intact families. Adults and children are more secure, productive, and happy when they are part of intact families.

Why go through so much pain and effort to redeem your marriage to someone who feels like the wrong person?

Because God has a stake in your relationship, even if you made an unwise choice of a mate. He values covenant relationships so much that He sent His Son to die for human beings who spurned relationship with Him.

And it's worth it to do the work of trying to redeem your marriage because the consequences of not trying are so serious: for you, for your spouse, for your children, for the culture as a whole.

At the beginning of this book, I asked you to temporarily suspend your sense of hopelessness and open yourself to viewing your spouse, yourself, and your marriage in a new light. Given what's at stake, I hope you will continue to put your doubts on hold and make a promise to yourself that you'll do some "transformation work"—described in upcoming pages—that may not feel very comfortable, at least not at first. The next few chapters will move away from diagnosing the problems that exist in your marriage and start showing you how to do something about them. So hang on a little longer.

EXERCISES

The long view

Life tends to unfold in stages. Marriages go through definite seasons. More often than not those seasons correspond to broader life stages. Sometimes it's easier to deal with frustration and disillusionment in marriage when you have a clearer picture of each time of life and what it is likely to mean for your relationship with your spouse. This exercise is designed to help you take the "long view" of your marriage. The following chart lists some stages through which the typical marriage passes. Also listed are some aspects of life that tend to change as a marriage unfolds. As you look at each stage of marriage, reflect on its impact on the various aspects of life. Does this long view give you any hope that your marriage will improve as you enter another season of life? For example, is it possible that some of the stresses in your relationship will be alleviated after your children leave home? Or are they likely to get worse? What do your answers imply about what you need to do in response to painful patterns in your marriage?

Stage One: Newlyweds/new marriage

career	family
sex	extended family
friends	shared values
shared interests	spirituality
health	money
parenting	home
community	travel
church	companionship
mutual support	intellectual pursuits
creative pursuits	

Stage Two: Children arrive

career	family
sex	extended family
friends	shared values
shared interests	spirituality
health	money
parenting	home
community	travel
church	companionship
mutual support	intellectual pursuits
creative pursuits	

Stage Three: Children in school

career	family
sex	extended family
friends	shared values
shared interests	spirituality
health	money
parenting	home
community	travel
church	companionship
mutual support	intellectual pursuits
creative pursuits	

Stage Four: Adolescents at home

career	family
sex	extended family
friends	shared values
shared interests	spirituality
health	money
parenting	home
community	travel
church	companionship
mutual support	intellectual pursuits
creative pursuits	

Stage Five: Children in college

career	family
sex	extended family
friends	shared values
shared interests	spirituality
health	money
parenting	home
community	travel
church	companionship
mutual support	intellectual pursuits
creative pursuits	

Stage Six: Children married

career	family
sex	extended family
friends	shared values
shared interests	spirituality
health	money
parenting	home
community	travel
church	companionship
mutual support	intellectual pursuits
creative pursuits	

Stage Seven: Retirement/grandchildren

career	family
sex	extended family
friends	shared values
shared interests	spirituality
health	money
parenting	home
community	travel
church	companionship
mutual support	intellectual pursuits
creative pursuits	

Why stay married to the wrong person?

Following is a list of some divorce-related issues discussed in this chapter. On a scale of 1 to 5, rate the degree of concern you have about each issue in terms of the impact of a divorce. (1 = No concern. 5 = Serious concern.)

Low   High

1 2 3 4 5   Starting over
1 2 3 4 5   Children
1 2 3 4 5   Memories/traditions
1 2 3 4 5   Doubt
1 2 3 4 5   Guilt
1 2 3 4 5   Loneliness
1 2 3 4 5   Family
1 2 3 4 5   Friends
1 2 3 4 5   Stage in life
1 2 3 4 5   Relationship to God
1 2 3 4 5   Other _____

JOURNALING

Continue with your structured journaling. Write a "best case scenario" and "worst case scenario" for each of the issues you identified as being of high concern to you (4's and 5's) in the previous exercise. Which scenarios are most realistic?

SPIRITUAL DISCIPLINES

Contemplation

Take time to reflect on Psalm 27:4, 5, 13, and 14:

One thing I ask of the Lord, this is what I seek: that I may dwell in the house of the Lord all the days of my life, to gaze upon the beauty of the Lord and to seek him in his temple.

In this difficult journey, where so much is at stake, keep me fixed on what is most important. Turn my desires to You and the beauty and wisdom You are offering me in the midst of this time of my life. Help me receive what You are teaching and become what You are shaping.

For in the day of trouble he will keep me safe in his dwelling; he will hide me in the shelter of his tabernacle and set me high upon a rock.

"My courage so easily fails me. My struggle exhausts me. So frequently, I feel alone, unloved. Help me know that You envelop me with Your protecting presence."

I am still confident of this: I will see the goodness of the Lord in the land of the living.

"Strengthen my belief that You hold my future in Your hands—that there is a life of peace and growth in that future, even though I can't envision it right now."

Wait for the Lord; be strong and take heart and wait for the Lord.

Meditation

Envision the worst case scenario you wrote about earlier. Picture Christ being present with you and those you care about. What do you feel about His presence? What would you say to Him? Write those words in your journal as a prayer. End your prayer with these words: "Into Your hands."

Read 1 Corinthians 13. Then try to honestly evaluate yourself in light of this passage and the characteristics it describes. Select three of the traits you would most like to integrate better into your life and list at least one way you could exhibit each of these three traits to your spouse in the next week. If you are working on these exercises with your spouse, affirm him/her for the ways in which he/she displays some of these characteristics. Only mention the positive traits that you see in your spouse. Don't berate him or her for any failings.

How do I express this trait in my marriage?

- Patient (tolerant of frailties, imperfections, and shortcomings of spouse)
- Kind (tender, thoughtful toward spouse)
- Not jealous (of genuine friendships with others or of the special gifts and talents of spouse)
- Not boastful (about personal appearance or achievements in an attempt to compete with spouse)

- Not arrogant (not disdainful of spouse's looks or achievements; don't belittle spouse)
- Not rude (not inconsiderate of spouse's needs or feelings)
- Not insistent on own way (willing to compromise, to consider spouse's needs and interests)
- Not irritable (don't snap at spouse; approachable)
- Not resentful (don't hold grudges; forgiving)
- Don't rejoice in wrong (don't delight in spouse's misfortunes; don't keep score or tally perceived wrongs)
- Rejoices in right (truthful; don't try to conceal things from spouse)
- Bears all things (supports spouse in times of struggle)
- Believes all things (don't challenge words of spouse)
- Hopes all things (don't wallow in pessimism about the marriage; keep a positive attitude)
- Endures all things (don't give in to pressures of life; willing to stand by a spouse who is having personal struggles)

Seven

What You Think Is What You Get

E arlier in this book, I suggested that the journey of marriage in many ways resembles a spiritual journey. The object of a spiritual journey is to develop a closer relationship with God. One of the objectives of marriage is that the partners develop a closer bond to each other.

In marriage, as in a spiritual journey, developing a close relationship involves a certain amount of mental transformation. The apostle Paul knew that. That's why he instructed a group of Christians in Rome to ". . . be transformed by the renewing of your mind" (Romans 12:1). We modern-day believers have to transform our minds, too. Why? Because, in order to have a loving relationship with God, we have to think in ways that don't come naturally to us. Thinking about ourselves and our wants comes naturally. Thinking about God, His characteristics, and His desires does not.

Even in marriage most of us find it easier to think about ourselves—our own wants, needs, and feelings—than to think about our spouse's wants, needs, and feelings. That fact alone causes problems. But in addition, we often bring unhealthy thinking *habits* into marriage, habits that influence how we interpret everything that happens in relationship to our partner. In this chapter, I invite you to examine your thinking habits and the way they are affecting your marriage.

We humans are constantly evaluating, judging, labeling, and inter-preting. We think about ourselves and about other people. We speculate about what people think of us. We interpret the significance of events around us. We make projections about the future. But the way we think about ourselves, behavior, events, and other people often differs signifi-cantly from the way other people think about them.

A few summers ago, as I was attempting to launch my sailboat, I re-alized too late that I had somehow steered the boat's trailer onto the wrong access route to the ramp. The mast hit a tree, the head stay snapped and the mast fell on top of the boat. It then bounced onto the trunk of my car, back onto the boat again, and came to rest half on the road and half on the boat. There was only minimal damage to my car, but the boat couldn't be sailed without major repairs. I wasn't happy—with the event, the consequences, or myself.

My boat accident was a fact. But there were several different ways I could have interpreted the significance of the incident. Depending on my habitual ways of thinking, I might have said, "This is a catastrophe. My summer is going to be a disaster because I won't be able to sail. I've had other bad experiences with this boat. The evidence is clear—with my luck, something like this is probably going to happen next summer, so I'll be unhappy again. I should probably just sell the boat and be done with it."

If that had been the way I chose to interpret the boat incident, I would have allowed it to make me miserable, make the people around me mis-erable (it's no fun to be around someone who pouts), and shape the fu-ture.

I could have even allowed this incident to affect my view of myself. One of the thoughts that went through my mind after examining the dam-age to my boat was, *What a stupid thing to do.* Stupid indeed. If I had been concentrating, the incident never would have happened. But consider where my thoughts could have taken me if I had chosen to make judg-ments about myself based on the day's events:

"This was a stupid thing to do."

"I am stupid."

"I'm too incompetent to rig and sail a boat."

"I can never do anything right."

"There's no use in trying."

"I'll never do anything again where there's a possibility of an accident."

There were some onlookers who witnessed the boat incident that day. No one likes to feel stupid. No one likes to feel stupid in front of others. But depending on my thinking habits, I might have drawn some weighty, ongoing conclusions about what they were thinking:

"Only a complete fool could do what he just did."

"He looks like the type who would do a dumb thing like that."

"He's liable to wreck someone else's boat."

"We don't want an idiot like him keeping a boat at this marina."

The boat incident is an example of how an ingrained thought pattern can affect someone's view of reality. As unpleasant as it was, the accident didn't have to undermine my view of myself, my relationships with other people, or my outlook on the future. But it easily could have.

In the same way, our thoughts can make us miserable in marriage. All too often, we allow ourselves to draw permanent negative conclusions about ourselves, our partners, and our relationships based on a single incident or trait. In fact, the main cause of unhappiness in marriage isn't a spouse's thoughtless, cruel, or unacceptable behavior—but how the other partner interprets behavior.

I'm not saying that thoughtless, cruel, and unacceptable behavior doesn't exist in marriage—of course it does—or that it is something we should quietly accept. (You'll remember that throughout this book I have mentioned talking troubles through *in a noncombative way* with your spouse.) Sometimes marriages are destroyed because of such behavior. But don't miss the point: Many, many more marriages are needlessly reduced to misery because of unhealthy thinking habits on the part of one or both partners.

Many psychologists and psychiatrists have studied the ways we think ourselves into unhappiness. They have developed a high degree of consensus on the faulty thought patterns that create mental distress and wrenched marriages. Here are some of these patterns:

- Either/or thinking
- Overgeneralization
- Filtering out the positive

- Dismissing the positive
- Mind reading
- Negative expectations
- Exaggeration
- Emotional reasoning
- Shoulds/musts
- Labeling
- Personalizing

I've already talked about three of these patterns—mind reading, emotional reasoning, and either/or thinking—in earlier chapters. In the following pages, I'll elaborate on how these and the other patterns can damage your relationship and cause you to conclude you married the wrong person.

Either/or thinking

Chapter 4 pointed out that the expectations we bring to marriage often lead to an either/or thinking pattern: *Either my life works out the way I pictured or I'm going to be miserable.* The same is true of expectations on a smaller scale.

My wife and I enjoy ballroom dancing. Sometimes, one of us (usually me) will forget an important step and squash the other person's toes. We might even stumble over each other and, in my interpretation, look pitifully foolish in front of the other dancers and onlookers. When that happens, I am sometimes tempted to fall into an either/or thought pattern: *Either we dance well or the evening is a disaster.* My wife, on the other hand, tends to think it's fun to dance whether or not we're dancing at our best.

Here's how our thought patterns might look:

Me:
"I can't believe we missed that step."
"That hurt, and besides it was extremely embarrassing. People must think we're idiots."
"We've had three lessons now and we're getting nowhere."
"Tonight is a disaster."

My wife:
"We made some mistakes. Not as many you think we did."
"I had fun. Relax."

Like other negative thinking patterns, either/or thinking can be applied to trivial matters like dancing or to important issues. In either case, it can make life miserable, especially in marriage.

Fran and Jake had been married for thirty-five years. He was a successful businessman who had started out selling industrial tools out of his basement. She was a homemaker. They had three beautiful and talented daughters and all the accoutrements of an affluent lifestyle: a breathtaking house in a prestigious neighborhood, a fancy car, frequent vacations.

While the outward circumstances of Fran and Jake's life were enviable, their family life was not. Fran was thoroughly unhappy with both her husband and her daughters. At any given time, she wasn't speaking to one of them, sometimes to all three.

The cause of Fran's unhappiness was classic either/or thinking. If her daughters phoned her once rather than twice a week, in her eyes they hadn't called her at all. Either they were loyal and devoted or they weren't. Two phone calls equaled loyal and devoted. One phone call equaled disloyal and rejecting.

She carried the same pattern into her relationship with Jake. Fran wanted him to cut off all ties with his parents because of his mother's habit of expressing negative opinions about what Fran and Jake did. Jake offered to see less of his mother. He suggested that Fran stay home when he and the girls attended family gatherings. But there was no compromise. For Fran, either her husband broke off his relationship with his mother or he was being disloyal to her.

The same pattern of either/or thinking shows up in the husband who insists that if his wife really loves him, she'll lose twenty-five pounds. Either she loses the weight or she admits that she doesn't really care about him.

It shows up in the wife who demands that her husband earn as much as her college friends' husbands. Either he provides a level of comfort that she thinks she deserves or he proves that his marriage is unimportant to him.

It shows up in the spouse who measures love on the basis of the frequency of sex. Either the less aggressive partner agrees to sex a certain number of times a week or there's no love in the marriage.

Either/or thinking creates unbearable tension in a relationship. It creeps into every facet of marriage, making unrealistic demands that cause frustration, anger, and alienation. The more extreme it is, the more dangerous it is.

Overgeneralization

People who overgeneralize tend to think that if one thing is wrong, everything is wrong. Take Peter, for example. He would get furious with his wife, Shannon, because of her inability or unwillingness to balance their checkbook. Based on this one factor, he declared her to be incapable of handling money. Since she was clearly, in his view, financially inept, he would have to take charge of every aspect of their household economy. In fact, he wasn't going to trust her to handle any money at all. He wasn't even sure she could be trusted to make decisions about their children, because she clearly didn't care about their financial future. The fact that Shannon had one flaw meant that everything about her was flawed. Peter was *overgeneralizing*.

Filtering out the positive

After years of conflict, Anna and Nick finally broke down and went for marriage counseling. Anna was the one who was most unhappy in the relationship. She complained that Nick was too busy to give their marriage any attention. There was no romance between them. They had sex, but it was always on Nick's terms, to meet Nick's needs. In the process of counseling, Nick began to see the validity of some of Anna's complaints. He began to make some changes—for him, big changes. He phoned his wife from time to time while he was at work. He would put his arm around her or give her a kiss at unexpected times. He began to be more tender and romantic during sexual intimacy. But when Nick cited these specifics during a marriage counseling session, Anna claimed she hadn't even noticed. She was so fixated on Nick's old, negative patterns that she couldn't even recognize his attempts at change. Positives didn't register because she had filtered them out.

Dismissing the positive

Some spouses have an even more active way of filtering out positives. Instead of simply not recognizing positive traits in a spouse, people who engage in this thinking pattern acknowledge their partner's good points, but insist they don't count.

Mark was a historian who achieved prominence in his field at an early age. Extraordinarily talented in writing and research, he was held in high esteem by his students, colleagues, and professional peers. But he got no respect at home.

Carla, Mark's wife, had grown up with a carpenter father and two brothers who eventually became electricians. She assumed that all "real men" were like the men in her family—that they instinctively knew how to troubleshoot small appliances and do little repairs around the house. But when she and Mark bought a "fixer-upper" house, it soon became evident that Mark didn't even notice what projects needed to be done, much less know how to do them. When Carla called his attention to a particular task, he quickly forgot. His mind was on history—his work and his love.

This was extremely frustrating to Carla, who accused her husband of living in the past. Mark's greatest gifts—reading, writing, and teaching about the past—became a reminder to Carla of all the things her husband failed to do in the present. On the rare occasions when Mark would try to tackle a home repair or improvement project, it usually ended in failure—like the time he tried to install an electrical outlet and almost burned the house down. Carla never let him forget about it, or any of the other episodes that proved to her that he was an inept excuse for a man. She dismissed Mark's achievements as a historian, his kindness as a husband, and his genuine attempts to learn how to do more projects around the house. Carla rejected these as insignificant in the face of his failure to be a "real man."

This pattern of dismissing (often even disdaining) any positive traits is one I see all the time in my counseling practice. Del is a prime example. After thirteen years of marriage and three children, he suddenly announced to his wife, Meg, that he wanted a separation. A shocked and confused Meg dragged him into my office, where he wasted no time beating around the bush. "I want out because our sex life is no good and never has been," he said bluntly. I decided to hold that issue for a while and asked Del to recall what it was that attracted him to Meg in the first place. When I asked Meg the same question, she responded with a long list of Del's good points. Del couldn't think of anything except Meg's appearance. I tried to help him out a little bit. What about Meg's intelligence, spiritual values, commitment to home and family? Del greeted each suggested strength with a "Yes, but . . ."

"Yes, she does take good care of me and the kids, but she makes no effort to make me proud of her looks. I need a woman who looks good. She looked great when we first got married. I can't figure out what happened."

"Yes, she's smart, but she's too demanding. I don't know why she can't be satisfied just staying home and watching TV on weekends. She keeps pushing for a 'night out.' What's the big deal?"

I've heard this pattern of disqualifying the positive from people who've been married six months and those who've been married twenty-five or more years. They become so focused on the perceived negatives in their spouse that they exhaust themselves with frustration. They use up all their energy marshaling arguments for why their partner's flaws outweigh all the strengths.

Negative expectations

When you have negative expectations, you try to convict your spouse before she or he commits a crime. Consider this exchange:

"I'm getting a baby-sitter."

"For what?"

"I have to go to church for a committee meeting."

"Why get a baby-sitter? I'm going to be home."

"You won't put Tommy to bed on time."

"What do you mean, I won't put Tommy to bed on time?"

"You never get him to bed on time."

"Are you kidding?"

"No, last time you stayed with him, he didn't get to bed until after 9:30."

The wife in this vignette insists that since her husband failed once in getting their son to bed on time, he will fail again. She has developed negative expectations based on one incident. When negative expectations become a pattern, the spouse with the expectations becomes chronically angry and the object of the expectations chronically frustrated and discouraged.

Ben and Sue fought the battle of negative expectations for eighteen years before they finally came for counseling. Their problems actually started before they married. When Sue met Ben, she had been dating Rick for several years. Sue wanted to marry Rick, but he wasn't ready for a commitment. So she started going out with Ben. But it took a year before Sue was able to break things off completely with Rick. Ben was extremely frustrated. He felt like he never knew where he stood with Sue. Eventually Sue and Ben got married, but Ben continued to feel vulnerable and off-balance. He assumed Sue still had romantic feelings about Rick. Despite her attempts to reassure him of her commitment, he assumed she really wanted to be married to Rick. His negative expectations caused him so much anger and frustration that he became verbally abusive. By the time they came for counseling, they were on the verge of divorce.

Exaggeration

This common thought pattern is an extension of "filtering out the positive." If you are guilty of exaggeration, you overemphasize the importance of your spouse's faults and minimize his or her strong points.

Richard nearly ruined his marriage to Brenda by magnifying her faults and minimizing her strengths. Richard was like Felix Unger in *The Odd Couple*, always fussing about cleanliness and propriety. Brenda was no slob, but it didn't take much to be more casual about their environment than her husband. Hard-working and energetic, she expended more of her energies on her work and community activities than she did on housekeeping. Her co-workers and fellow community volunteers widely admired her for her many accomplishments, but at home she received only criticism. Richard harped constantly about Brenda's "messiness." She wanted to please him. In fact, she desperately wanted to please him, but he couldn't be pleased. As far as Richard was concerned, Brenda's domestic shortcomings were the central issue in their marriage. Despite the accolades she got from others, Brenda was devastated by her husband's constant disapproval. Her self-esteem plummeted, and she developed an anxiety disorder so severe that she had to take medication to control it. Fortunately, her anxiety also drove her into counseling, where she and Richard eventually confronted their problems. One of the biggest was Richard's pattern of magnifying Brenda's failings and minimizing her many strengths.

Emotional reasoning

Remember Marie and Ed from chapter 5? Marie's basic assumption was, "If I feel it, it must be true." She felt Ed didn't care about her, so it must be a fact. Like Marie, people who engage in emotional reasoning often draw negative conclusions about their spouse and assume those conclusions reflect the way things really are.

Linda assumed that her husband, Gary, didn't like her appearance. Despite being an attractive woman, she was quite self-conscious about her looks. She had never gotten over her insecurities about being a tall and somewhat heavy teenager. Early in their marriage, Linda asked Gary's opinion about everything she wore. If he didn't express great enthusiasm about her outfit, she felt he was finding fault with her clothing and her looks. When he was enthusiastic, she accused him of giving compliments just to make her feel good. Eventually, he stopped bothering to compliment her—the ultimate proof to Linda that he was lying all along.

Shoulds/Musts

Although "should statements"—as in "you should do this" or "you should not do that"—have gotten a bad reputation among therapists, people of faith know there are some legitimate shoulds in life. However, it is the *unexamined* shoulds and should nots, musts and must nots, that create havoc in marriage. When you apply these words to yourself, you tend to feel guilty. When you apply them to your spouse without testing their fairness or appropriateness, you tend to feel angry. In either case, they can cause problems.

James and Nell came for counseling because they had decided to get a divorce but wanted to minimize the impact on their children. When I suggested they reconsider and try to work on reconstructing their relationship, Nell said she was willing to try for the sake of their children, but she honestly couldn't muster any hope for their marriage. She was fed up with living a life ruled by James' *shoulds.*

James came from a wealthy aristocratic family. Nell came from a middle-class, blue-collar family. His father was a physician who had inherited family money. Her father was a machinist. James' family enjoyed all the symbols of their upper-class culture: an elegant home, expensive cars, fine linens, silver, opera, ballet. Nell's family enjoyed a happy family life in a three-bedroom, immaculately clean bungalow.

After marrying Nell, James refused to accept any money from his family. But he also refused to give up the lifestyle he was used to. He insisted on joining the country club, driving a Mercedes, and living in a large house in a prestigious community—none of which they could afford on his engineer's salary.

Nell put up with these excesses because she knew that if their cash flow problems got really bad, James could always draw on the trust fund his grandparents had set up for him. Her problem was with all the things she was expected to do to live by James' shoulds: They should attend the opera and the symphony because that's what aristocratic people do. They should buy pricey clothes at expensive stores. They should send their children to a private school. Should eat certain foods. Should drink certain beverages. Their entire lifestyle was dictated by a tradition that had been established by several generations of James' family. None of these traditions was necessarily wrong, but Nell began to feel that her preferences didn't matter, that her husband's shoulds were an implicit statement of her family's inferiority.

The tyranny of shoulds can show up in a variety of ways in marriage. A husband might assume that his wife should know what his emotional needs are without his telling her. If he's tired, discouraged, or angry about something at work, she should figure out what's going on and do something about it. A wife might assume that her husband should know she wants him to help out around the house, show a greater interest in the children, or be more responsive to her needs. Often, we don't even know for sure what our needs are, but still feel our spouse should know.

The problem with shoulds and musts is that life never delivers on all of them. People and circumstances are too unpredictable.

Labeling

Another common thought pattern in marriage is labeling—focusing on one of your spouse's behavioral patterns and branding your partner with a negative tag because of it. If your husband doesn't confront his boss about injustices at work, he's a "wimp." If your wife forgets to hang up her clothes, she's a "slob."

Anthony was the youngest man ever to receive a Ph.D. in physics at his university. He was chosen from an international pool of several hundred outstanding candidates for a coveted position on the faculty at Cambridge University. In short, Anthony was brilliant. But he was also remarkably forgetful and easily disoriented. If his wife wanted him to pick some things up from the store, she had to write him a note and give him a list, even if all she needed was a gallon of milk. What's more, she had to write down explicit directions for getting there. Anthony was notorious for getting lost.

It would have been tempting for Anthony's wife to label him as the "absentminded professor," a laughable buffoon worthy of derision. Instead, she chose to view his forgetfulness as part of his charm. Instead of focusing on his absentmindedness, she valued him for his impressive mind and delightful sense of humor.

Unfortunately, Kathryn wasn't able to take the same view of her husband, Brian. Annoyed by his habit of leaving tools and equipment lying around the basement or garage or wherever he happened to be using them, she labeled him a "scatterbrain." In applying that label, she was essentially saying that he couldn't be trusted to do anything right because of his "spaciness." But Brian was an outstanding civil engineer and involved community leader. Taken to extremes, Kathryn's label could undercut his other achievements and relationships. Why would Brian's clients want to hire a "scatterbrained" civil engineer? Why would his children seek his advice, or look to him as a mentor, if their mother convinced them that their dad was a scatterbrain? And why would Brian want to have a close relationship with a woman who labeled him this way?

Pinning a permanent negative label to your spouse on the basis of one incident or even a series of events is not only unfair, it's destructive. It creates negative expectations and locks in negative roles.

Personalizing

Personalizing is thinking you caused a negative event when you may have had nothing to do with it. Let's go back to the example of ballroom dancing. When my wife and I dance, I can usually sense her moods. If she isn't showing her usual enthusiasm, especially if she looks a bit stressed or distracted, I might conclude she is angry about something. I could assume she's angry with me and start racking my brain trying to figure out what I'm doing wrong. *Maybe she's upset because I'm not leading her with enough strength and certainty. Maybe she's mad because I stepped on her foot a couple of minutes ago. Maybe she's ticked off about the way I drove on the way here.*

This kind of personalizing is actually a form of emotional reasoning. I interpret my wife's facial expressions and apparent lack of interest in dancing on the basis of my feelings. If I feel she is angry with me, then she *is* angry with me.

These are some of the common thinking patterns that undermine happiness in our lives and marriages. It's helpful to remember that most of us engage in these patterns at times. What's dangerous is when these patterns become habits, determining the shape of our relationships—especially our marriage relationship.

If you recognize yourself in any of these patterns, there's a good chance your faulty thinking is contributing to your disappointing marriage. There's a good chance that the cause of your unhappiness isn't a wrong spouse, but a wrong way of thinking about your spouse. If that's the case, you need to transform your thinking. How? Chapter 8 offers some help.

EXERCISES

All of us, at some time and to some degree, fall into the unhealthy thinking patterns described in this chapter. Before we can change them, though, we have to be able to recognize them. Following is a list of unhealthy thought patterns. Check the ones that you think apply to you, at least part of the time.

_____ Either/or thinking
_____ Overgeneralization
_____ Filtering out the positive
_____ Dismissing the positive
_____ Mind reading
_____ Negative expectations
_____ Exaggeration
_____ Emotional reasoning
_____ Shoulds/musts
_____ Labeling
_____ Personalizing

After reviewing this list, pick three of the thought patterns that most apply to you. Write a few sentences about how each of these patterns has affected your relationship with other people, especially with your spouse.

Pattern 1:

Pattern 2:

Pattern 3:

JOURNALING

Use column 3 of your structured journal to record some of the thoughts you've had during and after difficult interactions with your spouse. Note both positive and negative interactions, but pay particular attention to whether or not you've exhibited any of the negative thought patterns discussed in this chapter. Your journal will look something like this:

Interactions	Feelings/ Sensations	Thoughts
John and I snapped at each other at breakfast. His mother's one-hour phone call kept him up. I don't remember what was said, but it wasn't pleasant.	angry, frustrated, tense	John's mother is the most intrusive person I know. And he lets her get away with everything. He is more her little boy than my husband. I wish I were as important to him as his mother is.

Perhaps you can see from this example what an important role our thoughts play in stirring up our emotions—and ultimately creating alienated relationships. The conflict over breakfast occurred not only because John was tired but also because Ellen was angry. She was angry with her mother-in-law because she interpreted the phone call as intrusive. She was angry with her husband because she interpreted his actions as being those of a little boy instead of a grown man.

Later on, I'll offer some strategies for managing your thoughts and testing your perceptions. For now, though, just record your thoughts in response to the "incidents" in your marriage and pay attention to any evidence of the patterns discussed in this chapter.

SPIRITUAL DISCIPLINES

Contemplation

Take some time to meditate on a favorite Psalm or hymn. Remember that repeating portions of the Scriptures or the great hymns of faith can refresh your spirit and bolster your strength. Psalm 40 is especially good for this purpose:

I waited patiently for the LORD;
    he turned to me and heard my cry.
He lifted me out of the slimy pit,
    out of the mud and mire;
he set my feet on a rock
    and gave me a firm place to stand.

He put a new song in my mouth,
    a hymn of praise to our God.
Many will see and fear
    and put their trust in the LORD.

Blessed is the man
    who makes the LORD his trust,
who does not look to the proud,
    to those who turn aside to false gods.
Many, O LORD my God,
    are the wonders you have done.
The things you planned for us
    no one can recount to you;
were I to speak and tell of them,
    they would be too many to declare.

Sacrifice and offering you did not desire,
    but my ears you have pierced;
burnt offerings and sin offerings
    you did not require.
Then I said, "Here I am, I have come—
    it is written about me in the scroll.
I desire to do your will, O my God;
    your law is within my heart."
I proclaim righteousness in the great assembly;
    I do not seal my lips,
    as you know, O LORD.
I do not hide your righteousness in my heart;
    I speak of your faithfulness and salvation.
I do not conceal your love and your truth
    from the great assembly.

Do not withhold your mercy from me, O LORD;
    may your love and your truths always protect me.
For troubles without number surround me;
    my sins have overtaken me, and I cannot see.
They are more than the hairs of my head,
    and my heart fails within me.
Be pleased, O LORD, to save me;
    O LORD, come quickly to help me.

May all who seek to take my life
  be put to shame and confusion;
may all who desire my ruin
  be turned back in disgrace.
May those who say to me, "Aha! Aha!"
  be appalled at their own shame.

But may all who seek you
  rejoice and be glad in you;
may those who love your salvation always say
  "The LORD be exalted!"
Yet I am poor and needy;
  may the LORD think of me.
You are my help and my deliverer;
  O my God, do not delay.

Prayer

As you pray about your marriage, keep in mind that you are working on a relationship not only with your spouse but with a personal God who enters into and understands your experiences. Before speaking the words of your prayer, the ones suggested below or those from your own heart, offer a wordless prayer to God. Pray through a mental picture of bringing your spouse to meet Jesus. Imagine what the surroundings would look like the day you brought _____ to the Lord. What would the temperature be? The color of the sky? Imagine how Jesus would greet your mate. What words would He say? What tone of voice would He use? Would He say anything to you? Would He give you advice?

Lord, I don't want to be controlled by patterns of thinking that alienate me from those around me. Give me the wisdom to see these patterns, the courage to face them, and the strength to change. By your grace, liberate me from thinking about _____ in ways that are unfair or unrealistic. Help me always to realize that _____ belongs to You. I submit to You all the thoughts I have toward _____. Amen.

Eight

Thinking Your Way to the Right Person

I hope I've convinced you that how you think about your spouse matters. The whole of this book is aimed at helping you heal your marriage by developing healthy patterns of thinking toward yourself, your spouse, and your relationship. Why? To a large degree, your thoughts determine your emotions—how you interpret your spouse's actions shapes how you feel about your mate. And your interpretation of your spouse's actions is influenced by the tendency we all have to distort what we see and hear because of flawed thought patterns.

One of the challenges before you is learning how to test your perceptions. To do that, you need to deal with any faulty habits of thinking you may have developed. No one's perceptions of self or a spouse or a marriage are fully accurate, but there are specific steps you can take to bring your thoughts in line with reality. And those new thoughts have the power to reshape your feelings and build a stronger marriage.

STEP 1: ACKNOWLEDGE RELATIONSHIP REALITIES

Your first step is to accept several realities about the situation you face:

Reality: Relationships are hard. Relationships take work, because it's easier to be distant than to be close. This isn't just your problem, it's everyone's problem. Humans have been struggling with broken relationships ever since Adam and Eve. That's the tragedy of sin. It's important to understand the fact that alienation, whether in marriage or in other relationships, is a spiritual condition. To overcome it, you will need every resource at your disposal, including spiritual resources. *Especially spiritual resources.* Working on your relationship with your spouse means working on your relationship with God, too. It means that one of your tasks as you attempt to restore your marriage is to become a channel of reconciliation in all aspects of your life.

Reality: The more psychologically vulnerable you are, the more likely you'll be to fall into unhealthy thought patterns. When you struggle with self-esteem, for example, you're vulnerable. When you have low self-esteem, relationships become more difficult. It's harder to recognize your faulty thinking habits; you'll tend to cling to them more tenaciously than you would have otherwise.

If you are one of the many people in rough marriages who struggle with low self-esteem, you need to be doubly suspicious of your feelings of anger and hurt. You have likely developed deep-seated patterns of negative thinking—about yourself, your relationships (especially your relationship with your spouse), and your future. Working on self-esteem is usually a lifelong battle. But take heart. God, who has a special place in His heart for the "meek of heart," has special resources available to you. He loves you more than you can love yourself. Allow yourself to tap into that love. Start paying attention to what builds up your self-esteem and what detracts from it. And consider whether a therapist or support group might be part of God's plan of healing and growth for you.

Reality: The more important a relationship is to you, the more difficult it is to be objective about it. This is why it's so easy for most of us to fall into unhealthy ways of thinking about our mates. Our marriage is the most important relationship in our lives, and we fear being hurt. As we anticipate the possibility of being hurt and try to avoid it, our thoughts often become skewed.

Reality: You're not alone. If you allow yourself to talk with other people about your struggle with negative thinking habits, you'll find these patterns are quite common. There is no reason to feel ashamed and different because of your struggle. You're no different from anyone else.

Reality: You might be right—at least about a lot of your perceptions. Just because you become aware of unhealthy habits of thinking doesn't mean you're completely out of touch with reality. If you assume you distort everything, you will become immobilized with self-doubt. What's important is to consider the *possibility* of distorted thinking when you're feeling upset or angry or disappointed. Also, remember that dealing with your faulty thinking habits is *your* responsibility, not your spouse's, and vice versa. Don't use your new awareness of various negative thought patterns against each other, as in, "There you go again, 'mind reading.'" That type of verbal bludgeoning obviously won't help your relationship heal.

Reality: Some of your spouse's actions and attitudes evoke powerful emotions in you because of their symbolic importance, not their real importance. In most marriages, certain behaviors become symbolic of acceptance, rejection, love, or indifference. Because these behaviors have so much power to provoke feelings of joy or pain, sometimes marriage partners start seeing these behaviors and attitudes even when they're not there.

This pattern was evident in the issue Iris had with Bud less than eighteen months after their wedding. Bud's career often placed him in situations that were extremely stressful. He knew when the stress was beginning to get to him, and he had developed a fairly effective way of dealing with it. He went "soaring." I had never heard of this and thought that he was jesting when he first mentioned it. Soaring involves piloting an aircraft that has no engine—a glider. Bud would go to the local airport, rent a glider, and arrange for a twin-engine plane to tow him aloft. As I recall, at about 3,000 feet he would pull a release mechanism that freed him from the towing craft. He then depended on wind currents to keep him airborne and to carry him over miles of landscape. Steering the craft into one wind current after another, he controlled the glider's direction, lift, and dives. The exhilaration he felt from this incredible ride in a cloudless sky was unlike anything he experienced on the ground. At the end of the flight, his nerves were completely "unfrazzled" and his energy restored. No question about it: soaring was an excellent way for him to achieve immediate relief from his stress. "The best medicine money can buy," was the way he described it.

But this home remedy had its side effects. It infuriated and depressed Iris. She wouldn't talk to him for hours, sometimes days, following his flights. He would ask her what was wrong. "Nothing." "Don't you want me to go soaring?" he would persist. "That's really up to you." It was like a dance. Each partner verbally swirled in circles around the other while frustations and anger mounted. It took weeks of counseling for Iris to come out with the facts that revealed how Bud's soaring symbolized that she was an "inadequate" wife. If she were a good wife, she thought, he wouldn't need to go soaring. Time spent with her would be enough to relax and renew him. She didn't hint at this, perhaps didn't realize herself that she was thinking this way, until the layers of painful thoughts and feelings were peeled back during counseling. And there it was. It was a dazzling revelation to Bud. He couldn't believe his ears. But he received it with sympathy, and was able to explain the difference between his need for soaring and his need for her in a way that provided balm for her wounds. They were able to move on with their marriage, but not without dealing with an accumulation of bad patterns of thinking and behavior that had begun to poison their relationship.

There are also simple, everyday behaviors that take on special negative significance. Failing to replace the cap on the toothpaste suggests disrespect for the other partner who uses the same tube. Overspending communicates disdain for the spouse who is trying to control the budget. Being late for dinner signals lack of appreciation for the efforts of the one who prepared it. There are hundreds of little things that serve as time bombs because of the symbolic meanings that a spouse might attach to them. When frustration, anger, and disappointment build to a combustible level, some small misstep by one or the other spouse produces the explosion. And each explosion causes fissures in the relationship. These accumulate and jeopardize the marriage. The fissures will not re-cement until the symbols are identified and neutralized.

How can you know when certain behaviors are becomeing negative symbols? Get suspicious if the emotions you're feeling, especially negative emotions, are unusually strong, or if they trigger the kinds of thinking patterns we discussed in the last chapter. Once you become aware of the symbolic power of your spouse's behaviors, remind yourself that they don't necessarily have significance in themselves—that their significance may lie solely in the meaning you attach to them.

Reality: Unhealthy habits of thinking tend to predetermine what you hear and don't hear. It's a fact. The only way to deal with this problem is to be aware of it and try to be open to all the information coming your way.

Reality: You might need help. Faulty thought patterns, especially deeply in-grained thought patterns, are hard to correct. You may want to ask a close, trusted friend to help you recognize and overcome some of your negative thinking habits. Or you might want to consider getting help from your pastor or a professional therapist.

Once you've recognized some of the realities about thinking habits, you can move on to practical strategies for derailing negative patterns.

STEP 2: STOP NEGATIVE TALK

When you start feeling overwhelmed by negative feelings—anger, fear, disgust—deliberately tell yourself, "Stop!" Then think: "What am I saying to myself that is causing these powerful feelings? Is it possible that I am perceiving this situation incorrectly, that I'm falling into an unhealthy thought pattern? What information have I unintentionally screened out?" Determine within yourself that even if your perceptions are correct, you won't allow your feelings to control you or direct your actions.

STEP 3: TAKE A STOP WALK

When you find yourself becoming overpowered by your emotions, you may find it necessary to remove yourself from the situation. You can do this physically or mentally. Take a walk, work out, say a prayer, make a phone call, window shop—anything it takes to cap your feelings long enough to calm down and gain perspective.

STEP 4: HAVE A FACT TALK

After you've stopped reacting emotionally to a situation, your next task is to get the facts. This means challenging your interpretations of what

is going on. It means thinking through the evidence you already have but
may not have considered. It may mean gathering additional facts, or consulting your spouse about his or her real viewpoint or intentions. Fact talk
boils down to talking to yourself about the *facts* instead of just brooding
over your *perceptions*.

STEP 5: REINTERPRET YOUR SITUATION

Once you've considered the facts, think through all the possible interpretations of the situation you're reacting to. Temporarily assume your
initial way of thinking about your spouse or the incident is wrong. Then
take your negative conclusions to their logical extreme (sometimes this
can reveal the absurdity of some thought patterns). Counter your negative
thinking with positive assumptions and conclusions.

STEP 6: TEST YOUR REINTERPRETATION

Just as it's possible that your negative conclusions are wrong, it's also
possible that your positive conclusions are wrong. Test your reinterpre-
tation according to the facts at hand or facts you assemble. But remember,
the more you struggle with low self-esteem, the more likely you are to be
guided by distorted interpretations. So be careful. If you're not sure about
your interpretations, share your dilemma with one or two strong and
trusted friends who you know can be honest and objective with you.

STEP 7: ACT ON YOUR NEW INTERPRETATIONS

Once you develop a new view of your spouse and your marriage
through a continual process of interrupting old thought patterns and challenging old interpretations, you still need to establish new ways of relating
to your partner, ways consistent with your new perspective. You'll otherwise fall back into your old thinking habits and be back where you
started. Teri and Dan are proof of that.

Teri and Dan came to counseling because they had "drifted apart."
Despite their problems, they were both willing to work on their relationship, and at least initially their efforts paid off. One of the assignments
their therapist gave them was to spend more time together. They took his
advice and really enjoyed it. They felt closer as a result.

Eventually, though, Dan started feeling pressure from his job and his active schedule of volunteering for several worthy causes. He started to get anxious about how his increased time with Teri would affect the other side of his life. How could he be responsible at work and in his church and community involvements if he kept spending so much time with his wife?

Meanwhile, Teri found herself wanting to spend still more time with Dan. The more of him she got, the more she wanted. She was hurt and confused when she started feeling resistance on Dan's part. She concluded that the steps they were taking to rebuild their marriage weren't working. She started holding back on some of the therapist's assignments. She adopted an either/or pattern of thinking: Either she and Dan would spend as much time together as she wanted, or they would have to go back to the distance and alienation they had been feeling before.

What could Teri have done to break this pattern of thinking? What should she have done?

First, she could have tested her interpretation of what was going on. Her line of reasoning was:

"Our relationship has improved tremendously."

"We are getting along so well that I would like to spend more time than our assignments call for."

"Dan obviously doesn't want to spend more time than we've been assigned."

"Clearly, he doesn't care as much about the marriage as I do."

"If he doesn't care as much as I do, what's the point?"

"We should go back to where we were before we started counseling."

"If necessary, we might as well get a divorce and get it over with."

What Teri might have done instead was to get the facts, that is, find out why Dan was reluctant to go beyond the agreed upon amount of time they were spending together.

Dan would have explained that he also enjoyed the new arrangement, but that the increased time they were spending together was making it difficult for him to keep his other commitments. He couldn't commit to more time right now, but he would try to adjust his other obligations to allow them more time together in the future.

As it was, when Teri asked and eventually demanded more time, Dan engaged in some skewed thinking of his own. He assumed that Teri didn't care about the outside pressures he bore (mind reading). When Teri pressured him, he felt she was being insensitive to him and his situation and concluded she didn't care about him (emotional reasoning).

What could Dan have done to avoid the downward spiral that resulted from his misinterpretations?

He could have initiated a conversation with her about his real feelings. He could have told her he would gladly spend more time with her but the demands on his time where just too great right now. He could have asked her to help him think through what he might do to make changes in the future, like cutting back on his involvements or including her in some of his outside activities. Dan and Teri were on their way to thinking themselves into a transformed marriage, but they gave up too soon.

It doesn't have to be that way. Adopting new ways of thinking—and acting on those new patterns until they become ingrained habits—can truly bring marriages back from the brink, as Cal and Lisa discovered.

Although Lisa didn't know it, Cal had begun to view her as a very uninteresting woman. She seemed to be tired all the time. She had few interests. She no longer sparked any sexual passion in her husband who, in contrast to Lisa, had one of those enthusiastic, scintillating personalities that keeps people entertained no matter what the situation. By the time Cal and Lisa came for counseling, Cal had already emotionally exited from the marriage. He wanted a divorce, but was haunted by guilt at the prospect of breaking his marriage vows. He was also worried about the effect a divorce would have on their four-year-old son, Austin. Cal adored Austin and agonized about the hurt he knew a divorce would inflict on him. After months of internal struggle, Cal came to see me at my office. The conversation soon turned to his perception of Lisa: Sexless. Frumpy. Couch potato. Zombie. Pitiful. Cal was embarrassed by the labels he had pinned to his wife, but he honestly couldn't think of anything positive to say about her.

I suggested to Cal that he look for just one trait he could admire about Lisa. The following week he came in and reported that after our last session he had watched her interact with Austin for a few days and had noticed how tender, nurturing, and patient she was. He compared Lisa to his own mother, who had always been too distracted to pay much attention to him. He wished he could have had a mother like Lisa.

I asked Cal if he could label Lisa in a way that would give her credit for her mothering skills. With tears in his eyes he said, "Loving." He immediately insisted, however, that one positive label wasn't enough to overcome his negative feelings toward his wife. "It takes the edge off," he said, "but it doesn't turn me around."

I asked Cal to think about his mother. What if she had been like Lisa? How would he express his appreciation to her today? "I guess I would thank her for being a good mom." I suggested that perhaps Lisa deserved some sign of appreciation from him. Cal reluctantly but dutifully approached his wife the following week: "Thanks for being such a wonderful mom to our son." With those words, there was a small but significant breakthrough in Cal and Lisa's relationship. It became apparent when I asked Cal to repeat to me the labels he had used to describe Lisa in our first session together. He couldn't do it.

"What do I do now?" Cal said in frustration. "I'm not in love with Lisa anymore, but I do see her as being a very caring human being. Is there any possibility that the passion will come back?" "There's no guarantee," I told him, "but I've seen the rebirth of passion in many relationships— usually from non-passionate efforts to be caring and close."

"What would that look like in my case?" Cal asked. I asked Cal to think about what it was that Lisa needed from him—perhaps a break from caring for Austin, perhaps some indication that he admired and respected her. Cal decided to accomplish both these objectives by taking Lisa out for ice cream at a restaurant they used to go to early in their marriage. Amazingly, many warm feelings returned for him there. Not immediate passion, but genuine affection. He and Lisa decided to repeat the outing on a regular basis. They started to talk again. Lisa opened up and told Cal about how painful it had been for her to see him drift away over the years and to detect the contempt in his attitude toward her. Cal realized that the root of much of the behavior he so disliked in his wife was probably depression. The labels he had put on her in his mind began to change. The two of them began working on a different kind of marriage.

Like Cal, you can change the way you *feel* about your spouse by changing the way you *think*. To diagnose the possibility of distorted thinking on your part, acknowledge the relational realities discussed earlier in this chapter. Test and retest your thoughts about your spouse and your situation. Practice your new thinking skills. And then ask God to help you use them to transform your mind—and your marriage.

EXERCISES

Throughout this process of transforming your thoughts, there are several things you can do that are likely to increase your motivation to change and enhance your perspective. One is consulting trusted friends or family members. You may have plenty of people around you who are willing to echo your negative thoughts about your spouse, fully backing up your side of the story. While their support is commendable, you don't need their blind support. Find someone who will be honest with you as you work through this process of being honest about your spouse. Show your friend or family member the descriptions of unhealthy thought patterns discussed in the previous chapter. Ask for truthful feedback about how you may be falling into some of those patterns. Invite suggestions for overcoming your faulty thinking habits.

"On the other hand. . . ."

You can also challenge your unhealthy thought patterns on your own. In the following exercise, try to seriously challenge your negative thoughts about your spouse—not because they are necessarily inaccurate, but because your marriage is too important to take your perceptions for granted. On the left side of this page, list the negative qualities or habits that bother you about your mate. Then, on the right side, list as many explanations or counterbalancing positive traits as you can think of.

Negative trait   Explanations/positive traits

"Exaggerate the positive"

Another way to transform your negative thoughts about your spouse is to exaggerate his or her positive traits. Once you start thinking negatively about a person, your thoughts tend to become exaggerated. Sometimes, the only way to counter those exaggerated thoughts is to exaggerate the other way, which is what I'd like you to do now. A warning: the following exercise isn't easy. It may feel like you're lying to yourself, and it isn't meant to be the final word on what your marriage really *is*. But it may also spur a breakthrough in understanding how far you've gone in overemphasizing your partner's negative qualities, and forcing you to recognize other, more positive traits. List some positive qualities you would like to see in your spouse:

Now try as hard as you can to find some small pieces of evidence that these traits are present in your mate, at least to some degree. If you're having trouble, try consulting with a friend.

Positive trait   **The evidence**

"Judge and Jury"

Think of one trait, theme, or statement that best describes your spouse—the one you think of when you're the most upset with him/her. Then imagine how others would challenge your description. What would they say in your partner's defense?

Who?   **How would they challenge your description?**

Your children:

His/her mother:

His/her father:

His/her siblings:

His/her friends:

Colleagues:

Jesus:

Finally, be the judge of these witnesses. Has listening to their testimony changed your mind? If not, why? If so, why?

JOURNALING

If you are continuing the structured part of your journaling, add a fourth column to challenge the thoughts/interpretations you are recording in column 3.

Remember that in column 1, you are writing descriptions of activities and events—what you are doing and what's going on around you, with a focus on interactions involving your spouse.

In column 2, you are recording your feelings and physical sensations in response to interactions.

In column 3, you are noting your thoughts about the activities and events you've recorded.

Column 4 is for challenging your perceptions of your spouse and the labels you've applied to him/her based on your perceptions.

As you journal, challenge yourself not only to test your negative interpretations, but also to look for positive interpretations of your spouse's behavior. Then think of new labels you can apply based on the new, positive interpretations. Use any insights you gained from previous exercises.

If you have stopped using the structured journal, use the unstructured portion of your journal to reflect in writing about how you might be able to interpret your spouse's behavior more positively—or at least be aware that this is the challenge before you now.

SPIRITUAL DISCIPLINES

Contemplation

Working on a weakened or collapsed relationship requires incredible stamina and endurance. The task before you will require not only physical and emotional stamina but also spiritual stamina. One key is learning the discipline of praise. Praise reminds us that God is in charge and that we are loved.

Allow the words of these Psalms to be your own. Let them capture your heart:

Psalm 9:1–2:
I will praise You, O Lord, with all my heart; I will tell of all your wonders. I will be glad and rejoice in you; I will sing praise to your name, O Most High.

Psalm 96 (NKJV):
Oh sing to the Lord a new song! Sing to the Lord, all the earth. Sing to the Lord, bless His name; proclaim the good news of His salvation from day to day. Declare His glory among the nations, His wonders among all peoples. For the Lord is great and greatly to be praised; He is to be feared above all gods. For all the gods of the peoples are idols, but the Lord made the heavens. Honor and majesty are before Him; strength and beauty are in His sanctuary. Give to the Lord, O families of the peoples, give to the Lord glory and strength. Give to the Lord the glory due His name; bring an offering and come into His courts. Oh, worship the Lord in the beauty of holiness! Tremble before Him all the earth. Say among the nations, "The Lord reigns; the world also is firmly established, it shall not be moved; He shall judge the peoples righteously." Let the heavens rejoice and let the earth be glad; let the sea roar, and all its fullness. Let the field

be joyful, and all that is in it. Then all the trees of the woods will rejoice before the Lord. For He is coming to judge the earth; He shall judge the world with righteousness, and the peoples with His truth.

Be open to the transforming power of God in Proverbs 4:23 (NKJV):
Keep your heart with all diligence, for out of it spring the issues of life.

Prayer

Lord, there are thoughts, feelings, attitudes, and habits that come from deep within me, so deep I feel like they are me. Without them, who would I be? So much of what I think and feel bubbles up from a sea of pain. Old pain, new pain—I don't always know the difference. At times I want to erect a wall around me, seal myself off from others, deny access to anyone—people who seem to want to hurt me and even people who want to love me. Other times I reach out in panic, clinging to people around me as though they are my only hope.

Who am I? Lord, be my salvation. Be my health. Be my healing. I hear your voice in your Word:

And do not be conformed to this world, but be transformed by the renewing of your mind, that you may prove what is that good and acceptable and perfect will of God (Romans 12:2, NKJV).

Lord, be my transformation. Amen.

Reflect on the notion that our thoughts can alienate us from God. When we live in alienation, we are very much conformed to this world. We need the transforming power of God to free us from alienating thinking.

Lord, I confess that I often feel like a prisoner to my thoughts and emotions. I know I can never fully understand any other person, including _____. I know all too well how easy it is to misjudge and unfairly label another person, especially when that person has hurt me, most especially after I have made myself vulnerable and offered my trust. Help me to be open to new ways of seeing others. Help me especially to be open to new ways of seeing _____, to whom I have made a promise of lifelong faithfulness. Amen.

Nine

Intimacy 101: Learning the Secrets of Passionate Friendship

A weary mother of four was speaking wistfully of the early weeks of her romance with the man who later became her husband. "I remember when I used to feel this *electricity* from just touching his hand," she mused. "It's too bad those wonderful feelings don't last, isn't it?"

This young wife isn't alone in her mourning a loss of passion in marriage. Some alteration in the level or nature of passion is common in marriage. As the years pass, it's difficult to sustain the emotional sizzle and crackle of courtship. When the electricity goes—or when the lights at least dim—some spouses conclude they married the wrong person. They mistakenly assume that if the intense feelings are gone, the marriage must not be right.

Many of us, of course, have outgrown that notion. Thanks to a plethora of sermons and books, we've learned that love is more than a feeling and that it's natural for emotions to change over the years. Some passions subside. Others take their place. What's confusing for most people is that *sexual* passions are no longer as insistent as they were in the earliest stages of their relationship.

While it's true that love is more than a feeling, sex is an important barometer of the health of a marriage. One measure of a marriage is the degree to which the people involved can maintain a balanced sexual relationship—one that meets each partner's needs without violating the personhood of either.

Sex is much more than merely giving and receiving physical pleasure. It's a promise. It's a way for you and your spouse to say you belong to each other. It's a gift that opens you to vulnerability as well as to pleasure. If your partner says or does hurtful things after you've given of yourself through sexual intimacy, the wounds cut far deeper than they would in a less intimate, nonsexual relationship.

If you begin to withdraw from your spouse because of tensions in the marriage—especially if you withdraw from sexual contact and other forms of physical affection—it feels to your spouse like you're breaking a promise. You feel the same way if your spouse begins to withdraw sexually from you. Sexual withdrawal spells *rejection*. It causes hurt and confusion. It intensifies conflict. It makes passion a mere memory from the past. It confirms—at least apparently—the feeling that you married the wrong person.

Given the power of sex to both reflect and affect our whole relationship, it's no surprise that the apostle Paul wrote, "Let the husband render to his wife the affection due her, and likewise also the wife to her husband. The wife does not have authority over her own body, but the husband does. And likewise the husband does not have authority over his own body, but the wife does. Do not deprive one another except with consent for a time, that you may give yourselves to fasting and prayer; and come together again so that Satan does not tempt you because of your lack of self-control" (1 Corinthians 7:3–5).

Of course, temptation comes in many forms, including the urge to surrender to anger and alienation that often follows sexual rejection. Sexual alienation tends to influence everything else in the marriage. Paul's words can't be taken lightly.

It's both strange and unhealthy the way many couples respond to any inkling of feeling alienated and distant. They do exactly the opposite of what they should do in response to conflicts and disappointments in their relationship. At the time when they most need to start working on ways to regain their sense of closeness, they begin withdrawing from each other. They stop spending time together. They stop saying, "I love you." They stop touching, hugging, and caressing. They stop having sex. Eventually they make the fatal diagnosis: We must not have been meant for each other.

Ryan and Sue are an example. They hadn't touched each other in at least a year when Sue came to me for counseling. She had almost no feelings left for her husband and little desire to become close to him again, but she was worried about the effect of Ryan's increasing withdrawal from the family on their girls. He was working seventy hours a week and practically ignoring their daughters, something that was out of character for him. He had always been an involved father, but the stresses of his work were beginning to take a toll. A sociologist with a Ph.D. from a prestigious university, Ryan had chosen to start his own business instead of following a traditional academic career. Unlike his peers, who had started out as lowly assistant professors on tiny salaries, he hired himself out to universities for special projects. At first, he made a lot more money than his friends in academic careers. But they were on tenure tracks and he wasn't. Every time a project ended, he had to move on.

Twelve years into his business, funding for Ryan's kind of work started to dry up. Because he hadn't done any research or publishing, no university was interested in hiring him as a faculty member. Money started getting tight. As their financial situation deteriorated, Sue became increasingly angry and frustrated. She took an "I told you so" attitude toward Ryan and began to withdraw. At first she just spent less time with him, choosing instead to focus on their four girls and a variety of volunteer activities. Gradually, she stopped making the little affectionate gestures that had always been part of their relationship. Then she started avoiding sex. Ryan, who was already depressed about his career situation, was devastated by Sue's withdrawal but felt powerless to redeem himself. Over time, his self-recrimination turned into bitterness and resentment toward his wife.

Why is this such a common scenario? Because too many people go into marriage without having learned the basic skills required for a friendship, much less a lifelong, passionate friendship.

Research has shown that good marriages, the kind that remain vital over the long haul, are based in large part on an ongoing friendship. The reason? The qualities that make for satisfying friendships are the same qualities that contribute to satisfying marriages. In marriage, friendship skills are the building blocks of intimacy. Yes, even passion.

There's a logical conclusion here: If you want to recover the passion in your marriage, you need to learn how to cultivate a deep friendship with your spouse. That won't happen without developing in three areas, the most important ingredients of a satisfying friendship: acceptance, shared activities, and shared talk.

We all naturally seek out people who seem to accept us and make us feel good about ourselves. Likewise, we tend to keep our distance from people who verbally belittle us. Criticism does have a place in friendship, but only when it's offered sparingly and in the context of mutual support and affirmation.

One of the challenges of friendship, and of marriage, is to communicate acceptance. (That may sound like an impossible goal, but it's sometimes true that you have to communicate acceptance before you actually feel it. In chapter 12, you'll learn more about how to accept traits in your spouse that drive you crazy but aren't likely to change.)

The reason continual criticism erodes friendship is because it communicates lack of acceptance. More often than not, the cause of criticism isn't one person's imperfections, but the critic's own shaky self-esteem (that again!). People with low self-esteem tend to criticize their mates because it takes the focus off their own feelings of inadequacy. If you find yourself being overly critical, take an honest look at your sense of self-esteem.

Fortunately, you don't have to completely solve your self-esteem problems before you can start acting in loving ways. It's difficult, but not impossible, to concentrate on saying and doing things that will make your spouse feel valued and special, even when it doesn't come naturally.

When couples come to me for marriage counseling, I often give them an assignment. I tell them, "Make a list of things you can say or do to make your spouse feel good about himself or herself." I often get back a short, vague list. For example: "I should do more to show her I care." A statement like that is almost meaningless, but at least it defines a category of activity. So I start a dialogue in an effort to produce more specific responses.

"What kinds of things can you do to show your wife you care?"

"Well, I should compliment her more."

"That's good. But compliment her how and about what?"

We continue working until both partners have listed at least twenty-five things they can say or do to make their spouse feel good about himself or herself.

When these lists are finished, I ask both partners to list what their *spouse* could say or do to make them feel good about themselves. It's quite interesting to compare the first and second lists. Sometimes they match closely, and sometimes they are completely contradictory. When they are contradictory, I ask each spouse to revise the original list and turn it into an action plan. As I've worked with couples on this assignment over the years, I've found that the items they list tend to fall into certain categories. Based on their responses, I've concluded that what most people want from a spouse are words and actions that indicate COMMITMENT, CARING, AFFECTION, and RESPECT.

COMMUNICATING COMMITMENT

For most of us, the knowledge that someone is committed to us enhances our feeling of self-worth. So one way to make your spouse feel good about him/herself is to say or do something that indicates your commitment.

What communicates commitment? My youngest daughter, Danette, found a unique approach. Early in her marriage to Jeff, she started celebrating his birthday *week*. During that week she engineers small surprises—little gifts, cards, notes, special meals, and the like—every day. Jeff would have to be incredibly thickheaded to miss the commitment message in that kind of extended celebration (fortunately, he's very appreciative of her efforts!).

I think Danette's birthday extravaganza is a wonderful approach, but we all differ in how we express or receive symbols of commitment. To get you thinking about how you could demonstrate commitment to your spouse, I've listed some examples generated by one group of couples. They shared ways they try to communicate commitment—or how their spouse communicates it to them:

- Holding my hand in church.

- Seeking out my company at a social gathering.
- When he initiates "dates."
- Hearing, "I'm glad I picked you."
- Saying, "I'm committed."
- Listening to each other's dreams.
- When he tells me he loves me.
- When we walk through the house model together and dream out loud about the future.

It's obvious from these responses that commitment can be conveyed in a vast variety of ways. What symbolizes commitment to one person may mean nothing to another. That's why it's so important to find out what words and actions signify commitment to your spouse, and in turn to let your spouse know what communicates *commitment* to you.

The same is true about communicating *caring, affection,* and *respect.*

COMMUNICATING CARING

Caring is about saying—and living out—the words "I love you." Both men and women say they wish they heard these words more often, especially from their marriage partner. It's not surprising, because most of us hear these words from only a handful of people in the space of a lifetime. The fact that we hear them so rarely and from so few sources makes the "I love you's" in our lives priceless. They have the power to make us feel safe, supported, and encouraged.

Ironically, "I love you" is something many people find hard to say, even when they desperately want to hear the words themselves.

Do you tell your mate, "I love you"? If there are long-standing tensions in your relationship, chances are these words have disappeared from your marriage vocabulary. There's nothing harder to say when you're feeling angry or resentful or disappointed. But there's also nothing more powerful you can say to bridge a relational chasm.

As important as they are, though, loving words are not enough. To truly communicate caring, words have to be reinforced by little daily acts that show your spouse how important he or she is to you.

Here are some things men have said they can do to communicate caring to their wives:

- Thank her for the tie she gave me and tell her about all the compliments I got on it.
- Share the housework.
- Be the one who thinks of fun things to do together.
- Bring her a small gift—like one rose—that expresses tenderness.
- Arrange my schedule to take care of the children so she can go out with friends.
- Plan a date regularly.
- Ask her when I leave the house if there's anything she needs while I'm out.
- Clean up the kitchen.
- Leave tender messages on the answering machine.
- Fill up her car with gas.
- Take her shopping (I hate shopping).
- Tell her to take her time when she's getting ready for an evening out even though I have a real thing about being on time.
- Turn up the heat in the morning when I get up.
- Vacuum the rugs for her.
- Listen understandingly when she needs me.
- Enjoy her family.

What men have said they wish their wives would do to communicate caring:

- Be pleasant in the morning, even when I'm not
  (and I'm usually not).
- Ski with me.
- Do my laundry.
- Give me space for private time at home.
- Refill my coffee cup.
- Let me read late at night.
- Encourage me in my profession.
- Prepare my favorite foods.
- Share my concern for my parents.
- Say thank you when I do the little extras.
- Ask me how my running went today.
- Make surprise phone calls just to talk and see how I'm doing.

What women say they can do:

- Be ready to turn my attention on him when he comes home at night.
- Cook a huge Italian meal.
- Help the kids make a big WELCOME HOME DADDY sign when I know he's had a rough day at work.
- Go camping with him.
- Leave him notes on the stairway railing.
- Show interest in the political things that interest him.
- Keep in close touch with his parents and siblings.
- Send him a box of his favorite nuts via UPS to his office.
- Celebrate his ethnic heritage with the kids.
- Get up even earlier than he does to make the coffee.
- Listen to his golf stories.
- Call him every day just to say, "I love you."
- Ask him if he wants me to pick up the baby-sitter.
- Listen to his dreams about his work and the future.

What women want their husbands to say or do:

- Tell me this was the best meal he's ever had, even when it's round steak.
- Hire a baby-sitter and take me out sometimes.
- Ask me about my work.
- Get some special food we can share after the kids go to bed.
- Go to bed early together.
- Notice my efforts to look good.
- Ask me if I'm warm enough.
- Give me a birthday gift with thought and planning instead of just obligation.
- Go for cappuccino with me.
- Help me move my car into the garage when it's late or the weather's bad.
- Fix me an avocado and cream cheese sandwich.
- Be willing to visit a fine art gallery.

Did you notice something about these lists? Few of the items listed are grand, heroic gestures. They are small, daily, seemingly trivial acts that marriage partners can engage in to show they are thinking about each other. That they value each other. That they *care*.

Consider the powerful effect of saying one simple phrase to your spouse: "You look good." Few of us escape adolescence unscathed when it comes to our body image. We carry the wounds throughout life. But a compliment or word of support to your mate can go a long way in counteracting the lingering effects of adolescent self-consciousness about physical appearance.

Some examples of what men have said they can say or do to make their wives feel good about their looks:

- Tell her her dress looks great.
- Tell her she's the classiest woman in the place.
- Compliment her for her hair.
- Compliment her that she can eat so much and look so thin.
- Tell her she looks really good.
- Compliment her appearance before going out.

What men have said they'd like their wives to say or do to bolster their confidence in their appearance:

- Tell me I look handsome in that suit or shirt.
- Purchase an item of clothing because she thinks I'll look good in it.
- Comment on my haircut.
- Tell me I was the best-looking guy at the party.
- Insist that I'm improving with age.
- Tell me I look great in my beard.
- Tell me I have broad shoulders.

Women respond about what they can say or do:

- Tell him how handsome and fit he is.
- Tell him he looks nice when he gets dressed up.
- Notice and comment on new clothes he wears.

What women have said they'd like their husband to say or do:

- Notice my attempts to look good.
- Go shopping with me and hold something up off the rack that he thinks I'd look good in.

These examples of seemingly insignificant words and actions, repeated in the dailiness of life, have a powerful impact in marriage. They convey a message that you care.

Sometimes caring means going beyond mere thoughtfulness. Sometimes it means being present during times of serious struggle. My son-in-law Mike is one of the best examples I know of this kind of caring.

Mike is married to my daughter Donna. One afternoon a few years ago, Donna was rushed to the hospital with severe abdominal pain. By the time she arrived, she was going into shock from internal bleeding. The doctors discovered her uterus had ruptured. It was cancer. Donna required emergency surgery and then six months of chemotherapy. She would check into the hospital every Friday evening and stay there until Sunday afternoon when her treatments were completed. Throughout each stay, she was groggy from the drugs and extremely nauseated.

The hospital staff took good care of Donna, but that wasn't enough for Mike. He took her to the hospital every week and stayed by her side all night throughout her stay. Family and friends offered to spell him, but he refused. He wanted to be with Donna to attend to any need the professional staff might miss. He brought in nonhospital food for her, read to her and with her, prayed with her, held her hand when she was feeling especially discouraged, brought her tapes they could listen to together, read the Bible with her. As wonderful as these little gestures were, none of them would have meant as much—or elevated her spirits as much—if they had come from anyone but Mike.

After her initial set of treatments, Donna had a four-month remission. Then the cancer reappeared. She went through six more months of chemotherapy. This time, the doses were even heavier and the side effects more serious. The weakness and nausea persisted beyond the weekends of treatment. She lost her hair. She felt too sick to follow her normal routines. Throughout this period, the only time Mike left her side was for work.

Now Donna is cancer-free. There is no question in my mind that Mike's caring presence throughout her months of treatment contributed to her healing.

As exemplary as Mike's continued caring was in the face of Donna's crisis, it's even harder to be caring when a spouse has a chronic illness—

unending, energy-draining, an illness that drags two people into depression, that guarantees their marriage will never be what they envisioned on their wedding day.

When I was a pastor, I met a man whose wife was suffering from an advanced case of rheumatoid arthritis. She was completely bedridden, her body horribly misshapen by the disease and the disfiguring effects of twenty years' worth of powerful medications that both bless and curse. When I first met Brad, he was in his wife's hospital room, giving her a drink of water. He cradled her gently in his arms as he held the glass to her lips. Nell greeted me with a smile as broad as her puffed-up face would allow. I later learned that the caring I saw that afternoon was just a glimpse of a caring relationship these two had maintained throughout years of a painful, destructive disease. After Nell died, I saw a picture of her taken early in their marriage. Before arthritis ravaged her body, she had been a beautiful woman. An evil disease had crushed both Brad and Nell's marital hopes. But the caring between them prevented the disease from destroying their love.

Mike and Donna. Brad and Nell. Their situations were extreme. It's easy for us to recognize the need for caring in the crucibles of their lives. What's hard is recognizing the need for caring amidst the small but blistering crises of daily life—the need for small yet highly symbolic, immensely sustaining acts of caring in the middle of daily busy-ness.

You might never face cancer or chronic illness, but virtually all couples go through periods of crisis. How you react to crisis speaks volumes to your spouse about how much you care. So do your words and deeds in the dailiness of life. Do you say and do little things to lift your mate's spirits? Do you show your spouse in little ways that he or she is important to you? What do you do when life is hammering at your partner's stamina, self-esteem, and sense of hope? Are you communicating that you care?

COMMUNICATING AFFECTION

There is something about touch that conveys affirmation as no words ever could. We humans take immense pleasure in physical contact. And not just sexual contact. As important as sex is in a marriage, it is rarely sustained without other forms of physical affection. Conversely, unless there are medical problems, marriages devoid of sexual affection are usually also devoid of other forms of physical contact.

Loving touch between two people who have promised themselves to each other is like the seal and signature on a legal document. Without the appropriate seal and signature, a legal document is null and void. Without physical touching, a marriage is essentially void. It may exist on paper, but it doesn't have any real-life validity.

Remember Sue and Ryan? The stresses in their relationship didn't take a really serious toll until they withdrew physical affection from each other. And their marriage didn't begin to heal until Sue courageously re-initiated loving touch. Fearful of her daughters' future if her marriage fell apart, Sue came to me for advice. As she told the story of her alienation from Ryan, Sue realized that she had initiated that alienation, moved by her terror of what endless financial struggle would mean for their family. She became extremely remorseful about the way she had inflicted emotional punishment on her husband for his career mistakes. As her attitude changed, she suddenly wanted to restore her marriage, but didn't know how. I explained that in a relationship where such severe alienation has set in, one partner has to be willing to "go to the cross," to allow his or her ego to be crucified in order to redeem the marriage. For Sue, going to the cross would mean reaching out to Ryan with loving touch, even though there was a risk that he would reject her.

At first, Sue didn't think she could do it. But with prayer and my encouragement, she mustered up her courage. Late one evening, she asked Ryan if he would like to go for a walk. It was something they had done every night for the first decade of their marriage. They would walk the streets of their neighborhood, holding hands and dreaming about the future. But they'd long since given up this routine. So it took all the bravery Sue could muster to suggest a return to a symbol of a happier time.

Ryan's first response to Sue's invitation was predictable. He glared at her and snarled, "Are you kidding?" It wasn't a question. It was a definite, "No!" But Sue gently persisted. "No, I'm not kidding," she said softly. "Let's go." For some reason, Ryan relented, but not without letting Sue know that he was doing so under protest. As they left the house, he jammed his hands angrily in his pockets. There would be no hand-holding. But Sue had made up her mind to go to the cross. She put her arm on Ryan's—the first time she had touched him in months—and said, "I pray to God He will forgive me for destroying what you and I once had together."

Ryan stopped abruptly, visibly shaken by her words. Because he had so little trust left for his wife, he was about to respond with a sarcastic barb. But before he could say anything, Sue put her arms around him. Pressing his arms, still shoved deeply in his pockets, against his sides, she whispered, "I believe God can forgive me, and I pray He will help you to forgive me, too. I love you and want our marriage back more than anything else in the world."

There were many tears that night, along with hours of talking. Sue learned that Ryan felt like an abysmal failure. He hated himself for letting her and the girls down. But he was also furious at her for failing to see his despair and for withdrawing from him when he needed her most. The forgiveness and restoration that took place that night came about in part because of the words of confession Sue spoke. But the words weren't enough. Sue could never have broken through her husband's bitterness without a courageous act of loving touch. In marriage, touch, affectionate physical contact, is an instrument of healing.

Over a period of many months, Sue and Ryan restored their marriage. Their passion for each other came back slowly, but it did return. Their family was reborn.

The alienation in this marriage could have been avoided if Ryan and Sue had known the importance of maintaining physical affection—both sexual contact and the little loving gestures that speak so powerfully of commitment and caring—in the face of life's stresses. The greater the stresses, the more important loving touch becomes.

Here is what some couples have said about how they want their spouses to express physical affection to them:

- Kiss me when I least expect it.
- Rub my back for a long time.
- Give me a squeeze.
- Make the first affectionate gesture.
- Hold my hand in church.
- Touch me affectionately during the day.
- Give me a neck rub.

- Initiate sex.
- Give me at least one hug a day.

Here are some examples of what they said they could do to express affection to their spouses:

- Wear sexy stuff to bed even when I'm not seeking physical intimacy.
- Talk a lot before we have sex.
- Hold his hand when we're walking.
- Give her a kiss on the forehead when she's still in bed and I'm leaving for work.

Do you validate your marriage commitment with loving touches—not just sexual contact, but with small embraces, spontaneous kisses, pats on the arm or hand—that communicate genuine affection?

COMMUNICATING RESPECT

Most of us want to be respected. We especially want to be respected by the people who know us best—our friends, colleagues, and family. The unique value of respect from people who are close to us is that it is *informed respect*. Not to mention that it flies in the face of the too-often-true observation that "familiarity breeds contempt."

But what does it mean to show respect for your spouse? It means acknowledging that your mate is an individual apart from you. Recognizing that he or she possesses unique gifts—and that some of the traits that look to you like flaws are really gifts, or potential gifts, in disguise. It means opening yourself to the knowledge of what it is that your partner contributes to your life together.

Acknowledging your spouse's individuality

The promises you made to your mate at your wedding were not conditional. You didn't vow to love and cherish your spouse "if he/she changes in ways I shall designate right after this ceremony ends." But many of us act as if we have a right to "improve" our partner.

Trying to change your spouse's basic character is inconsistent with respect. Respecting your mate's individuality means admitting to yourself that it's not necessary or even desirable for you and your partner to share all the same interests, tastes, or points of view. It means accepting some annoying idiosyncrasies. It means that with a few exceptions, ultimatums to your spouse—as in "either you stop such and such, or . . ."—are out of line.

Recognizing your mate's gifts

Your spouse needs reinforcement from you that he or she is a capable, talented person. This is true even if your mate is successful and from all outward appearances confident. The assaults of life are such that most of us have at least some secret doubts about our abilities. Even if we've achieved a measure of success, we all know somebody else who is more successful, more talented, than we are. So we all need reminders that we're pretty good at what we do, that we're competent in fulfilling our life tasks.

Most of us have few people we can go to for the reinforcement we need. Positive feedback is rare in the workplace. Friends can provide it at some level, but the kind of affirmation we all crave comes only from those who know us intimately. For most of us, the person who knows us best is our spouse.

You need affirmation from your spouse that you have talents and accomplishments. *Your spouse* needs the same kind of affirmation from you. As you consider this, remember: It's a law of nature that those traits that get attention are accentuated. When you affirm your mate's talents and strengths, he is empowered to build on them even further. When you diminish your spouse or harp on her weaknesses, you demoralize her—and usually achieve the opposite of what you intended.

Paula had always loved her work, but was forced to resign her job when her company was bought out. When she came to me for career counseling, I took on the role of vocational cheerleader. I coached her in how to identify her skills, define her job search objectives, and network to accomplish those objectives. As part of our work together, Paula wrote a detailed work history. We looked at her history together and examined the evidence that Paula was indeed a gifted person who had every reason to feel proud and confident as she approached prospective employers. We put together a resumé that told Paula's story and highlighted her accomplishments. After completing her resumé, Paula was energized and enthusiastic about her job search. But then she made a critical mistake.

When Paula came for her next appointment, she was a different person. Instead of the confident, energetic woman I'd seen the week before, she was depressed and filled with self-doubt. After some probing, I found out why. With great hope and excitement she had shown her husband her resumé. But instead of encouraging her, or acknowledging her accomplishments, or even giving her a tiny crumb of affirmation, he had laughed. He told her she didn't have the skills she had listed. That she had exaggerated her achievements. That the level she had achieved at her previous job was a fluke. That she had only looked good in contrast to her inept boss. That she was, in effect, a no-talent person with extremely limited prospects. He urged her to take a low-level job with a temporary agency.

Her confidence completely destroyed, Paula took his advice. Within a few months, one of the companies she worked for as a temporary file clerk offered her a full-time job in sales. In three years she rose to vice president at a salary significantly higher than her husband's. It's not clear whether her husband ever acknowledged that Paula's gifts were real.

You can't make your spouse respect or even recognize your talents and abilities if he or she is determined to diminish you. It's more likely the case, though, that your partner just doesn't know how to communicate respect for your capabilities and accomplishments.

One of the most important steps you can take to develop or rebuild a passionate friendship is to actively look for each other's gifts. To make a point of acknowledging them. To celebrate them.

Here are what some couples have said they can say or do to affirm each other's gifts.

What men have said they can say or do for their wives:

- Compliment her abilities as a professional.
- Tell her how organized she is.
- Tell her she's done a great job with the kids' piano.
- Tell her she's better at the math homework than I am.
- Tell her I am proud of how well she handles her various volunteer activities.
- Express confidence in and approval of her childrearing abilities.

- Acknowledge and appreciate the fact that she makes more money than I do.
- Compliment her ability to make good financial decisions—she's better at it than I am.
- Acknowledge projects she's working on around the house.
- Express appreciation for the way she organizes an evening for guests.
- Tell her she has a great sense of color and compliment her on how well she has furnished our home.

What men have said they'd like their wives to say and do to affirm their gifts:

- Give me words of encouragement about my work.
- Acknowledge the projects I do around the house.
- Tell me I have "wonderful ideas."
- Tell me, "I know you can do it."
- Support my professional goals.
- Flatter my abilities.

What women say they can say or do to affirm their husbands' gifts:

- Comment on his computer expertise.
- Be supportive in his attempts to accomplish something for our house (remodeling, wiring, repairing, etc.).
- Tell others in his presence about his career accomplishments.
- Compliment him on specific things he has achieved at work.
- Ask, listen, respond about his work.
- Speak out in defense of him in a world that is often hostile to his profession.
- Show enthusiasm for his special talents and allow him to take time to pursue the interests that relate to them.
- Praise his parenting skills.
- Tell him I'm proud of him.

What women would like their husbands to say or do to affirm their gifts:

- Come to performances I'm in.
- Show interest in my work (ask questions about it and listen to the answers).

- Share my career experiences with me.
- Consider my career as important as his.
- Come and watch my team compete.
- Accept the fact that I cannot balance the checkbook.
- Tell me I'm attractive and competent.

The principles discussed in this chapter are all part of intimacy work, the process of building intimacy. Intimacy means different things to different people, but a key ingredient of intimacy for most of us is a feeling of closeness. The suggestions contained in these pages are aimed at promoting that feeling.

Realistically speaking, though, intimacy work is extremely difficult for couples who have been at odds with each other. The more alienated they feel, the more difficult it is to make an effort to achieve intimacy.

Saying and doing the things that promote closeness feels risky. Your spouse might not even notice your efforts. He or she might even notice your attempts at closeness but dismiss them as irrelevant. You did something, but in your partner's eyes it wasn't what you should have done. When you ask what you can do to help bridge the chasm between you, you may be told, "You should know." Or, "You figure it out. It's your problem." Your spouse may even respond to your efforts with anger—by questioning your motives or accusing you of being manipulative and controlling.

These responses hurt. They make the prospect of putting a lot of energy into the possibility of a passionate friendship daunting.

As you consider whether or not to take on the challenge of intimacy work, consider this reminder: It's a lot easier to be alienated in your relationships than it is to be close. The reason is very simple: sin. Sin IS alienation—alienation from God, from yourself, and from others.

It will be easier to continue being alienated from your spouse than it will be to take measures to bring you closer together. It will be easier for your mate to overlook, dismiss, and misinterpret your efforts than to acknowledge and accept those efforts.

So recognize it: Taking steps toward intimacy, toward passionate friendship, will be hard. But the payoff could be transforming.

Most of this chapter has been devoted to communicating acceptance as a way to develop a passionate friendship with your spouse. But there are two more critical components of intimate friendship in marriage—shared activities and shared talk. To find out more about these important relationship builders, read on.

EXERCISE

Intimacy Report Card

In this chapter, I've outlined ways in which couples achieve intimacy. I've suggested that intimacy in marriage depends on some of the same factors that need to be present in any friendship: acceptance, commitment, caring, affection, and respect.

If you were to get a report card on the degree to which you exhibit these intimacy factors, how do you think you would do? This exercise gives you a chance to rate yourself. Assume you are a teacher in an elite school. You are grading someone who performs exactly the way you do. Do your best to be objective: Don't hesitate to give yourself the recognition you deserve, but be willing to acknowledge mediocre or poor performance if it's warranted.

- Circle your grade, adding any pluses and minuses that you think apply.
- Name five things you can say or do to raise your grade.

A B C D F   Acceptance
1.
2.
3.
4.
5.

A B C D F   Commitment
1.
2.
3.
4.
5.

A   B   C   D   F   Affection
1.
2.
3.
4.
5.

A   B   C   D   F   Respect
1.
2.
3.
4.
5.

A   B   C   D   F   Caring
1.
2.
3.
4.
5.

Develop a plan for infusing your marriage with multiple little acts of acceptance, caring, respect, commitment, and affection. Plan to introduce one small act each day.

JOURNALING

(1) Record your efforts to implement your plan for showing acceptance, commitment, caring, affection, and respect. If you are using structured journaling, use column 1 for these notes.

(2) Make notes in column 2 about what you're feeling as you carry out your small daily acts of intimacy.

(3) Use column 3 to record your thoughts.

(4) Pay attention to how your spouse responds. Did he/she notice your efforts? Did he/she behave differently toward you? Use column 1 to record your spouse's reactions.

(5) One week after starting to implement your plan to show more accep-

tance, commitment, caring, affection and respect, evaluate the following:

Your feelings toward your spouse:

- More negative
- No change
- More positive

Your feelings about your marriage:

- Less hopeful
- No change
- More hopeful

Your understanding of intimacy:

- More clear
- No change
- Less clear

Repeat your efforts for at least a few weeks, evaluating as above at the end of each week. Remember that building a new marriage takes planning, effort, and time!

SPIRITUAL DISCIPLINE

This is the time to draw on every resource you possess. Pour your heart out to God in prayer. Focus your thoughts in your journal. Draw on support from trusted friends in the community of faith. Don't be afraid to seek understanding and support from a pastor or spiritual mentor who views marriage as a sacred covenant—and who is sympathetic to your struggle.

Contemplation

Meditate on the words of Psalm 84:1–4, 10–12

How lovely is your dwelling place, O Lord Almighty!

Lord, I'm trying to take new risks, but I need to know that I am surrounded by Your presence on all sides. My marriage has felt very lonely at times. Each day is a reminder of the closeness, the partnership, I crave.

My soul yearns, even faints, for the courts of the Lord; my heart and my flesh cry out for the living God.

The greater the risk, the more alone—the more empty, frail, and defenseless—I feel. I reach for the assurance that You are with me.

Even the sparrow has found a home, and the swallow a nest for herself, where she may have her young—a place near your altar, O Lord Almighty, my King and my God.

But You have prepared a place for me in the center of Your concern. I know I can be protected there when I am fearful and depleted.

Blessed are those who dwell in your house; they are ever praising you.

I could never walk without You. I am encircled on all sides by Your constant presence and love. Some small place within me will always glow in thanksgiving and praise, whatever the future holds. I put myself in Your hands.

Prayer

Lord, there are times when I'm afraid of closeness. The more I want to feel close to my spouse, the more vulnerable I feel. I'm afraid of being hurt. I know You understand the depth of my feelings. You know how I have been hurt in my marriage, and how I have sometimes hurt my spouse. I'm afraid to work at being close again. But I made a promise before You in the presence of Your people. Give me the courage to fulfill that promise. Help me make something beautiful of my marriage—not necessarily perfect, but beautiful. Amen.

Ten

Advanced Intimacy

S atisfying relationships require an investment of time. They can't begin without it—and they can't survive without it.

A young man who is attracted to an intriguing young woman in chemistry class has to figure out a way to make his life intersect with hers. Chemistry class doesn't often lend itself to getting to know the opposite sex, so he alters his schedule. Instead of hanging out with his friends on a Friday night, he starts going to basketball games—certain she'll be there with her friends. He knows that unless he restructures his time so he puts himself where she is, he doesn't have a chance of connecting with her.

If the two chemistry students start dating, they may begin organizing their lives to spend time together. The more time they spend together, the better they'll get to know each other. At some point, they'll make a decision about whether they want their friendship to develop into a serious relationship. If they decide to get serious, they'll spend even more time together. Eventually, they will either decide to make the relationship permanent or break up.

It seems obvious that a man and a woman have to be in the same place at the same time in order to meet—and have to spend significant amounts of time together in order for their relationship to grow.

Here's the catch: It isn't obvious to many married couples that they have to invest significant amounts of time together in order for their relationship to thrive.

Erica and Kevin were in their mid-forties when they realized their marriage was in trouble. There were no dramatic issues between them, just an accumulation of minor grievances that had never been resolved in their seventeen years of marriage. Both Kevin and Erica were devoted parents to their teenage daughters, who were excellent students, outstanding athletes, and talented musicians. The girls were able to maintain a heavy schedule of school, social, and extracurricular activities because their parents went out of their way to support them. They helped them with homework, transported them to music lessons and athletic practices, and did all the little things necessary for the girls to be part of the adolescent social mainstream. The heavy investment of time and energy that Kevin and Erica gave to their daughters was in addition to their own career pursuits. Both architects, Kevin worked long hours at his downtown office and Erica worked part-time from home. Erica also volunteered for a number of charities and maintained an active social schedule with a large group of friends. Kevin spent most of his free time—what little he had—indulging his passion for basketball. He attended as many games as possible and watched as many as he could on television.

Over the years, the busy-ness of this couple's lives led them to drift further and further apart. They became complacent about spending time together. They lost interest in physical intimacy. They started bickering over little things. They began spending even less time together—and when they did talk, their conversations became increasingly mean-spirited. But it wasn't until their youngest daughter started crying during one of their bickering sessions that Erica and Kevin woke up to how estranged they had become.

Kevin and Erica had one main problem: They were leading separate lives. And as long as they continued in their isolation, there was no hope for improving their marriage.

A husband and wife living separate lives is an extremely common problem. Without exception, it is devastating to a marriage, though the effects might only be obvious to outsiders in the long term. It's no wonder so many marriages become dry and brittle when so many spouses hardly speak to each other except to ask, "How is Karen getting to her piano lesson tonight?"

Because the issue of separate lives is so crucial, it's one of the first things I deal with in marital therapy. Kevin and Erica's situation was no exception. Shortly after they came to me for counseling, I gave them the assignment I give most couples. I asked them to commit to spending thirty minutes talking to each other each day for thirty days. They were to have their conversations alone. Physically together—not over the phone. No kids allowed in the room. If they had had young children, I would have asked them to have their conversations after the kids went to bed. But because their children were teenagers, I told them to simply explain that mom and dad needed some private time together. Oh—and wherever they decided to go to talk should be TV-free.

Because Kevin and Erica had forgotten how to talk to each other about anything but their daughters' activities, I specifically instructed them to spend fifteen minutes apiece talking about how their respective days had gone.

They protested immediately: "What's there to talk about?" Erica couldn't imagine what would interest Kevin about her day. She liked the "very part-time" job she had taken on after the children started school, but it was mainly paper-and-pencil architecture. She rarely had a chance to do anything creative with her paid work. What she really loved most was being a mother and homemaker. She was a remarkably inventive and nurturing parent who never made her children feel they were an after-thought. She thrived on almost every aspect of raising the girls: listening to their troubles and triumphs, brainstorming activities to enhance their learning, volunteering at their school, even shuffling them back and forth from lessons and sports activities. Erica enjoyed her work and adored be-ing a mom, but she viewed her daily activities as routine. Only rarely did she feel she had accomplished something that would interest anybody else. Something "significant." Something interesting enough to fill thirty min-utes of conversation for thirty consecutive days.

Kevin likewise assumed there was nothing especially interesting about his typical day. He basically liked his work. He wasn't crazy about com-muting, but he had compatible co-workers and an above-average income. He got to travel a bit, which he enjoyed. But the routines that go with any job were what took up most of his time. For him it was going to meetings, talking about projects, and sitting at the drawing board dreaming up new designs. Like most people, he rarely received any feedback to suggest he was doing a good job or that his life was in any way significant. So what's to talk about for thirty minutes a day?

I had to reassure Kevin and Erica that their lives were no less interesting than for most of the rest of us. What we think of as trivia is really the stuff of our lives. Few of us have anything "significant" to share at the end of a day. If we can't find significance in the "trivial," we will find significance in nothing. Actually, there's more significance in the trivia of our lives than we often realize. But we won't realize it unless we talk about it with someone who values the whole of our life enough to listen. In fact, listening—and seeing value in the small things that make up our lives— is one of the most caring and important roles a spouse can play.

Actually, the importance of talking and listening has little to do with the content of a conversation. It's the process that counts most. When Erica talks about the trivia of her day, she bestows her life with new meaning and value. She suggests that it serves a purpose. And talking about it with Kevin includes him in her purpose. It's a scary proposition, because she has to trust him to see the worth in her life, a worth that will never be recognized if it remains unspoken. The same is true for Kevin. His workplace, like most, isn't exactly affirming. By taking the risk of talking with his wife about the small stuff of his daily life and trusting her to see value in it, he has an opportunity to get the approval missing in his work environment.

Some miraculous things can happen when a couple takes the "thirty minutes for thirty days" assignment seriously. When Kevin listened to Erica, he discovered some facets of his wife and her life that he hadn't known before. He started asking questions. He made comments. He expressed feelings and asked about Erica's feelings. He inquired about her relationships with other people. He asked about the meaning of her experiences. Erica began listening to him. Small talk became big talk. The commonplace in their lives became significant.

As the commonplace becomes worth hearing about, it becomes worth having feelings about and hearing more about. For Kevin and Erica, thirty minutes soon stretched into an hour and at times longer. Buried issues began to come out, were discussed and resolved.

Unlikely as it may sound, it's a fact that Erica and Kevin started feeling passionate about each other long before the thirty-day assignment was over. Romantic feelings that had been dormant for years came back in a flood of positive emotions. They became lovers again. It all started with a tiny bit of warmth that flickered during their first conversations. The warmth was fed as they stayed with an assignment that made them uncomfortable and neither thought would do much good. But as they hung in with the assignment, they saw new signs of commitment in each other. The chasm between them gradually narrowed. New life poured into their relationship.

Of course, this isn't what happens with every couple. Some spouses find their conflict actually increases when they pursue the thirty-minute dialogues. When the silences that had kept them from attacking each other are broken, previously unexpressed resentments come out in the open. Painful fights may erupt. But even these fights can be seen as a sign of hope—they mean that the two partners in the marriage are still trying to communicate. As uncomfortable as conflict can be, it is less dangerous than withdrawal. And sometimes it brings issues to the surface so they can be resolved.

Sadly, not all conflict is productive. In their anger, some people lash out with an intent to hurt and alienate their partner even further. That's why it's so important to learn how to deal with conflict—a major piece of which is learning how to solve problems. (More about this later.)

Fortunately, most couples I've worked with have found that the thirty minutes for thirty days assignment is a bridge across their silence. It allows them to take more steps toward reconciliation and renewal.

MONTHLY CELEBRATIONS

Celebration is an important part of a healthy marriage. Celebrating a wedding anniversary, for example, is a good way for two partners to signify to each other the value of their relationship. But a once-a-year celebration isn't enough. I strongly urge couples to celebrate their marriage promise at least once a month. It isn't necessary to spend a lot of money on these mini-celebrations, but they are powerful acts in bonding couples together when they've been invested with thought and planning—and observed faithfully.

Here are some suggested ground rules for establishing and making the most regular celebrations:

Plan an outing at least once a month for just the two of you. Have someone else take care of the kids. *Don't invite your friends. Gatherings with other people don't count!* For some reason, couples have a hard time with this concept. They recite all the things they do in each other's company—attending church potluck suppers, visiting friends and relatives, going to parties and dinners, cheering their kids at athletic events—and think they've offered proof of their attempts at togetherness. But think about it: how much do you actually talk to your spouse at these kinds of events? For that matter, how much do you actually SEE your partner at group gatherings? Let's not even talk about any expressions of affection in group settings. Again: *gatherings with other people don't count for these once-a-month outings!*

Take turns planning the event. One month it's your responsibility, the next month it's your spouse's. Realize that planning and implementing the outing is an important part of expressing your appreciation for your partner.

When it's your turn to plan the celebration, make arrangements to do something that you know your spouse would particularly enjoy. This is critically important. For a husband to take his wife to a hockey game, when she hates hockey, defeats the purpose of the celebration. For a wife to take her husband shopping, when he breaks out into a cold sweat at the sight of a mall, is not exactly a bonding experience. The idea behind monthly celebrations is to provide an opportunity for self-giving. So when it's your turn to plan, try to take the attitude, "I am willingly doing this for you to show you I care." Participate in the chosen activity cheerfully, not grudgingly. You may even discover that your spouse's interests are worth pursuing yourself, that they're something you can explore together. And you may find that planning activities with your spouse's interests in mind has another unexpected payoff: vicarious pleasure. There is joy in seeing another person's joy. If you plan a celebration with the express purpose of delighting your mate, you may well experience a delight of your own.

Keep your celebrations as simple as your time and budget requires. The critical variable in these events is spending time together. Spending money is optional. Almost every community has something affordable going on, even if it's an activity sponsored by the local high school. Don't be stuffy. Open your tastes to amateur productions. Investigate local theater groups, community symphonies, and sports events. And if at all possible, save up your money to splurge on an occasional extra-special celebration. It's a good investment.

Be creative. Never repeat an activity more than once a year. This may seem like an unduly rigid standard, but there's a purpose behind it. It's all too easy to get into a rut with monthly outings. If you go out to eat or go to a movie every month, the specialness of your celebrations is lost. They're no longer celebrations, they're habits. Or worse yet, obligations. Habits become boring. Obligations become irritating. Another reason for planning different events each month: Eventually, you'll probably have to look for activities you've never participated in before. Doing something new gives you something different to talk about, which can liven up your thirty minute dialogues! Also, as you start talking with your friends about your new activities and interests, you'll soon discover what boring lives many of them lead compared to you and your spouse. And you'll probably realize how boring your life was before you started your monthly celebrations. You may look back at when you thought renting a video and ordering pizza was having a good time and think, *Did we actually live that way?* No wonder you had doubts about whether you had married the right person. You and your spouse were boring each other to death.

If you can't imagine how you'll ever come up with enough ideas for a year's worth of monthly celebrations—and initially most people can't—read your local newspaper. You'll be amazed at what it will reveal about what's going on in your community (and how little you're currently taking advantage of). My wife and I have a home on Michigan's Upper Peninsula. Having lived in the Chicago area all of our lives, when we first bought the house we wondered what people did with their time up there. Our place is thirty miles from the nearest "city," Escanaba, which has a total population of 15,000. Over the past five years, we've learned that there is an incredible variety of activity going on in Escanaba and the little communities surrounding it. We've found that people in small towns are just as creative and motivated to keep life interesting as any in larger cities. Awaken to the possibilities—together!

Kevin and Erica took to the monthly celebrations right away. One of the first activities Erica planned was a basketball night—dinner out and a professional basketball game. The expense was well worth the investment. Kevin was thrilled, and completely hooked on the idea of monthly celebrations. Although Erica didn't become a basketball fan, she developed a better appreciation for the game and thoroughly enjoyed being able to make Kevin so happy.

In an amazing turnaround, Kevin took Erica to the ballet. Amazing! Although Erica loved ballet, Kevin detested it. When we first talked about the ground rules for monthly celebrations, Kevin said he'd do anything but go to the ballet. He couldn't explain his disgust, except that to him ballet represented the most boring and noxious of all possible activities. He swore he'd never waste money on it or anything like it. Not even a *movie* about ballet. But after Erica took him to the basketball game, he changed his mind and bought tickets to a local production of Swan Lake. I'd like to report that he became an enthusiastic fan of classical dance, but that's not what happened. Actually, he vowed afterward that he'd never go again—but not quite as forcefully as before. And Erica saw through his bluster to the intent behind his actions. She knew the only reason he would force himself to go to a ballet was because he wanted to please her.

One final ground rule for planning your celebrations. When it's your turn to make the arrangements, don't tell your spouse where you're going ahead of time. Just tell him or her how to dress for the occasion. The element of surprise is part of the fun, as Myra discovered. She and her husband worked out three evenings a week at the local YMCA. One Friday, without telling her husband, Myra packed two bags with enough clothes for the weekend—one for Rob and one for herself. After hiding the bags in her trunk, she suggested taking her car to the YMCA that night. When their workout was over, she got behind the wheel and headed for a hotel, which happened to be in the opposite direction of home. Rob pointed out that she had taken a wrong turn. Myra told him she wanted to stop at a store. When they pulled up to the hotel, Rob still didn't have a clue what was going on until Myra announced her surprise plans for the weekend—to Rob's delight. It was an expensive celebration, but what made it special was the thoughtfulness and the element of surprise, not the cost.

WEEKLY "VACATIONS"

If you've ever been frustrated by the standard advice to married couples to indulge in frequent "getaway weekends," don't despair. Your marriage can thrive without the expense of prepackaged hotel romance. But you do need to get away—from the TV, from children, from work, from the distractions of everyday life. Fortunately, any time away together counts, even if it's only for an hour. Go out for coffee. Take a walk. Ride bikes. Do anything that's enjoyable—as long as it's just the two of you.

Ironically, the couples who most need to "get away"—those with young children—are the ones who find it most difficult. Lack of time, lack of available baby-sitters, lack of money—these are just a few of many potential barriers to the idea of weekly getaway time. But the new tensions and conflicts that come to a marriage when children arrive make couples' together time even more crucial. Fortunately, many young couples have found that, while they can't necessarily go out for weekly dates, much less for getaway weekends, they can carve out times to be alone together on a daily or weekly basis. Here are a few suggestions:

Read together in bed after the children have been tucked away for the night, even if it's just for fifteen minutes. Many couples say that while they have widely different reading interests, just lying next to each other and reading makes them feel close. Also, try to share a story, idea, or incident from what you're reading.

Choose a book or books you think you'd both like to read. If you choose more than one book, read one of them while your spouse reads the other. Then talk about what you've read. You may or may not decide to read at the same time, as suggested above. The key here is to select some books that are likely to interest both of you.

Set aside a special time for sharing a cup of coffee or tea together. This may be as simple as lingering at the dinner table to talk while the kids go play in another part of the house, or reserving a half hour after the children go to bed, for conversation and refreshments. The point is to relax and talk.

Watch a favorite television program together once a week. Take a shared interest in sports. Try to find a sport and a team you both care about and then tune in each week to watch your team on TV. Be sure to sit together while you watch.

Become movie buffs. Rent a movie once a week and watch it together, after the kids are in bed or while they're busy in another part of the house. If the children are awake, tell them it's time for mom and dad to be alone for a while.

Have a special meal together once a week. If you do this at home, work together on preparing it. Make an effort to create "atmosphere" with music, candles, and a fresh tablecloth. Feed the kids first and then send them to bed.

There are endless possibilities. But before you can explore them, you and your spouse need to agree that it's important to spend time together enjoying something that pleases you both. Including these shared micro-vacations in your life can pay off handsomely in the form of marital satisfaction, but it takes planning and determination. In the busy-ness of life, the easiest thing to neglect is your marriage. But neglecting your relationship puts it at great jeopardy.

FAMILY TIME

One of the most telling signs of the status of a marriage is the way couples spend time with their children. Many couples who have drifted apart end up developing separate lives with their kids. Perhaps Mom takes them shopping and chauffeurs them to all their activities. Dad may take them to ball games and out for pizza. Only on rare occasions do they do things together as a family.

Even very young children are aware of these patterns and what they imply. And their awareness makes them feel deeply insecure.

It's important not only for your children, but for your relationship with your spouse, that you have regular time together as a family. Family time is a sign of your common commitment to your children, of what you've created together, of what you have to celebrate. It is also a powerful reminder of what you have to lose if you let your relationship wither up and die.

Whether you're trying to rebuild your marriage or simply enrich it, establishing a pattern of regular family outings is a good habit to adopt. One family activity a week is ideal, but one a month may be all that's possible. Family outings can follow a pattern similar to the monthly spouses-only celebrations. Each member of the family gets a turn at being the "chosen one"—the person the rest of the family tries to make feel special by planning an event he or she will particularly enjoy. These times together are what families, especially children, tend to remember. They build a sense of belonging and create images of what love looks like.

In this chapter, I've tried to suggest some ways you and your spouse can spend more time together, especially talking and engaging in activities together. It's true: Shared activities and shared talk, bolstered by a sense of unconditional acceptance, are the building blocks of friendship. And friendship is the foundation of marriage. Marriage is more than a friendship, of course. But marriages that last tend to be those in which friendship is at the core of the relationship.

One final note. This chapter is titled "Advanced Intimacy," but it could just as easily be called "Advanced Risktaking." If you and your mate have been drifting apart or are having serious conflicts, one of you has to take the risk of trying to turn things around. If you're the one taking the initiative to suggest some of the strategies offered in this chapter, there's a possibility that your partner may turn you down. If so, it's not going to feel good. But not taking the initiative also poses a risk—that your marriage will continue its downward slide.

The risk of reaching out is worth taking.

EXERCISE

Following is a list of the intimacy building blocks discussed in this chapter. Evaluate the degree to which you and your spouse already take advantage of these marriage builders. Use a scale of 1 to 10, with 10 being the highest. Then develop a plan for introducing some of these ingredients into your relationship.

	Evaluation	**Plan**
Time together		

Celebrations
    Frequency:
        Monthly
        Weekly
        Daily
    Alone together:
        Planning
        Creativity
        Done for the other
        Element of surprise

Vacations

Vacations at home

Family time

During the next few weeks, pay special attention to when and how you spend time with your spouse. Commit yourself to making room for the thirty minutes for thirty days plan discussed in this chapter. Consider establishing monthly celebrations, regular "getaways," and regular family times. Think of one thing you can do to prevent work, children, church, or recreation from crowding out time for your marriage.

JOURNALING
(1) In column 1 of your structured journal, record your efforts to implement your advanced intimacy plan. Include notes about how your spouse reacted.
(2) In column 2, note how you felt when preparing, initiating, and carrying through your plan, as well as how you felt about your partner's reaction.
(3) In column 3, record your thoughts through this process.

(4) In column 4, chronicle how you dealt with negative thoughts before, during, and after your efforts. Remember the strategies from chapter 8.

SPIRITUAL DISCIPLINES
Reflect on Psalm 63:1–8.

O God, you are my God, earnestly I seek you; my soul thirsts for you; my body longs for you, in a dry and thirsty land where there is no water.

Lord, each step I take, each new risk, brings hazards to deplete me. Where can I turn to be refreshed and renewed?

I have seen you in the sanctuary and beheld your power and your glory.

In Your presence is rebirth. Among Your people I find sustenance. Open me to every reminder that You are with me—in the people who support me, in the stirrings of strength within me, in yet-to-be revealed surprises.

Because your love is better than life, my lips will glorify you. I will praise you as long as I live, and in your name I will lift up my hands.

What would I do if I were truly alone in this journey? But You have given me Your people and Your hidden self. I journey with thanks.

My soul will be satisfied as with the richest of foods; with singing lips my mouth will praise you.

You have promised sustenance. Help me receive strength when my path is steep, when I can only measure my progress in inches. Or when I can't see any progress at all.

On my bed I remember you; I think of you through the watches of the night.

When I feel most alone and abandoned, You are with me.

Because you are my help, I sing in the shadow of your wings.

I will rest in Your care, and the care of Your people, knowing You are always faithful.

My soul clings to you; your right hand upholds me.

Each small step, every little risk, holds its own terrors. But my future is with You. I will let You lead me. I will take strength from Your strength. Into Your hands.

Prayer

Lord God, as I think of the minutes and hours that make up each day, I realize that they are a gift You present to me as I wake up each morning. Help me be a good steward of this gift. Help me use my time to fortify my marriage. Help me remember that the way I use my time will determine the shape of my relationship to my spouse for months and years to come. Help me make room in my life for my partner, to think and to plan for how we can become as close as You want us to be.

Eleven

Solving Long-Standing Problems

B oth good marriages and difficult marriages have problems. The difference is that in difficult marriages the problems tend not to be resolved. Hurts collect, building a reservoir of resentment and alienation.

The purpose of this chapter is to teach you some problem-solving skills to help you and your spouse improve your relationship. Among these are some communication techniques that lead to problem-solving, because problem-solving and communication are intertwined.

Why in the world would I wait until this far along in the book to talk about solving problems? Why would I waste my time talking about intimacy, for example, when you may have long-standing, unresolved conflicts in your marriage? For a very good reason: The effectiveness of problem-solving techniques are greatly enhanced by feelings of closeness.

Having said that, I have to add this plea: Please don't give up on problem-solving just because your marriage isn't yet as intimate as you'd like it to be. You can work on both at the same time. Just don't forget the important role that feelings of closeness play in solving problems.

STARTING THE PROCESS

There are actually two parts to problem-solving. The first step is defining the problem. The second is finding and working on solutions. It's a serious mistake to try to skip right to the second step without first working hard to identify the core issue. Often, the real problem isn't what it first appears to be. That being the case, if you and your spouse try to launch into problem-solving before you both agree on what the problem is, you'll both get frustrated and discouraged.

To help you think through what the problem is, I've listed some common areas of disagreement in marriage. These include

- Controversial attitudes
- Controversial behaviors
- Conflicting expectations
- Differing interests
- Finances
- Incompatible child-rearing styles
- Extended family disagreements
- Differing values/priorities
- Religious beliefs/practices
- Role definitions
- Practical responsibilities in the home
- Career demands
- Recreational pursuits
- Sex
- Friendships

There are many other issues couples disagree on, of course, but going through this list may help you start the process of defining the problems in your marriage. Once you've identified a few general issues, move on to a more specific problem-definition stage, taking into account the following "rules":

RULE ONE: Pray.

If possible, start this process by praying with your partner. If your spouse won't pray with you, pray on your own. If you find it hard to pray because the words don't come to you, or you're too weary from dealing with the tensions in your situation, try using a written prayer like the one included at the end of the chapter. Or pray through a psalm or hymn. The words will become your own if you speak them sincerely.

What should you pray about? First, pray for forgiveness. Admit to yourself and to God that you are struggling—as we all are—with a tendency to be alienated instead of reconciled. Pray for the ability to recognize instances in which you contribute to alienation from your spouse, and from others. Next, pray for courage: Courage to admit to ways in which you may be wrong. Courage to risk closeness. Courage to risk the vulnerability required for reconciliation and growth. Finally, pray for release from self-involvement, for new understanding, and for stamina to stay with the task of being drawn more closely to your spouse.

RULE TWO: Do your best to stay attuned to something positive about your relationship.

As you work with your spouse to define the problems facing you, don't be so focused on a problem or problems that you forget each other's good traits and the good aspects of your relationship. If you start to forget the good side of being married to each other, go back to the work you did in the early chapters of this book.

RULE THREE: Be specific.

In problem-solving nothing is more destructive than generalization. If my wife tells me that the problem between us is that I'm "not thoughtful enough," I might respond by saying, "No, the problem is that you don't appreciate me." What is the reality here? The only way to decide is to cite specific examples. Otherwise, we're in danger of a shouting match: "You're not thoughtful." "Yes, I am!" "No, you're not!" "Yes, I am!"

Who "wins" in a situation like this? The person who can shout the loudest, or who can outlast the other in what is guaranteed to be an exhausting game.

What if my wife skipped the generalizations and offered some specific examples of my thoughtlessness? She could come up with a long list:

- I don't offer to do the dishes enough.
- I don't pick up after myself.
- I don't help with the gardening.
- I don't go shopping with her.
- I don't do the laundry.

There are several courses of action I could take in response to these specific examples. For example, I could

- Explain away her example.
- Deny everything.
- Admit she's at least partially right but refuse to change.
- Agree with all or some of her examples and work at changing.
- Tell her she should have married someone else.
- Tell her to pray about it.

By offering specific examples, my wife provides options we can negotiate around, specific choices around which we can sanely make a decision. Without specifics, we get nowhere. We either wrangle to the point of exhaustion or we withdraw from each other.

RULE FOUR: Express your feelings—but in an appropriate way and without blaming your spouse.

For many years now, practitioners of feelings-based psychology have been telling us that the truth of every matter lies in our feelings. Supposedly, all we have to do to resolve our problems is to "get in touch with" our feelings and then express them. We've been told that the most healing act we can perform is to vent our feelings as forcefully as we feel them. Unfortunately, as is so often the case with psychological dogma, there is no research evidence whatsoever to support this notion. To the contrary, much evidence points to psychological conflicts resulting more from the way we *think* about things than the way we feel about them—and as much from the way we *behave* as the way we feel. Furthermore, studies have shown that venting negative emotions without constraint simply heightens those feelings. For example, if you indulge yourself by erupting in anger, your feelings become less controllable, you become less able to hear others, and you become less capable of rational thinking. None of those, I think you'll agree, is a good scenario—and we can all identify people who have destroyed their relationships by "letting it all hang out" or unchecked "emoting."

Expressing your feelings doesn't mean giving in to hysteria or rage. It doesn't mean you have permission to blame and attack. So how do you communicate intense feelings to your spouse without losing control and making things worse?

Concentrate first on expressing your feelings in a way that makes it clear that you are responsible for them. Contrast these two statements, for example:

"I'm feeling very unimportant to you."

vs.

"You really don't care about me."

The second statement is accusatory. It is almost guaranteed to be interpreted as an attack—and to provoke a defensive response. The first statement expresses strong feelings—negative feelings—but avoids blame. When it's followed by specific examples offered without hostility, it can be the start of a productive conversation.

Express your feelings, but admit that they may be out of proportion. Acknowledge the possibility that there may be a misunderstanding between you. Give your mate the benefit of the doubt and as much latitude as possible to respond without defensiveness.

RULE FIVE: Accept responsibility for your role—or possible role—in the problem.

It's possible, of course, that you don't have a role in the problem. But it's more likely that you are so angry or distressed that you find it difficult to recognize how you may be contributing to the situation. As a practical matter, if you want to make any progress toward a solution, you need to let your spouse know that you're open to considering the possibility that you're as much at fault as he/she is.

Reed and Trish are a good example of how responsibility for a problem is often shared, even when that isn't obvious from the beginning. Reed was an avid archer. A competitor in high school and college, he continued the sport as an avocation after he married Trish. Because she knew how much Reed enjoyed archery and how it relieved some of his work stresses, Trish felt guilty about resenting the time he spent with it. She especially resented his signing up for a major tournament that began within days of when their first child was due to be born. She needed him—for the tense days leading up to the delivery and, if the birth ended up being early, for the delivery itself. Furthermore, why did they have to plan every vacation around archery—contests, club rallies, training events? When Trish finally expressed her feelings about these things to Reed, he was shocked—with good reason. Up until then, Trish had seemed as excited about archery as he was. She acted proud when he won competitions, showed off his trophies when guests visited their home, showed every sign of approving of his participation in the sport. As for his cluelessness about Trish's desire for him to be around for the birth of their child, Reed protested, "I knew she was in the hands of a good doctor, and I didn't think there was much more I could do. In fact, I *asked* her if there was anything more I could do. She always answered that she was fine and I should go ahead with my plans."

Who's at fault in this situation? Most objective observers would say that Reed was clearly overinvolved in archery and insensitive to his wife's needs and desires. But Trish's behavior contributed to the problem. She never complained about Reed's neglect, at least not without a half-laugh or in a clear-cut way. Once or twice she said something like, "Why don't you skip this competition, Reed, so we can go up to see my sister in Minneapolis?" His typical response was, "But this is a really important tournament." He was obtuse, no doubt about it, but Trish never pressed her point. If she had been clear and firm about her preferences, Reed probably would have honored them. As it was, he dropped archery altogether after Trish finally confronted him and expressed how she felt.

The lesson in this story: Take responsibility for your part in a conflict, and for your own feelings. Otherwise, you may never come to resolution.

RULE SIX: Define the problem as briefly and simply as possible.

It's common for marriage partners to cloud the issues during a conflict by complicating them to the point that neither party remembers what he or she is upset about. It's also common for spouses to verbally speculate on the psychological and theological causes of each other's objectionable behavior. Resist this temptation! It's hard enough to agree on the nature of a problem without dragging in theories of why it exists.

When Marti left her husband, Chuck, after six years of marriage, she said she needed a temporary separation to get away from her husband's dominating ways. And she told anybody who would listen about her theories of why Chuck was so hard to live with: He had grown up in a family where the father was opinionated and domineering and the mother was mousy. He was just following in his father's footsteps. But she, of course, was no "mouse" like Chuck's mother. Had she shared her psychological theory with Chuck? "Oh yes, many times." How did he react? "He flies into a rage."

No wonder Marti had never been able to get through to her husband during their many arguments. She was confusing the issues by bringing up Chuck's relationship with his parents. He had stored up a lot of anger toward his father and mother, and Marti's theory only stoked that anger.

Marti and Chuck's situation was further complicated by the fact that Chuck had a theory for why Marti took the kids and left him. His theory was theological: It was Satan's doing. Since it was all the devil's fault, Chuck, of course, didn't need to take any responsibility for the problems in their relationship.

There was nothing inherently wrong with Marti developing a psychological theory for why her husband behaved the way he did or Chuck having a theological theory about why his wife left him. In fact, as we explained in a previous chapter, trying to understand the reasons for your partner's attitudes and actions can help you view him or her in a more sympathetic light. But as a practical matter, it's best not to share your theory with your spouse, at least not while you're in the process of defining the problems between you.

Both Marti and Chuck were using their theories to shield themselves from taking responsibility for their own actions. Chuck wanted to believe that Marti was pushed out the door by Satan, not his bullying behavior. Marti wanted to believe that she wasn't responsible to stand up to Chuck because their marital script had been written by his parents. Eventually, they both temporarily suspended their theories and defined the basic problem: Chuck needed to be less controlling, and Marti needed to be more direct in her communication with him. Once they were able to agree that was the problem, Marti came home and Chuck changed his ways.

RULE SEVEN: Discuss one problem at a time.

This is a hard rule to follow, since most married couples have more than one problem. People in troubled marriages tend to be trapped in a whole web of problems. It's tempting to try to solve them all at once. But that doesn't work.

As you and your spouse start this process, remember that conquering one problem will help give you the motivation and confidence to work on others. Be patient. Work for one success. It will lead to more.

Remember, too, that sometimes one problem will point to another. That was the case in Meg and Tony's situation, for example. Meg tended to be a bit flirtatious. Tony knew that, but assumed she would straighten up after the wedding. And she did. But shortly after the birth of their first child, Meg began flirting again—and not with Tony. He became furious. He ranted and raved, even accusing her of unfaithfulness. When they came to counseling, Meg's response to Tony's anger was quite simple: "You don't pay any attention to me anymore. Why shouldn't I flirt? It keeps my spirits up. It makes me feel good about myself as a woman."

There was a problem behind the problem. Meg's flirting was wrong and shouldn't be *excused*. But it can be *explained*. Tony had never learned how to be attentive or nurturing toward another person, including his wife. And Meg had never learned how to ask for the attention she wanted from Tony.

How does the principle of dealing with one problem at a time apply here? It still stands: When one problem was addressed—Meg's flirtatious ways—another problem was uncovered—Tony's inattentiveness. By sticking to one issue at a time, this couple was able to deal with both problems successfully.

RULE EIGHT: Don't bring up the past.

This is another hard rule to follow, because so often the problem at hand is, or seems to be, part of a long-standing pattern. But pointing that out doesn't help change the pattern. It just intensifies the emotion surrounding the problem. Especially if your spouse has been working on changing the pattern but has temporarily lapsed, he or she will be discouraged that you're not giving credit for progress made—and may even give up trying. It's also possible that you have completely misread your mate's behavior. It may not be connected to the past at all.

Sometimes bringing up the past is used as a smokescreen to avoid taking personal responsibility for problems in a marriage. Faced with a spouse's pain or anger, it's tempting to defend yourself against a criticism of your current behavior by counterattacking with a criticism from your spouse's past. "Okay, I didn't clean up like I said I would, but you didn't go grocery shopping last week. That's the fifth time you've promised to do something and . . ." If you're any good at this diversionary tactic, you can turn things around and quickly have your spouse defending his or her actions of last week—while what you said or did this week is completely forgotten. Clever ruse, but it doesn't help you work through problems.

RULE NINE: Practice the art of paraphrase.

This technique is one of the most commonly taught communication enhancers, for good reason. It works. Use it to make sure you understand your spouse's point of view. When your partner states a problem, repeat what you think he or she said in a summary statement. Say something like this: "What I think you are saying is . . ." Then listen to your spouse's feedback on whether or not you're on target. Be patient. Your mate may not agree with your summary, and it might take several tries before you get it right. Try to understand the feelings behind what your spouse is saying. Test your understanding of the feelings. "My impression is that you feel . . . Am I right?" One of the side benefits of using this approach to make sure you understand your partner's point of view is this: If you truly understand your mate's view, you'll probably become more sympathetic to it. And having some sympathy for your spouse's view can create a much better atmosphere for working on a solution.

RULE TEN: Don't read motives behind your spouse's words.

Don't try to make something more of what your partner is saying than his/her words signify. You can't read someone else's mind. If you try to, or give the impression that you think you can, you'll have an angry and frustrated spouse on your hands (make that an even more angry and frustrated spouse).

RULE ELEVEN: Listen to your spouse with an open mind.

This is another difficult rule to follow because it's hard to ignore past hurts, experiences that have predisposed you to interpret your partner's words negatively. Even hurts from outside your marriage can skew the way you hear your mate. But if you approach an issue with negative thoughts, you'll expect that there's no solution to the problem—and you'll get what you expect.

RULE TWELVE: Don't interrupt.

Let your spouse finish statements, no matter how strongly you feel about what is being said. When your mate is stating his or her view of a problem, your job is to listen and understand. You can't listen if you're concentrating on your comeback. You certainly can't listen if you're interrupting. Even if you think your spouse is totally off base, wait your turn to speak.

RULE THIRTEEN: Start with the least-threatening issue first.

If you have multiple problems to define and solve (and who doesn't?), it makes strategic sense to begin with the one that is least likely to cause bad feelings in the process of dealing with it. Solving a simple problem can give you momentum and trust to tackle more difficult ones.

RULE FOURTEEN: Try to agree on a written statement of the problem.

Why would you want to do that? Because all kinds of strange things happen in the problem-solving process that may force you back to the problem-definition stage: Side issues may get introduced. Additional problems may be added in. You may forget the original problem entirely. A written problem statement will give you something to return to periodically to help you keep a clear focus. As you and your spouse gain experience in problem-solving, your trust level will increase and you may be able to drop this technique.

RULE FIFTEEN: Treat your spouse the way you want to be treated.

Suppose that your spouse is upset with you about a recurring sore spot in your marriage. How would you want your spouse to approach you? Go back and review each of the other fourteen rules. How would you react to being confronted in this firm but loving way? Likely much better than if met with an all-out assault. This is the one rule to come back to when anger or hurt threatens to take hold of you once again.

SOLVING THE PROBLEM

Once you and your partner have worked through the process of defining a problem, you've developed some skills—and an attitude of cooperation—that will take you a long way toward actually solving the problem. The problem-solving stage has several distinct steps, which are listed below. One caution as you start this phase: Remember, don't go backward. Once you've started problem-solving, don't go back to defining the problem unless you've come to a complete impasse. Problem-solving is stressful enough without prolonging the process. If you prolong the process too much—and create too much stress—you'll undermine your confidence that your problems can be solved.

STEP ONE: Create a list of alternative solutions and consider them all.

If you can't finish your list of options in one session together, reflect on your accomplishments so far and then add to the list at a later date.

STEP TWO: Evaluate the alternatives.

Consider the pros and cons of each option on your list. Discuss the options until one of them makes the most sense to both of you.

STEP THREE: Develop an action plan.

After you've selected an option you both agree on, "operationalize" your choice. What steps will be required to implement this option?

STEP FOUR: Assign responsibilities.

Agree on who will do what. Discuss how you will maintain a cooperative and mutually supportive relationship while implementing your plan.

STEP FIVE: Evaluate the result of your action plan.

Your plan should include a method for assessing how well the plan worked. If one or both partners' behavior is the issue, for example, you might want to agree on a rating system. Perhaps you'd establish a scale of 1–10 to measure how much a particular behavior has changed. If you use a rating system, both partners should chart their perceptions. Be sure to work this out together or you'll risk starting a new problem.

STEP SIX: Plan for how you're going to celebrate your solution.

This is important. Solving a problem is a tremendous boost to marital morale. It builds confidence that you'll be able to work together to overcome problems in the future. So make the most of your successes. Go out on a date. Make love. Give your spouse a gift (it doesn't have to be expensive, but it should reflect some thought).

STEP SEVEN: Put your chosen solution, action plan, and celebration plan in writing.

Then sign it (both of you) as a statement of commitment and clear indication of your mutual responsibility for carrying out the plan.

If you follow these steps, you'll grow much more skilled at solving problems in your marriage. But successful problem-solving isn't a guarantee of marital happiness. Couples rarely draw closer together just because they've become more effective at communicating and solving problems. I'm not saying the problem-solving skills aren't important. They are. But it's necessary to be realistic about how these skills fit into the overall mix of skills you need to make your marriage work. Again, that's why it's critical to work on developing intimacy before you start problem-solving. But if you and your spouse can't solve problems, your sense of closeness will eventually erode.

EXERCISE

Assess your problem-solving style

(1) Write an account of your last argument/conflict with your spouse. What was the problem? How did you define it? How did you try to solve it?

(2) Now go through each of the rules and steps associated with defining and solving problems and grade yourself on how well you followed

them. Give a letter grade as if you were in school.

Defining the problem

A	B	C	D	F	1. Pray
A	B	C	D	F	2. Focus on the positive
A	B	C	D	F	3. Be specific
A	B	C	D	F	4. Express feelings appropriately
A	B	C	D	F	5. Accept responsibility
A	B	C	D	F	6. Keep it simple
A	B	C	D	F	7. One problem at a time
A	B	C	D	F	8. Leave the past behind
A	B	C	D	F	9. Paraphrase
A	B	C	D	F	10. Don't mind read motives
A	B	C	D	F	11. Listen with an open mind
A	B	C	D	F	12. Don't interrupt
A	B	C	D	F	13. Solve easier problems first
A	B	C	D	F	14. Cooperate on a written statement
A	B	C	D	F	15. Treat each other as you want to be treated

Solving the problem

A	B	C	D	F	1. List alternative solutions
A	B	C	D	F	2. Evaluate options
A	B	C	D	F	3. Develop action plan
A	B	C	D	F	4. Assign/carry out responsibilities
A	B	C	D	F	5. Plan evaluation
A	B	C	D	F	6. Plan celebration
A	B	C	D	F	7. Write celebration plan

Now look at how you graded yourself. Decide how you need to change. Make a note of that in the column next to your grade. Keep in mind that, however you think your partner scored in this exercise, you can't change him/her except by modeling good problem-solving. You can only take responsibility for your own actions.

JOURNALING

(1) Use column 1 to record your efforts to use a new approach to solving problems. Document what you did and what happened as a result.

(2) Use column 2 to record your feelings about the new approach.

(3) Use column 3 for notes about your thoughts throughout the process.

(4) In column 4, identify any negative thoughts during your problem-solving attempts and write some notes about how you might counteract these thoughts using suggestions from the chapter on faulty thinking patterns.

(5) Decide whether the new approach was reasonably successful. Would you try the same techniques again? Is there anything else you could do? Anything different?

SPIRITUAL DISCIPLINES

Contemplation

Meditate on Ephesians 4:31–32; 5:1–2; 5:15–16; 6:10–13, NKJV.

Let all bitterness, wrath, anger, clamor, and evil speaking be put away from you, with all malice, and be kind to one another, tenderhearted, forgiving one another, just as God in Christ also forgave you. . . .

The conflicts in my marriage make me so frustrated and angry that sometimes I feel like being deliberately hurtful toward _____. Sometimes I *am* hurtful. Can You soften my heart, Lord? Can You remove my anger? Can You make me more forgiving? Don't let me become a hard and uncompromising partner. Don't let me lose hold of my dream of a marriage that works. I turn my anger over to you.

Therefore be followers of God as dear children. And walk in love, as Christ also has loved us and given Himself for us, an offering and sacrifice to God. . . . See then that you walk circumspectly, not as fools but as wise, redeeming the time, because the days are evil. . . .

I know that Christ has forgiven me at great cost. Through Him, I have been given a way of healing and wholeness. Help me walk in that way. Help me live with the dignity Christ bestows, the dignity of a forgiven sinner. Help me wisely decide between what is true and what is not. Help me invest my life in what is good. Give me sufficient love to work at the give-and-take of my marriage.

Finally, my brethren, be strong in the Lord and in the power of His might. Put on the whole armor of God, that you may be able to stand against the wiles of the devil. For we wrestle not against flesh and blood, but against principalities, against powers, against the rulers of the darkness of this age, against spiritual hosts of wickedness in the heavenly places.

I need Your strength to overcome the problems in my marriage and to achieve what You have called me to be. Show me where I can find the resources I need to be Your person. Help me recognize the sources of strength available to me.

Therefore take up the whole armor of God, that you may be able to withstand in the evil day, and having done all, to stand.

Into Your hands, Lord.

Prayer

Reflect on the words of Psalm 37:5–6, and then pray the words that follow:

Commit your way to the Lord, trust also in Him, and He shall bring it to pass. He shall bring forth your righteousness as the light, and your justice as the noonday.

Lord, help me to commit myself totally to Your hands. As I work on solving some of the long-standing problems in my marriage, help me remember that it is Your role to assure justice, not mine. Help me give up my need to prove the rightness of my own cause. Forgive me for all the ways I have contributed to the conflicts in my marriage. Help me recognize when I am selfishly seeking my own good, when I am refusing to see another point of view. Give me the courage to admit when I'm wrong. Take away my fear of being vulnerable so that I can risk closeness. Give me new understanding and enough stamina to stay with the task of solving problems. Thank you for Your promise of strength and comfort. Amen.

Twelve

Acceptance: Coping With Your Behavioral "Allergies"

W hen all is said and done, a lot of what improves marriage satisfaction boils down to one issue: *acceptance.* One of the biggest
factors that will determine whether or not your marriage thrives—or even
survives—is how much you can accept about your spouse.

At this point you may be thinking, "No kidding! That's exactly the
problem—I *can't* accept such-and-such about my spouse. And with good
reason, because such-and-such is unacceptable! That's why I'm questioning whether I even married the right person."

It's possible that you're right, that your partner's attitudes and/or behavior are simply unacceptable. If your spouse is having an affair or abus-
ing you mentally or physically, for example, you cannot and should not
accept such behavior. I'll be talking about what to do about clearly unacceptable behavior later. But for now, just consider this: If I were to draw
a continuum of what's acceptable and unacceptable in marriage, adultery
and abuse would be at the far end—in the "red" zone of attitudes and
behaviors that are without question unacceptable. But short of adultery
and abuse, few other behaviors are so clear-cut. That's because perceptions
of what's acceptable are extremely variable. What is acceptable to you may
be unacceptable to your best friend and vice versa.

Complicating the acceptance issue is the fact that while all of us are capable of change to some degree, most of us have basic traits that are essentially unchangeable. We can make superficial adjustments in ourselves and our behavior, but we can never become completely different people.

Of course, most of us aren't concerned about changing ourselves. We want to change our spouses! If we could, we wouldn't have to worry about acceptance. But the reality is this: While we can sometimes ask our mates to modify the attitudes and behaviors that drive us crazy, their defining qualities and characteristics are going to remain the same. That's where *acceptance* comes in.

When Nancy first met Dan, she was immediately attracted to his looks, athletic ability, and spiritual commitment. As they began dating, though, she was somewhat put off by his shyness and limited range of interests. Aside from sports—especially football, baseball, and tennis—Dan didn't seem to have many interests. Nancy found sports boring. And she was bothered by Dan's bashfulness in public. She liked a man to be outgoing— not necessarily the life of the party, but a strong, "take charge" presence around other people. To her, shyness was the same thing as weakness. She didn't have anything against "weak" men, but she didn't want to be married to one.

As their relationship progressed, Nancy decided to talk to Dan about her concerns. To her surprise, he took no offense. In fact, he told her he was willing to change. She was thrilled. Given time, and with her help, Dan would almost certainly become more outgoing and "interesting." He'd be a perfect husband.

So they got married. True to his promise, Dan did try to make some changes. Despite his shyness, he agreed to socialize with her friends. And even though he found them embarrassing, he took dancing lessons because Nancy loved to dance.

But Nancy wasn't satisfied. Dan wasn't changing as dramatically as she had expected. Even though he was attending parties and social gatherings with her, he was too quiet to please her. He would talk to people, but usually after they initiated the conversation and made a special attempt to draw him out. Friends who had known Dan before he got married were surprised by how much more sociable he was—he had never gone to parties when he was single—but Nancy was disappointed. She couldn't understand why he couldn't just snap out of his shyness. How could someone so handsome, so athletic, so masculine, be so . . . weak!

She was similarly disappointed with Dan's attempts to expand his interests. Okay, so he had taken up dancing, but why couldn't he be more enthusiastic about it? And why couldn't he be more eager to try other new activities?

Nancy was frustrated because Dan hadn't changed as much as she believed he had clearly promised to change. But for him to alter himself that much, he would have had to undergo a total metamorphosis. By expecting Dan to virtually become a different person, Nancy was setting herself up for disappointment. Recent research suggests that shyness, for example, is often an inborn trait. People who are born shy aren't necessarily doomed to a life devoid of social interaction—they can moderate their shyness, but only within limits.

The same is true of many other traits. If you're born without a natural gift of music, you can still learn to play the piano. You can read notes and move your fingers, but you'll probably never play as well as a natural musical prodigy. It wouldn't be fair to expect you to.

Fortunately, Nancy finally realized that it wasn't realistic to expect Dan to become an outgoing, gregarious adventurer. She made up her mind to accept him as he was.

If you want your spouse to be the right person for you, consider this: Perhaps it's time to stop focusing on what you can change about your mate and start thinking about how you can be accepting.

Learning to accept traits and behaviors that drive you crazy—almost as if you were allergic to them—isn't easy. But here are some strategies:

LEARN TO UNDERSTAND

Understanding why someone behaves the way he or she does doesn't automatically translate into acceptance, but it's a good first step. So ask yourself what influences—family, friends, school, environment—have been at work on your spouse to produce the traits and habits you find so unacceptable.

A note here: Remember what you learned in the last chapter. If you receive a flash of great insight into your spouse's behavior, it isn't your job to wave it in his or her face.

A second note: Don't confuse *understanding* irritating behavior with *excusing* irresponsible or unacceptable behavior. When you find excuses for irresponsible behavior, you're condemned to live with those excuses. The point of trying to understand your spouse is to determine first, whether change is necessary; second, whether it's possible; and third, if it's possible, to what degree. Also, understanding the forces that shaped your mate can help you develop the empathy to accept behaviors you can't honestly label unacceptable or irresponsible.

Some spouses become remarkably tolerant once they understand why their partners act a certain way. I assume that's why my wife accepts some of the annoying quirks in my personality—like my tendency to be a spendthrift. When I shop for groceries, I always come home with more than we need. I'll bring home so much fruit that some of it will inevitably spoil before we can eat it. And I'll sneak in a lot of snack foods that I'm not supposed to have. My wife is amazingly accepting of this irritating behavior, perhaps because she understands where it comes from. I grew up poor. My family lived in a low-income housing project on the south side of Chicago. We couldn't just go to the store and pick out whatever we wanted. We had to be careful about every purchase. And we almost never had enough. So now that I have more financial flexibility, I tend to go a bit overboard.

Just as my wife has become more accepting of my overenthusiastic grocery shopping, so has she learned to accept my passion for books. In the past, she justifiably complained that I bought too many books. Many of the books I buy I could just as easily borrow from the library. Why must I own them? Maybe it's because I'm trying to live down my miserable performance as a high school student. Maybe the books that line my office are my way of proclaiming to visitors that I'm not as dumb as my early school record would suggest. It's been forty years since I almost didn't graduate from high school, and I've collected four degrees since then. But somehow my book collection feels like a badge of intelligence to me. My wife seems to understand that. I'm sure it also helps that I read and make use of them all.

Sometimes acceptance grows out of better understanding yourself.

Why is it that some of your spouse's behaviors trouble you so much?

When Nancy asked herself that question, it made a big difference in her ability to accept Dan. When she reflected on what it was that bothered her about Dan's shyness and narrowly circumscribed lifestyle, she realized that she was concerned about what other people thought of Dan—and therefore what they thought of her. It was an issue left over from her adolescence.

In high school, Nancy was part of a group of girls who were, in her words, "crazy over boys." They competed with each other to go out with the cutest, most popular guys. At the time, Nancy was gawky and not terribly attractive. She couldn't begin to compete with her friends. At school events, she would end up with the boy that her friends wouldn't dream of being seen with. She felt humiliated. The impact on her fragile ego had lasting consequences, even though she evolved from an awkward teenager to a poised and beautiful young woman. Gradually, Nancy became aware that because of her high school experiences, she was expecting Dan to become the man that ALL the women wanted but couldn't have.

As she became aware of the adolescent pattern that had carried over into her adult life, Nancy was able to become more relaxed about Dan's shyness and narrow interests. She realized that she was trying to use her husband to satisfy her immature desires. She recognized that the real need in this situation wasn't for Dan to change but for her to grow up.

Although understanding yourself and why you react the way you do to your spouse's behavior can be another step toward acceptance, self-understanding may still not be enough. You may need to understand how your reactions affect your spouse.

As I've already pointed out, our reactions to the behaviors we don't like sometimes actually intensify those behaviors. Dan's shyness, for example, actually got worse as Nancy's frustrations with him escalated. Early in their marriage, Dan perceived Nancy as a supportive presence at social gatherings. He began to feel more at ease. He started taking more risks. But as he became aware that Nancy was watching everything he said and did, he became more and more self-conscious. He started perceiving Nancy as a hostile presence. When she was around, he couldn't be at ease—even with people he already knew. He became so anxious he'd occasionally garble his words or misunderstand another person's comments.

He also became secretly angry with his wife. Sometimes he would be deliberately silent at parties just to aggravate her. She in turn would become even more upset, and the cycle continued.

Once Nancy developed a better understanding—of the origins of Dan's shyness, of why she was so upset by his shyness, and of how her reactions to his shyness only made it worse—she was better able to accept the fact that Dan could only change so much and probably didn't need to change too much.

Change your labels

If someone's behavior is annoying enough, we tend to begin thinking of him or her as a bad person. Often we focus on and eventually exaggerate a person's negative qualities while overlooking good qualities. We may perceive negative traits as being more significant and pervasive than they really are. When we begin to think that way about a spouse, it spells trouble.

I urge you to temporarily reconsider the labels you've put on your spouse. Give your partner the benefit of the doubt. Try to think of your mate's negative behavior as an aberration—one or two bad traits among many not-so-bad traits or perhaps even a few good traits. Try to view the crazy-making habit(s) as a result of ignorance or lack of know-how. It may be that your spouse really can't help it, that he or she was born with a particular temperament and can't really do much about it. Some people, for example, will never be good at nurturing relationships. They just don't get it—they can't "read" other people. They can't see someone else's point of view no matter how simple and concrete you get with them. People like that aren't necessarily evil, but they may be handicapped.

Natalie and Scott, a couple in their mid-thirties, are an example of how a relational handicap can affect a marriage. Natalie came to see me, complaining that her husband was driving her crazy. She described Scott as a highly gifted industrial designer who received top awards in his field, made a lot of money, and enjoyed the respect of colleagues who viewed him as a brilliant, up-and-coming star in his industry. "But I can't stand living with him anymore," Natalie said, choking back tears. "He plays these colossal mind games with me. And no matter how I try to tell him what I need from him, it doesn't sink in. In fact, he usually ends up doing just the opposite of what I ask. I feel like a fool, a complete discard."

At Natalie's request, Scott reluctantly made an appointment with me. He arrived in my office already antagonistic, obviously expecting me to tear into him on his wife's behalf. Instead, I invited him to tell me his side of their marriage story. Not only was his side very different from what Natalie had told me, it didn't make a lot of sense. To keep him coming in, I reacted as sympathetically as I could, adding that I wanted to help him and his wife make something more of their marriage than trench warfare. I emphasized that I would be giving them *both* guidance about what they could do to improve their relationship. And over the next several weeks, that's just what I did. I gave both Scott and Natalie weekly assignments and asked them to report back to me on how they went.

Each week, Natalie would dutifully report to me that she had carried out her assignment, describing specifically what she had done. Almost always, her description matched the assignment almost exactly. Not so with Scott. He would say that he had done the assignment, but his descriptions of his actions were often quite different from what I'd asked him to do. Natalie's reaction was usually either anger or confusion. I began to see why she was convinced that Scott was playing "mind games," that he was deliberately trying to confuse and manipulate her. But it was obvious to me that Scott truly wanted to please Natalie. He thought he was doing what she wanted and was in genuine agony over the fact that her reactions were exactly the opposite of what he expected. He was so frustrated, in fact, that he was starting to sink into a serious depression.

It became clear to me that Scott just wasn't wired to connect empathetically with other people. He couldn't read the nuances in another person's words, emotions, and body language. Specifically, he couldn't read Natalie. When he tried to carry out my assignments, he would perform as though Natalie were an object he was designing. When she reacted negatively, he either forgot all I had told him or became confused about how to implement my suggestions. Natalie's anger and his own good intentions combined to make him extremely anxious and all the more confused.

After explaining to Natalie what I thought was going on with Scott, I suggested that the only realistic way to salvage their marriage was for her to acknowledge Scott's good intentions and understand his limitations. She had to be more patient and more specific in what she wanted—and she had to reinforce every positive attempt on his part. Hard as it would be, she had to overlook his missteps. Individually, they weren't major, but there were honestly so many of them that they felt overwhelming. And Natalie took each one to mean he didn't really care about her. As we worked together for a few more months, Natalie was able to become more accepting of Scott and their marriage. The relationship improved. It wasn't perfect, but much better.

I've seen relational handicaps like Scott's many times in the troubled couples who come to me for counseling. They seem to occur more often in men than women. I think they're much like dyslexia in the sense that they seemed to be a pre-wired condition (and, in fact, I've often seen these relational handicaps accompanied by learning disabilities). Just as you can't expect some people to be good readers of books, you can't expect some people to be good readers of other people.

How can you tell if your spouse has a relational handicap? A real diagnosis can only be made by a professional, but one sign is if you're able to detect some genuine love behind all the confusion and "mind games." Another sign is when other people besides you experience similar confusion or frustration in their relationship to your spouse.

If you just can't make sense of your spouse's behavior, it's important to consider the possibility that he or she has a genuine relational disability. They're more common than most people realize.

DON'T TAKE IT PERSONALLY

Why does a spouse's behavior tend to affect us so deeply? Because we take it personally.

Let's assume, for example, that Nancy personalizes Dan's shyness. She concludes that he deliberately acts shy because he wants to embarrass and annoy her. If she truly believes this, her anger and anxiety will be heightened and she'll stop thinking logically about the situation. She certainly won't be able to help him grow. If she can challenge her tendency to personalize Dan's behavior and assume it has nothing to do with her, she can see Dan in a different light.

Depersonalizing by setting aside your assumptions can pay off enormously in marriage. It can give freedom where once there was bondage to frustration, resentment, anger, disaffection, and alienation.

LOOK AT THE WHOLE CONTEXT OF YOUR LIFE

When you have a tiny pebble in your shoe, it can eventually seem like a boulder. There's more going on in your life than that little piece of rock, but after a while everything else is obscured. That's the way it is with a spouse's irritating trait or behavior. There's a lot more going on in your life and marriage, but the negative characteristic may be capturing your thoughts and emotions so totally that you can't see or feel anything else. If that's what's happening to you, your challenge is to free yourself enough so that one habit or characteristic doesn't consume you—and blind you to all the good aspects of your spouse and your life together.

Set the objectionable traits in your partner aside for a moment. Look at the total picture of your marriage and family life. What do you have to lose if you allow a pebble to become a boulder that consumes your mind and heart?

LOOK FOR THE GIFT IN THE WEAKNESS

Is it possible that your partner's frustrating characteristic may actually be a gift? It may be your spouse's gift that he or she is overusing, or it may be a gift to you, to help you grow as a person.

Setting aside the question of whether a particular trait of your mate's is actually positive or negative, consider first the impact it has on you. Most likely it makes you frustrated. If you are like most people in American society today, you probably have a low tolerance for frustration. We Americans possess so much that we don't know how to do without. We have so much control over our lives that we can't stand it when something seems beyond our control. It may be that the frustration you experience over your spouse's objectionable behavior actually represents an opportunity for you to grow—to learn, for example, how to tolerate frustration.

What's more, this situation may be forcing you to reflect on the meaning of your life and marriage in ways that would never happen if you had the "perfect match." (Not that there is a perfect match.)

It may even be that what your spouse lacks, or you perceive that he or she lacks, gives you a chance to develop a side of yourself you might otherwise neglect. Janis says that's clearly been the case for her: "When I was growing up," she explains, "my father tended to be the dominant personality in our family, at least as far as public situations were concerned.

My dad taught the adult Sunday school class at church, served on the
board, and was generally an acknowledged leader in our congregation. He
also had certain specific roles within the family. When it was time to buy
a new car, for example, it was usually my dad who handled the negotiations—and did he negotiate! Car salesmen are probably still telling stories
about him. Consequently, it came as a shock to me when my husband,
Paul, didn't automatically assume the roles my father had played. Paul
hates negotiating for anything, particularly cars. And while he's recently
started teaching a sixth grade Sunday school class, he hasn't taken on the
same degree of leadership in our church that I once assumed he would.
Although Paul's laid-back style disoriented me for a while, it eventually
forced me to think about my assumptions—and consider some new roles
for myself. It used to irritate me that Paul wouldn't even try to negotiate
for a car. Now I just handle the negotiations myself and feel pretty proud
when I think I've gotten a good deal. I've accepted some leadership po-
sitions—serving as a board member for some nonprofit organizations,
teaching an occasional adult class at our church—that once seemed a
man's domain to me. These have been wonderfully satisfying involvements I might have missed if Paul had played the parts I once expected
him to play."

Looking at Nancy and Dan's situation again from the vantage point of
Janis's experience, we might conclude that Dan's shyness gave Nancy an
opportunity to express herself in a way she never could have had she married a more outgoing person. Many women complain to me that their
husbands have nothing to say at home, but dominate conversations in
public. Rather than making an issue of Dan's laid-back social style, Nancy
could have chosen to view it as a gift to her—an opportunity to be more
talkative and outgoing herself.

LOOK FOR GOD'S AGENDA IN YOUR SITUATION

Do you look for the hand of God in your personal history? It's interesting that so many of us, even those of us who have a deep faith, tend to
ignore the reality that God is working in our lives. We accept the psychological notion that what we become in life is a product of early family
influences. We accept the sociological idea that we are influenced by our
cultural environment. And—on a theoretical level—we believe that God

has an agenda for us that He is working out on a daily basis. But on a practical level, we don't act as if we believe that.

Have you ever thought about how God is using your spouse to sculpt you into the person He wants you to be? Have you considered the possibility that God is using your spouse's personality and behavior patterns to shape you for His service? Have you considered whether your spouse's traits, even the ones that irritate you, are precisely what make him or her usable to God?

Dan and Nancy again: To Nancy, Dan's shyness was a weakness, a negative. But shyness can also be a spiritual gift. Dietrich Bonhoeffer wrote that the first ministry of any believer is to listen. Often, shy people are much better listeners than people who are perfectly confident to voice their opinions—whether or not anyone else wants to hear them. By categorizing Dan's shyness as a fault, Nancy was actually negating his potential for a rare and needed ministry.

It would be ridiculous to suggest that every one of your spouse's irritating traits and habits has a place in God's purposes for the world and for you. Dan, for example, may actually be a good listener. Or he may be as deaf as a stump to people's real needs. Please do, however, consider the *possibility* that God is trying to get your attention through your spouse—even through that behavior you find annoying.

One of my patients used to complain to me about his wife's nagging. "She's always after me about getting enough exercise and going to church," he said disgustedly. Were these things bad for him? I asked. "No," he replied. "But I'll get around to them in my own time." How long had his wife been nagging him about these things? "About eight years," he admitted, a bit sheepishly.

Now, I don't want to recommend nagging as a good strategy in marriage. But it's possible that God was willing to work with this wife's very flawed strategy to nudge her husband a little bit. Can't blame the guy for being annoyed. But if he had been willing to see beyond his irritation to the message—and had adopted some physical and spiritual disciplines—the previous eight years would probably have been far more healthy and meaningful.

Ray and Tiffany's story is also applicable here. Ray accused his wife Tiffany of being "codependent"—a catchall term seemingly used to describe any and every kind of behavior these days. It's become more of a weapon than an explanation. In any case, Tiffany spent a lot of time trying to help women who were addicted to drugs. She saw this work as her ministry. Ray didn't see it that way. He insisted that Tiffany needed to have those women need her. He accused her of making them dependent on her and of neglecting her own family in the process.

As they talked about these issues, both Ray and Tiffany had some insights. Tiffany realized that she did, in fact, need to be needed by the drug-addicted women with whom she worked. She recognized that being needed helped to compensate for her deep-seated feeling that she was never good enough, that she had to prove to herself and others that she was a worthy person. She was taken aback to discover that her pre-teen daughters bitterly resented her "ministry," because she was never around when they needed her. So Tiffany cut back on her involvement. She still viewed it as her ministry, but she made certain she was more available to her family.

At the same time, however, she starting sharing more openly with her husband and daughters about why she was so passionately devoted to her work. She talked about the struggles of drug-addicted women, about the desperate conditions in which they lived. It began to dawn on Ray and the girls how privileged their lives were, how insulated they had become. They considered themselves to be people of strong faith, but they had defined their faith by their personal piety. Unlike Tiffany, they had made no effort to lighten the burden of people in the grip of despair. It certainly had never occurred to them to help her as she tried to balance the competing demands of homemaking and ministry. As they developed a new appreciation for why Tiffany was so dedicated to her work, Ray and the girls saw their wife and mother in a different light. After confronting their anger and frustration, the whole family made some new commitments. It seems that God used the irritations of life to nudge this couple and their daughters into a new relationship and a more mature understanding of the spiritual life.

ACKNOWLEDGE THE REALITY OF THE GENDER GAP

Bud is a "car guy." His business is towing cars and he loves it. He owns three trucks which he pampers like babies—paints them himself, does all his own mechanical work, washes and polishes them inside and out. When he isn't working, he loves to hang around garages watching the mechanics work on the cars he's towed. Although "car guy" stuff fills his life, Bud also has other dimensions to his personality. He is a devout Christian who attends church regularly and studies theology as an avocation. Well-known and well-liked in his congregation, he's always willing to help people out with their cars. Members of the church staff in particular have the equivalent of Medicare for their cars. Bud works on them for free. He makes their broken-down jalopies run like BMWs. All because he's a car guy.

Unfortunately, it is precisely Bud's car guy behavior that drives his wife Sandy crazy. "The first word my kids learned was 'car,'" she says in exasperation. "The second was 'transmission.' They're three and five and both of them look like grease monkeys. They hang around with their dad all the time while he's working on his trucks and they come in with grease all over their clothes and even in their beautiful blond hair! What can I do with this guy?!"

What CAN Sandy do with Bud?

If she's wise, she'll accept him.

Like many men, Bud has attached his identity to his work. He is a "car guy," but he could just as easily be a "carpenter guy" or a "lawyer guy" or a "doctor guy."

While more and more women are deriving their identities from their work, this has historically been a male pattern—and probably an annoyance to women as long as it has been around. But women have some "patterns" associated with them as well. One of the most characteristic female patterns has to do with talk. Men are often befuddled by their wife's need to talk—as a way of connecting and, seemingly, as an end in itself. I don't know how many times I've heard my male clients complain about their wives using talk as, in their husband's view, a substitute for problem-solving.

Chip, for example, sat in my office and recounted a telephone marathon his wife had conducted after being "demoted" at work. "Actually," said Chip, "it wasn't really a demotion. It was more of a temporary reduction in responsibilities until she could get a better grasp of the products she was supposed to represent. But Diane went ballistic." In this case "going ballistic" meant that Diane telephoned five of six or her friends, told them the whole story, cried, and got their reassurance that she was in the right and her boss was out of his mind.

"What would you have done?" I asked Chip. "I don't know for sure," he replied in disgust, "but I can tell you one thing, I wouldn't have blabbed it all over town. What would compel anyone to spend six or eight hours on the telephone broadcasting their troubles down to the last detail?" When I explained that there's a difference in the way men and women process stress—men tend to clam up and women tend to talk—Chip's jaw dropped in disbelief. His wife's behavior was normal?

The talk gap between men and women is real, and it's a huge issue in marriage. Men are generally better than women at public talk than personal talk. They're better at communicating facts and ideas than feelings. Men tend to talk about events and impersonal problems, while women tend to talk about relationships and personal problems. An example: Nikki and Fred were friends with a couple who were going through a difficult divorce. Nikki, knowing that the husband was really hurting, suggested that Fred get together with him to try to bolster his morale. So Fred took him to a ball game. Afterwards, Nikki asked how the friend was doing. "What do you mean?" Fred asked. "Well, how is he holding up during all this?" Nikki replied. "How should I know?" Fred grunted. "We were at a ball game. But he looked okay."

It's patterns like these that account for why women seldom know what's going on in their husband's mind, much less what he's feeling. Complicating the problem is the fact that men tend to think of home as a place where they don't need to talk, while women often think of home as a place where they can use talk to achieve closeness.

Perhaps the most disconcerting consequence of the talk gap between men and women is its effect on their styles of nurturing. A woman thinks she's showing love to her husband when she *listens* to him. But since he seldom talks—at least not at home—she's at a loss for how to nurture him. A man thinks he's showing love for his wife when he *does* something for her. But since both sexes tend to want the kind of nurturing they give, what his wife really wants is for him to listen to her. What the husband really wants is for his wife to do something for or with him. Both genders need nurturing, but they're often at cross-purposes.

Another source of some intense gender-based marital skirmishes is whatever trait it is that allows a man to happily exist in a house where the garage is a disastrous firetrap, the back door lock doesn't work, and the dishwasher leaks soapy water onto the floor. This same trait allows him to walk through a room so cluttered it would take a shovel to get through it. Many women think, "Any normal person wouldn't act like that." They're right, any normal person wouldn't—unless he's a guy.

A recent research project suggested why this happens. Two groups, one all men and the other all women, were ushered into a suite of offices. One office was designated as a waiting area, the other an interview room. The first office was set up with a variety of objects scattered about on a desk and table. There were several pictures hanging on the wall. Members of each group were seated in the waiting room, one at a time, for five minutes. Then they were taken into the interview room, where they were asked to describe the objects in the room and where they were located. The men were able to describe very little of what was in the waiting room. Often, when they recalled an object, they got the location wrong. In some instances they described objects that weren't even there. The women, on the other hand, had a high degree of recall of both the objects and their location. This gender difference, which seems to be pre-wired, has been supported by similar research.

One seemingly logical solution to this would be for a woman to take her husband by the hand, show him what needs to be repaired or cleaned up, hand him the tools, and stand there until he does what he should do (if she were to the leave the scene, he would likely forget, wander off to another room, and watch a football game—completely unconscious of the trouble he's creating for himself).

But this strategy won't work. Because men tend to have another characteristic trait: They don't like to be told what to do. Men tend to see the world as a hierarchy, and they know enough to try to be on the "up" side of it instead of the "down" side. This tendency starts early, as evidenced by the variety of one-upmanship games little boys play with one another. The maneuvering to make it to the top of whatever the hierarchy is defined to be can get pretty rough. I remember, as a teenager, getting into a pushing and shoving fight with one of my best friends over who sat in the front seat of another friend's car because in our minds the front seat was more "up" than the backseat.

This male sensitivity to who's up and who's down doesn't change with marriage. So when a guy's wife leads him around the house, pointing out all the tasks he needs to perform to keep the place from falling down around their ears, he has a knee-jerk reaction: *No way!* If he were to let her tell him what to do, she would be "up" and he would be "down."

Women find the male sensitivity to hierarchy hard to understand because they tend to want to affiliate rather than compete. Women will go to great lengths to make sure everyone in a group is at the same level. Often, women are so uncomfortable at the idea of being "up" that they give orders or make requests only very indirectly. Problem is, when a woman makes an indirect request of her husband, he often mistakes it for a suggestion and ignores it. That's when the fireworks begin.

Recognizing gender-based patterns is important in marriage for this reason: It keeps you from taking certain behaviors personally. Even genuinely annoying behavior can be easier to accept when you look at it as part of a characteristic gender trait. That's not to say that all men or all women exhibit the same attitudes and behaviors. But the patterns described here are common enough to require that you take them seriously as you look at issues in your marriage. As you consider these patterns, remember that neither the male nor female style is usually inherently good or bad. What's important is understanding some of the reasons your spouse may be predisposed to act the way he or she does. (For a more detailed explanation of the differing ways men and women communicate and behave, you might want to read *You Just Don't Understand* by Deborah Tannen.) A little knowledge of gender differences can go a long way in marriage. When you understand the way your partner has been put together, it's easier to accept the traits that irritate you.

WHEN YOU CAN'T—AND SHOULDN'T—ACCEPT YOUR SPOUSE'S BEHAVIOR

All this said, taking a marriage vow is *not* taking a vow of martyrdom. Consequently, you cannot and should not accept any and all behavior on the part of your spouse.

How can you judge what's not acceptable? There are two ways. First, you can evaluate what's acceptable according to external guidelines, especially the guidelines recorded in Scripture. Second, you can judge on the basis of what impact your partner's behavior has on you, your children, and those around you. The first method of judging is much more clear and reliable. The second method of judging is less clear and less reliable, but still important.

God places a high value on covenant-keeping, but it's possible that your marriage covenant has been broken through no fault of your own. Jesus came down very hard on divorce, but even He acknowledged that adultery is such a serious violation of the wedding covenant that it is legitimate cause for ending a marriage. Not all marriages need to end because of infidelity. When a spouse is truly repentant, as proven by an end to the adulterous relationship and a recommitment to the marriage, then learning to forgive is often best for all concerned—though certainly not easy. But a continual pattern of unfaithfulness is unacceptable. Continued infidelity destroys a marriage covenant.

Jesus didn't talk about abuse as a cause for dissolving a marriage, but He did speak of God's special concern for the poor and powerless in the world. Perhaps no one is poorer in spirit or more powerless than someone who is being physically or emotionally abused by a spouse. And in some instances the only way for a victim of abuse to avoid further harm—to oneself and any children involved—is to separate and end the abusive marriage.

While all forms of abuse are unacceptable, physical abuse is much easier to define than emotional and verbal abuse. The problem is that almost anyone who's severely alienated from a spouse feels to some degree "emotionally abused." So how can you distinguish behavior that is truly emotionally or verbally abusive?

First, try to objectively assess the *frequency* of the troubling behavior. Does your partner's objectionable trait or action occur: Rarely? Occasionally? Often? Consistently? The more frequent a negative behavior is, the more unacceptable it becomes.

Some assessments of the *impact* of your mate's behavior can also be helpful. How does your partner's behavior make you feel? Disappointed? Uncomfortable? Irritated? Frustrated? Insecure? Hurt? Oppressed? Fearful?

These are words I often hear my patients use to describe their feelings. There is a sense in which these words can be viewed as an emotional continuum. Feeling uncomfortable, for example, is far less threatening than feeling pain or fear. Thinking of your emotional responses as a continuum can help you reflect on both the frequency and seriousness of your spouse's objectionable traits, attitudes, and behaviors. For example, you might feel discomfort and irritation if your wife embarrassed you with an uncharacteristic verbal put-down in front of your colleagues at the office Christmas party. But if her put-downs became a continual pattern, your emotional response might eventually devolve into frustration, disappointment, and pain. The frequency of the behavior makes the impact on you more severe. There are some behaviors that are so unacceptable, though, that even one instance is enough to warrant a justified sense of fear and oppression. If your spouse were to threaten you with a gun, for example, that one act would constitute clear emotional abuse.

While looking at your emotional responses as a continuum can be helpful in diagnosing the seriousness of your situation, it doesn't always apply. Sometimes you can feel discomfort, irritation, frustration, disappointment, pain, oppression, and fear—or some combination of any of these—all at the same time. In some instances you may be putting inappropriate labels on your feelings. In a culture where we're encouraged to see ourselves as victims, it's all too easy to label discomfort as oppression, for example. Still, trying to clarify your feelings can often give you some perspective on your partner's alienating or hurtful words, attitudes, and behavior.

The emotional continuum is definitely not foolproof as an assessment tool. Our culture's desire for instant gratification, for example, makes it difficult for us to tolerate any level of emotional discomfort. But in general, I suggest the following guidelines: If your partner's traits or behaviors cause you only occasional discomfort, irritation, or frustration, you may need to do some significant work on your relationship—you may even need counseling—but you are probably not in an abusive marriage. If, however, you live with a constant sense of oppression or fear, your marriage is in a state of emergency. You need to take action. You need help.

What to do about a spouse's unacceptable behavior

If you are in a physically abusive marriage:

Tell your family and/or a few trusted friends about your situation. You need their help and support. Having a supportive network will be crucial to getting out of a dangerous situation.

Make a plan for leaving the marriage, at least physically, if not legally.

- Inform the people in your support network that you plan to leave.
- Find a temporary place to stay, preferably with family members or friends, but if necessary, at a shelter or motel.
- Squirrel away some money.
- Pack a bag with whatever essentials you will need to live elsewhere.
- Find someone in your support network who can help you with child care.
- Get a referral to an attorney through someone in your network.
- Make arrangements for transportation if you have none of your own.
- Think of someone you can call if a tense situation gets out of hand (don't hesitate to call the police).
- Identify someone who can be with you when you leave.

Don't put up with abuse in the hope that your spouse will change. Abusers rarely alter their ways without external pressure. Don't wait for your abusive partner to suddenly be transformed, even if he or she apologizes for a violent episode. After the first incident, either get out or start making plans to get out.

Ideally, you and your partner should both get counseling. Your spouse will probably be reluctant, make excuses, and insist that you can work it out between yourselves. Don't fall for that. Don't go back to your spouse until he or she has joined you in counseling and there has been significant progress. Remember, though, there is no guarantee that being in counseling will protect you from further abuse.

If you are in an emotionally abusive marriage:

- Tell your spouse very directly and firmly that you will not tolerate any further humiliation and will not subject your children to the damaging effects of a verbally abusive situation.
- Be prepared to leave, even if only temporarily, as a statement of your refusal to accept abuse.
- Tell your family and friends about your situation and accept their support.
- Find a therapist.

- Ask your spouse to join you in counseling, but go yourself even if he or she refuses to go with you.
- Recognize that your spouse's verbal abuse threatens your physical and mental well-being and that of your children.
- If your spouse refuses to participate in counseling, give serious consideration to leaving.

HOW TO FIND A THERAPIST

The best way to find a good therapist is to ask your friends or your pastor for a recommendation. Look for someone with recognized credentials—a psychiatrist, clinical psychologist, clinical social worker, certified social worker, or certified pastoral counselor, for example. If possible, find someone sympathetic to your spiritual values. Someone who shares your faith would be ideal, but that's not always possible. At a minimum, try to find someone who respects your faith and views it as a resource for your marriage instead of a problem to be overcome.

GETTING HELP WHEN YOUR MARRIAGE ISN'T ABUSIVE

Just because your marriage isn't technically abusive doesn't mean you don't need outside help to put it back on track. In fact, the earlier you seek help, the greater the chance for healing.

If you have come to a point where you seriously question whether or not you married the right person, you may well need an outside resource to help you gain perspective and support you in the work you need to do to either redeem your marriage or, if your relationship is clearly irredeemable, start a new life.

It's possible that the exercises in this book are actually stirring up more negative emotions than positive ones. If you and your spouse are working through the exercises together, you may suddenly find that you're having more, not fewer, conflicts. Don't let this development discourage you—it's a fairly common occurrence when two people start working to undo years' worth of ingrained patterns. Increased conflict may even be a sign of hope, because it means you're working on your relationship. If, however, the conflict becomes severe—and continues—you're going to need outside help. Serious conflict by itself doesn't mean you can't save your marriage. It's just a strong indication that you can't do it alone.

THE BOTTOM LINE ON ACCEPTANCE

The question of what you can or should accept in your spouse is fundamental to the health of your marriage and can be crucial to your emotional and physical health. God doesn't require you to be a marital martyr—if your partner has broken your wedding covenant through continued infidelity or abuse or oppression, you may need to leave for your own sake and the sake of your children. You may even need to leave for the sake of your spouse, who might not otherwise be able to face up to his or her behavior and seek forgiveness and healing.

Although marital infidelity, abuse, and oppression are much more common than many people recognize, *most marriages fall apart for other reasons*. And many marriages could be saved if one or both partners could learn the secrets of healthy acceptance (as opposed to unhealthy resignation or martyrdom).

For the most part, trying to change your mate's defining characteristics is an exercise in futility. Some attitudes and behaviors can be moderated. Some can't be changed and shouldn't be tolerated. Some can't be changed but can be viewed in a new light. If you can look at your partner's irritating attitudes and actions in new ways—perhaps even see them as part of God's agenda for both of you—you may find that the "wrong person" you married isn't as wrong as you thought.

EXERCISES

In the space below, write down three or four of the most frustrating acceptance issues in your marriage. Then evaluate each issue in light of the acceptance strategies discussed in this chapter.

Issues

(1)

(2)

(3)

(4)

Acceptance strategies

- Understand your spouse's background.
- Understand yourself.
- Change your labels.
- Don't take the problem personally.
- See the problem in the total context of your marriage.
- Look for a possible gift in what appears to be a problem.
- Look for God's agenda.
- Be aware of gender differences.

JOURNALING

(1) Continue your structured journaling as before, using column 1 to record troubling interactions and column 2 for your feelings.

(2) Use column 3 to reflect on your usual way of thinking about these kinds of interactions.

(3) Challenge your usual way of thinking in column 4, using the strategies presented here.

SPIRITUAL DISCIPLINES

Contemplation

Reflect on the words of 1 John 4:7–11, NKJV.

> *Beloved, let us love one another, for love is of God; and everyone who loves is born of God and knows God.*

What is it that you find unacceptable in your spouse? Picture that trait, attitude, or behavior in your mind. Try to think of a specific incident that illustrates it.

> *He who does not love does not know God, for God is love.*

Picture again what you find unacceptable in your spouse. Think of a specific incident. Look within yourself. How do you respond to the person to whom you made a promise before God, in the company of His people?

In this the love of God was manifested toward us, that God has sent His only begotten Son into the world, that we might live through Him.

Picture the unacceptable trait in your spouse and a specific incident. Look within. How do you respond to the person who has failed you? Does God have anything to say to you?

In this is love, not that we loved God, but that He loved us and sent His Son to be the propitiation for our sins.

Picture the unacceptable trait in your spouse and a specific incident. Look within. How do you respond to the person who has failed you—someone who is loved by God, whose debt has been paid as yours has been paid.

Beloved, if God so loved us, we also ought to love one another.

What is God calling you to do?

Prayer

O God, I am so fragile and limited. Knowing that no human frailties can separate me from Your love, I'm sometimes tempted to accept them in myself. But it's hard to accept them in others, especially those closest to me. Help me see myself and _____ through Your eyes. Give me the grace to see through _____'s limitations to his/her gifts. Help me celebrate the qualities that have irritated me, but that You are using as part of Your agenda. Help me to love without demanding more of _____ than I demand of myself. Amen.

Thirteen

Finding the Meaning in Your Marriage

T his chapter is a little different from the previous ones. Up until now, the emphasis of this book has been on practical techniques and spiritual disciplines for transforming your mind and marriage. If, as I suggested at the beginning, you read through the main body of this book before working through the exercises at the end of the chapters, I would encourage you once you finish this chapter to go back to the beginning and do the more concentrated work. I hope that if you have already been implementing these techniques and disciplines into your life that you're starting to see some positive results. But now I want to take a somewhat different tack.

The goal of this chapter is to help you find the *meaning* in your marriage—even if at this point you still question whether you married the Right Person. Through the years, I've found that people are better equipped—and more motivated—to overcome marital problems after they've brushed away their emotional cobwebs and achieved a clear vision of what their marriage means to them. Those who successfully tackle the problems in their marriage often find that the work they did to uncover their union's meaning gives it a richness they never could have imagined. Others are able to find meaning in a marriage that never seems to improve and are able to celebrate a relationship that has value despite its imperfections.

THE MEANING IN YOUR MARRIAGE

When you get right down to it, what's the purpose of marriage? What was *your* purpose in getting married? You could give a lot of specific reasons, and you'd be in plenty of company: To be loved. To leave loneliness behind. To have children. To have a sexual partner. To become more financially secure. To be part of the social mainstream. To divide up the tasks of daily living. To meet deep emotional needs.

These are all practical reasons for getting married, and all great reasons. But as marriage unfolds, many of us long for a deeper meaning. What could that meaning possibly be?

I have shocked a few of my married patients with the question, "How are you living out the promise of your wedding ceremony?" This question is especially shocking to the patients who begin every session with a litany of complaints about how their spouse isn't meeting their needs. I always listen to these complaints, because usually there is genuine hurt and frustration behind them. But at some point, I start to gently encourage these bitter and discouraged folks to face their own responsibility to live up to the promise they made when they got married. It's usually a hard mental transition to make. The habit of asking, "What's in this for me?" is deeply ingrained, starting long before the wedding ceremony.

Marian, an attractive woman in her late twenties, came to see me after the man she had been dating for several months broke off their relationship. She was crushed because she had hoped she and James might get married. When I asked her what went wrong, she responded with a long list of James' shortcomings, ways he had failed to meet her needs. I was surprised at how negative she was about James. After all, if her negative picture of him were accurate, why was she so grieved by their breakup? But not knowing anything about the man other than what she told me, I simply accepted her description of him, sympathized with her hurt, and tried to help her move on.

In a few months, Marian started dating again. At first she bubbled enthusiasm about Matthew, but after a few weeks, she started complaining about him too. Interestingly, her complaints about him were almost identical to what she had said about James. He didn't understand her. He wasn't attuned to her needs and interests. Soon, Matthew started to pull away from the relationship. Marian became desperate to keep him, even though she continued to be highly critical of his attitudes and behavior. One day, after listening to a long recital of Matthew's deficiencies, I asked Marian, "What do you think *he* is getting out of this relationship?" Marian was momentarily speechless. She didn't understand the question. I explained that for any friendship to become serious and lasting, both people in it have to concentrate on what they put into the relationship, not just what they get out of it. I suggested that her relationship with Matthew might be unraveling because they were both concentrating on the wrong thing.

Marian became irate. As far as she was concerned, Matthew had to prove that he could be sensitive and responsive to her needs before she would even think of exerting any effort to understand and respond to his.

Unfortunately, too many people go into marriage with Marian's narcissistic attitude. Sadly, when two people try to forge a marriage around the question "What am I getting?" instead of "What am I giving?" the result is likely to be continuing stress and conflict.

Will Marian ever find someone to marry if she continues with her selfish attitude? Probably. But until she learns to ask the question "What am I giving?" she will never have a deeply intimate relationship with anyone.

The problem is that few voices in Marian's world encourage her to think any differently. Her way of thinking is encouraged by our culture of "self-realization." It's a culture that suggests we should focus on pursuing personal happiness—however defined—without regard to the impact of our decisions on the lives of other people or the communities in which we live.

On the surface, this may seem like a perfectly innocent approach to life—perhaps even a wise and appropriate one. After all, people are inclined to pursue their own self-interest anyway. That's what "self-realization" is all about.

But prioritizing personal happiness at the expense of others is toxic, not only from a spiritual perspective but also on a purely human level. A society is sustained by commitments, by people willing to set aside their personal interests for the good of the whole community, willing to postpone gratification of their own real or imagined needs for a *larger* good. Without this cooperation and personal sacrifice, society cannot hold together. People become dangerously isolated. If everyone is out for self, how can communities ever work together to solve problems that affect us all—whether they have to do with building roads, preventing crime, or providing for those who can't provide for themselves?

Furthermore, there is ample evidence in psychological research and in the clinical experience of mental health practitioners to suggest that the self-realization myth is deeply inadequate. The most psychologically resilient and interpersonally connected people aren't those who focus on self-fulfillment, but those who live for larger purposes. Those meanings don't have to be grandiose, but they do have to go beyond preoccupation with self-interest and pleasure.

It's these people who are better able to cope with uncertainty. They're the ones who are best equipped to transcend life's inevitable crises. What's more, they tend to be deeply connected with other people, perhaps because they are able to listen and respond to the needs and concerns of others. In a society such as ours, where forces from all sides drive us to hermitlike existences, connectedness is ever harder to come by. Studies show quite clearly that the loneliness resulting from the self-realization myth is unhealthy both physically and emotionally.

Even so, the myth is ever popular. It pervades every avenue of our cultural life. The media is awash in it.

Recently, a popular morning television program featured an interview with a woman, call her Linda, who described what she went through in the process of divorcing her husband. There was nothing seriously wrong with her marriage, but she had the feeling that life owed her something more. Her children cried when she told them her decision. Her husband was devastated. But she "had to do what she had to do." At this point, the interviewer smiled and nodded approvingly at Linda's "courage." She became increasingly enthusiastic as Linda described the aftermath of her divorce. She was so much happier now, ten years later. She was remarried to a wonderful man. Her children had adjusted nicely. As for her former husband, well, he was a grown man.

In my years of counseling, I have met many "Lindas" of both sexes. And having counseled some of the children and former spouses of these people, I am thoroughly skeptical of her description of the results of her divorce. As we've already shown, the children of divorce may eventually "adjust," but they also go through tremendous pain. Their security is shattered. Their ability to forge trusting relationships is forever tainted. They become more vulnerable to anger and depression. They tend to underachieve. They themselves are more prone to divorce.

Former spouses eventually adjust as well. But they are never unscathed by divorce. In every broken marriage, a dream of home and family has been shattered. That was certainly the case in Linda's family. Her husband was apparently devoted to her. He loved his children. Her decision to pursue her own happiness separated him not only from her, but from their kids. Against his will, he became a weekend father.

But despite these implications of Linda's decision, the interviewer smiled and nodded, celebrating a success story. Linda is now "happy."

People of faith know better. People of faith acknowledge that they have been created in the image of a God who values relationships, who makes covenants in His relationships, and who asks us to do the same.

The meaning of a marriage, even a flawed marriage, can be found in reflecting on a God who keeps promises. Who came to earth as a suffering servant. Who loved without being loved in return.

This kind of meaning is incomprehensible to much of our culture. It crashes up against the self-interest/self-realization approach to life. It goes against feelings. It could, we quickly realize, involve pain and self-sacrifice. It takes into consideration the impact our behavior has on others.

Bev and David's tumultuous marriage has been troubled almost from the day they got married eighteen years ago. Looking back, they can hardly remember why they got together in the first place. They met in college. Bev, who was inclined to be very serious, was attracted to David's fun-loving nature, even if he sometimes did go a bit overboard. And because David had a difficult family background, she felt she could be a positive influence. David, on the other hand, was amazed that this pretty girl was interested in him. He was flattered by her desire to help him and liked the fact that she seemed to see through his party boy image to a deeper self. They got married with high hopes of a wonderful life together.

It seemed like a perfect match. David needed Bev, and she liked being needed. But almost immediately, David started to resent the fact that he needed his wife so much. As children came along and financial pressure began to mount, he tried to relieve the stress by seeking out his old party-loving friends. He took up gambling and squandered most of their savings. Then he lost his job.

Bev couldn't take it anymore. She gathered up the three girls and moved out of state, settling in with her parents while she pursued a master's degree to prepare for a business career. David came to visit every few months or so—as often as he could afford—but the visits were filled with pain. David hated to leave, and the girls were equally upset to see him go. Seeing the suffering that the separation visited on their children finally compelled Bev to take David back, but only after he vowed to get treatment for his gambling problem. It took several tries, but he finally conquered it. So he and Bev got back together.

But their life together was still dogged by troubles. David couldn't hold down a job. He became severely depressed. They went through a series of marriage counselors. No matter how hard they tried to get their marriage back on track, they always seemed to run up against a brick wall. David's lack of self-esteem and his chronic depression left him without the energy or will to work as hard on the marriage as Bev felt she was working. So, after eighteen years of pain and struggle and tears, their marriage is still very, very difficult.

Seemingly, Bev and David have tried everything they could possibly do to transform their marriage—prayer, counseling with pastors and Christian therapists, seeking advice from friends who share their faith, incorporating spiritual disciplines in their lives, reading books on marriage, practicing communication techniques, you name it. And yet, no breakthrough. No transformation.

In a situation like this, wouldn't it be better for them to acknowledge their brokenness and go their separate ways?

Perhaps. You might make a strong case that this is an oppressive relationship. But Bev sees a larger meaning in sticking with her marriage. "I made a vow before God, and I believe I am called to be obedient to that vow," she says. "Besides, when people divorce and remarry, they take half of their problems with them because they take themselves."

So, presumably, David and Bev have chosen the "gutting it out" option? "Not at all," says Bev. "To me, 'gutting it out' implies resignation, without any striving for growth or wholeness," she explains. "If you can't transform your marriage, God still has a work to do in your life."

Bev's experience suggests a meaning in marriage even when it's unsatisfying. She is convinced that God can help people grow toward wholeness, give them inner joy, even in an unhappy situation.

How can someone in an admittedly unhappy marriage possibly experience joy? *Seriously*—how is it possible? Isn't that just religious talk?

Once again, Bev says no. From her own experience, she believes there are several steps to finding joy despite marital disappointment. "An important step for me was to not only accept David for who he is, but also to accept our marriage for what it is—and perhaps will always be," she reflects. "But that was only half the step. The second half was accepting what that meant in my life. I thought I had done a miracle job when I finally accepted the way David is, but there was still a long process of grieving over what that would mean for me."

Through that grieving process, Bev says, she became cleansed of the bitterness and resentment that had gripped her for many years. Asking God for cleansing, she says, is the second step toward inner joy. "I had so much bitterness and resentment that our counselor told me he was afraid I was going to end up in an institution because of what it was doing to me. I had to ask God to cleanse me of that and give me a heart of compassion for my husband. I told God, 'Use the things in David that made me angry to make me weep instead.'"

In asking for acceptance and cleansing, Bev's marriage wasn't transformed, but she believes she was. As a result, she has some words of advice to others in her situation: "If you feel you're the one who's doing most of the giving in your relationship, you may need to consider whether your partner is giving a high or even higher percentage of what he or she is *able* to give and then try to have a heart of compassion. Ask yourself if you're willing to bless your spouse, whether or not you're blessed in return. If you're not, go to God and ask to be given that kind of love. Those are three things we have to pray for—cleansing, a heart of compassion, and more love for the times when our spouse is unlovable."

Bev firmly believes this approach is possible without becoming a martyr. "You're a martyr when you're staying with the marriage out of resignation instead of commitment or love," she says. Jesus wasn't a martyr, because He *chose* to offer His life as a sacrifice. "If I can't tell my husband about my feelings without him getting upset, I can choose to stuff those feelings, which is being a martyr. Or I can choose to express my feelings to the Lord or to a counselor—and not be a martyr.

"If my husband were incontinent because of old age or an illness, I could take care of him and change the sheets over and over again out of a sense of martyrdom and resentment, or I could do it with a sense of love and service. It would be crazy for me to be angry and resentful because of something he couldn't control, but some people act like martyrs because their spouse is doing the emotional equivalent of soiling the bed.

"I think we need to be asking ourselves some questions every day: What does God want to do in me? What does God want to do in my spouse's life through me? How does He want to love and bless this person through me? If we set out to bless our spouses—not pamper them or baby them when God wants them to grow—we can find peace in even a far-from-perfect situation. Now that I've been cleansed of bitterness and resentment, now that I have finally been given a heart of compassion, I can look myself in the face and feel inner peace."

Ironically, the process Bev talks about—asking God for cleansing of bitterness and resentment, for a heart of compassion, for acceptance, and for more love—should be the same whatever the status of a given marriage. The steps are identical whatever the results. God is interested in us being whole people, whatever the circumstances of our lives. If we're walking martyrs, if we're bitter, if we're resentful, we're not whole people. But God can bring us to holiness and wholeness in any situation.

Did you marry the wrong person? Maybe you did. Especially if your definition of the Right Person is someone who always understands you, inspires your passion, entertains you, reduces your loneliness, appreciates you, makes you feel good about yourself—in short, meets your expectations.

The fact is, in some sense, we all chose a "wrong person" to marry, because there's something wrong with all of us. We are all created in the image of God, but at the same time we are all afflicted with the same fatal condition. The idea that we are born sinful has become politically incorrect, but the evidence is too strong to ignore. We are all flawed. We are all broken. We are all "wrong people."

Bev understands this. It would be easy to label David as the wrong person in their marriage, but Bev knows she's been a wrong person, too—that she's contributed to the alienation in their relationship. She continues to work on those "wrong person" elements in herself in the hope that someday her marriage might get better—and the knowledge that, whatever the other outcomes, God can make her more caring and sensitive, more humble and prayerful. She is working toward wholeness and holiness.

A therapist, even a Christian therapist, can easily find problems with the way Bev has dealt with her marriage. She has possibly been an "enabler" of her husband's problems. She might have waited too long to set boundaries on his treatment of her and the way he lived his life. But ultimately, only she can judge what God is calling her to do. A therapist can make certain she's considered the impact of her decision on her children, her husband, and herself. A pastor can advise her on both God's value of covenants and the availability of His grace. Close friends can share their perspectives on her situation. But only she can hear what God is saying to her.

Bev has found meaning in her marriage. She sees herself as obeying God, caring for her husband, and becoming a better person. She is defying the culture of self-realization.

Is sticking with the marriage the only God-honoring solution in a situation like Bev and David's? To answer that question, we have to consider once again the fact that the marriage covenant can be broken. A partner who is sexually unfaithful has broken the covenant. A partner who is physically or emotionally abusive has broken the covenant. The one who has kept the covenant is no longer bound to his or her promise. The difficulty, of course, is in discerning what constitutes "abuse," especially emotional abuse. That's why it's so important, in a situation that isn't clear-cut, to consult with a respected advisor—someone who shares God's view of covenant-keeping, who is supportive, and who can be objective in giving input.

There is a sense in which, on a spiritual level, a marriage covenant is never broken. Relationships established by vows spoken before God don't end because of a legal action. The people who made the vows are intertwined forever in God's eyes, whatever the practical realities of life. They are bound on a human level as well. They will always remain fixed in each other's memories. They will always carry scars from their broken dreams. They will often have to deal with each other for many years, perhaps a lifetime, because of children, family, friends, and finances. Even these "ties that bind" stand as a witness to a covenant that was formed and remains in eternity.

But if Christian marriage is a ministry in which two people are called to help each other become the persons God created them to be, the partner whose destructive actions reduce that possibility has broken the covenant in a very real way. That person will have to answer for the devastation that results.

For some people, leaving a marriage *can* be an act of defiance against the culture of self-realization. It's possible to make an idol of marriage, to cling to it even more tightly than you cling to God. While God values the marriage covenant, He doesn't value it above all else. If, for example, an abusive or extremely oppressive marriage were doing irreparable harm to your children, it could be an act of sacrifice to give up financial security, the good opinion of others around you, and the social benefits of marriage in order to protect your kids. What's more, you would be doing a chronically abusive, oppressive, or adulterous spouse no favors by staying in your marriage and, in effect, allowing him or her to continue in sin. To do so would not only put you and your children in danger of great physical or emotional harm, it would put your partner's soul in great spiritual danger.

While there is meaning to be found in the ashes of a broken marriage, the vast majority of us are called to find meaning *within* our marriages. The real purpose of marriage, at least for people of faith, is this: For two people to help each other become the people God created them to be. To sacrificially minister to each other. To grow together in relationship to God, to each other, to the community of faith, and to the larger community.

In marriage, two people accept a ministry. The first ministry of marriage is to each other—to help each other grow emotionally, socially, intellectually, and spiritually in a journey to become what God has gifted them to be. Marriage partners grow emotionally by learning to give and receive care and nurture. They grow socially by learning all the little skills—listening, compromise, communication, conflict resolution—that make it possible to live with someone else, skills that readily translate into relationships in the larger world. They learn intellectually by sharing and testing ideas. They learn spiritually by praying for and with each other, by participating in a community of faith together, by working together in service.

If a couple is faithful to their first ministry, they are ready for a second ministry of marriage—ministry to children. The arrival of children almost always puts a strain on a marriage, so only if they have learned what it means to love unselfishly can two people support each other as parents. Once a couple receives the gift of parenthood, they have a new and first priority: doing what is necessary for their children's fullest growth and development. No ministry is more important for parents than seeing that their children become all that God has gifted them to be, combining efforts to nurture their spiritual, intellectual, emotional, and physical development.

Carrying out this ministry sometimes requires self-sacrifice. Several years ago, I was offered a tempting position. It was my dream job, and what's more, it was located in an area where I would have loved to live. But my wife and I had two kids in high school. One was just starting her senior year. The other was just starting out as a freshman. As we considered the adjustments our children would have to make—a new school, a new "small town" culture—we couldn't inflict a move on them. The cost of problems we foresaw—for our children, not for us—was too high. I hated turning down that job, but I've never regretted it. I've found other places for ministry, other career opportunities (in fact, better than my "dream job" presented), but there would never be any other kids.

While many people today are concluding that self-realization, including career advancement, is less important than their children, too much of secular culture puts self first and children second. And children know it. They are condemned to uncertainty about whether they're important to anyone.

This is especially the case when parents divorce to relieve their own pain. Just staying together is a powerful way to minister to children. Not only does divorce create permanent emotional trauma for its young victims, but it also breeds spiritual cynicism. Children are deeply troubled at seeing Christian parents violate a vow before God and behave toward each other in ways that contradict the spiritual values those parents have tried to instill in them.

For all these reasons, many people find that one meaning of their marriage—and one reason to stay with the task of trying to transform their marriage—is doing what's best for their children. Not just "gutting it out," but consciously making a choice to give their children the gift of all that their partner can bring to their kids' lives.

The third and fourth ministries of marriage are to the community of faith and to the world. It takes a lot of work for two people to get a marriage to the point where they have something to offer as a couple to others. Two people who haven't worked on the first ministries of their marriage, ministering to each other and to their children, are like an empty cup offered to a thirsty world. They have nothing to offer others.

How does all this relate to you? If you and your spouse have worked on your first ministries, it's likely you'll have something to offer to your church, your community, and your world. And working together in service may well deepen the connection between you.

Craig and Lynne are a good example of how a couple can work through multiple ministries in their life together. From the earliest days of their relationship, it was pretty obvious that they were quite different. Craig is a "numbers person." Well-organized, goal-directed, disciplined, practical, quiet, he is also, by his own description, a little bit "dull." Lynne, on the other hand, is charismatic, creative, spontaneous. Always alive with ideas, she's the person who makes things happen in their community and in their group of friends. While they have opposite personalities, Craig and Lynne share a vital faith.

As their marriage evolved, Lynne and Craig came to understand two things: Their differences could make them wonderful complements to each other as they carried out the many tasks and responsibilities of marriage—but if they weren't careful, their differences could also cause them countless problems.

They decided to celebrate their differing gifts and craft a plan for how they would use these gifts both to strengthen their relationship and pursue a shared mission in life. Part of that mission was nurturing children to reach their full potential and bringing them up to love and serve God. So they took a hard look at what that meant about their respective careers. Because Craig's vocation had greater potential to generate income than Lynne's, and Lynne had always looked forward to being a mother, they decided that Craig would be the primary wage earner in the family. They agreed that once they became parents Lynne would work part-time and become the primary caregiver for their children. They made their decision with an attitude of respect for each other's gifts and preferences.

They made subsequent decisions with a similar attitude. As their children arrived and grew, they had to decide how to divide up the various roles of parenting. It turned out that Lynne was the one who was best at comforting the children when they were sick or upset, stirring their creative impulses, and generating ideas for fun activities. Craig helped the kids with their homework, guided them through science projects, built shelves for their rooms, researched the best extracurricular sports programs, and accompanied them to many of their extracurricular activities.

Craig and Lynne were able to minister to their children because they first ministered to each other. They both gained individually from the marriage because they encouraged each other to develop unique interests and abilities. As a result, their kids got the best of both parents.

Craig and Lynne's marriage was never seriously conflicted, but even partners in a difficult marriage can carry out this second ministry. If you can't collaborate with your spouse in parenting, you can still recognize that he or she has something unique to offer your children—and find meaning in a less-than-perfect situation. And sometimes, committing to a marriage ministry even individually can create a kind of soul bonding that wouldn't otherwise be possible.

Because Lynne and Craig worked on their first ministries, they were able to move on to a larger ministry. People of strong faith, they put a high priority on contributing their talents to the life of their church. But they also wanted to make sure their church involvement didn't detract from their family life. So they decided to take on one church responsibility and do it together. They chose to teach third grade Sunday school as a

team. Not surprisingly, given their respective gifts, Craig was the one who
did the didactic teaching, while Lynne was the one who brainstormed activities to make learning fun.

The fourth ministry of marriage is to the world. Sometimes this ministry takes the form of organized, formal outreach projects to serve a broken world, but Craig and Lynne see themselves as living out this fourth
ministry by developing their children into healthy and productive
adults—and by functioning as salt, light, and leaven in all their daily interactions. Other couples find other ways. The key to this ministry is for
partners to find a need, identify the strengths they have between them to
address that need, and then immerse themselves in a shared mission. This
is an important part of the path to spiritual connectedness, part of the
journey to becoming soulmates.

CREATING A BOND OF THE SOUL

When you got married, you probably did so in the hope that you had
found a "soul mate"—someone who would understand you, someone to
whom you could be connected in a deep and spiritual way, someone
whose innermost being "fit" with yours.

Since then, there have undoubtedly been days, months, and perhaps
even years when the last thing you felt about your spouse was that kind
of connection. You may still be wondering whether you missed your soul
mate, whether you are doomed to a life without the kind of intimacy we
all crave.

But as previous chapters suggest, whether or not you have a soul mate
for a spouse depends less on whom you chose to marry than it does on
the journey you've taken in your marriage. Soul mates don't "find" each
other in a single choice to get married. Instead, they *create* a bond between
themselves in their many seemingly insignificant choices of daily living.

Throughout this book, I've tried to suggest how your daily choices
about the way you think and act can affect the kind of bond you have with
your partner. I've tried to show how your deep-seated thought and behavior patterns can make you believe you are married to the wrong person—or help you view your spouse as a "right person." I've offered some
strategies for seeing your mate in new ways, for accepting the seemingly
unacceptable, for overcoming tough problems, for learning basic friend-

ship skills, and for developing intimacy.

But becoming soul mates involves more. Because marriage is a union of two people in a covenant before God, marriage is at least partly a spiritual journey. So becoming real soul mates means in part working together on a relationship with God.

I've chosen to talk about this "soul work" after all those other topics, but for some couples, it is just this dimension that makes all the difference.

After five years together, Dennis and Rita just couldn't seem to get their marriage on the right track. They weren't sure exactly what was wrong, but they both felt hurt and they both blamed the other for their problems. One big source of conflict, they knew, had to do with when to have children. Dennis wanted to wait a few years until they were more financially secure. He worked hard, had advanced a bit in his company, and was making a decent salary, but he didn't want to take on the responsibility of children until he'd had more time to establish himself financially. Rita, on the other hand, didn't care how much Dennis was earning. She wanted to quit her job, start having kids, and deal with the economic impact as it came. She wanted a large family, didn't mind living modestly, and deeply resented what she viewed as Dennis's obsession with financial security. They were so divided on the subject that their entire relationship was deteriorating.

Then they went on a spiritual retreat. The purpose of the weekend gathering was to work on their individual relationships with God, but the result was that they began working on their relationship with God together. And unlikely as it may seem to some, it made all the difference in their marriage. As they became more prayerful, more committed to involvement in their church, and more connected to Christian friends, they found their mutual resentment melting in the warmth of a new experience of God's love. Not only was there a new warmth in their relationship, but a new light in which to see each other.

Dennis began to see Rita's point about family being more important than possessions and economic security. At the same time, Rita became less insistent on her own timetable and more sympathetic to the pressure Dennis felt to be a financially responsible breadwinner.

They both became more aware of the influence the surrounding culture was having on their values and attitudes. Dennis realized that one

segment of the culture was telling him that his value as a man was measured by the amount of money he earned and possessions he displayed.
He began to envision a different kind of life, one measured by the depth
and quality of relationships instead of the number of things they owned
and their cost. Rita realized that she had been accepting messages from
another segment of the culture, a segment that suggested she was incom-
plete as a woman until she had children. For the first time, they were able
to discuss their future in a loving way and eventually came up with a plan
that was comfortable for both of them.

As Dennis and Rita worked together on their relationship with God,
they became more resistant to the influences that were pulling them apart.
They developed a strong and unified bond. They became soul mates.

It would be naive to conclude from this story that being in right relationship with God automatically puts married people in right relationship with each other. Still, many couples have found that spiritual resources, especially shared spiritual experiences, give them new energy, new
perspective, and new commitment to struggle toward a meaningful and
satisfying marriage. It is precisely because of the power of spiritual resources in transforming marriages that I have suggested a variety of spiritual disciplines throughout this book.

What is it that you are working toward in incorporating spiritual disciplines in your life and marriage? A closer relationship to God, certainly.
But most likely, you are also working toward a marriage that has meaning.
Soul work is relationship work. Because we have been created in the image
of a God who seeks relationship, the desire for relationship is deeply
imbedded in us. We become soul mates with someone by working together
on the multiple relationships of life—relationship with God, relationship
with each other, relationship with children, relationship with extended
family, relationship with the community of faith, and relationship with
the larger community.

Soul mates are intentional about helping each other work on the many
relationships that make up a meaningful life. Soul mates recognize each
other's natural resources—their respective gifts, interests, and motiva-
tions. They help each other define, develop, and value these resources.
They support each other in the pursuit of their shared and individual ministries.

If you choose to do the work required for you and your spouse to connect at the deepest levels, the likelihood that you will bond together as soul mates is greatly increased. But as is so often the case in life, there's no guarantee. We humans are so flawed and our world is so broken that it's possible for you to pour your soul into your marriage without getting back the results you so deeply desire. Soul work is not like putting a coin in a gumball machine.

What is the meaning of your marriage when your spouse isn't a soul mate? What if he or she never becomes a soul mate? What is the meaning of your marriage when you realize that your mate may never understand you, never love you the way you want to be loved, never be the person you want your life partner to be?

Our culture offers answers to these questions. It says, "Listen to your feelings." "Act on your feelings." "If you hurt, do whatever you need to do to relieve the pain." "There is no virtue in suffering." "Whatever causes pain is evil." "Whatever relieves pain is good."

The irony is that the steps we take to relieve pain often create greater pain. It's like having a severe headache. Doctors say that headache patients who take too many pain-relieving medications for too long can actually create a cycle of "rebound" headaches. They recommend that instead of reaching too quickly for a bottle of pills, their patients should take a look at the root cause of their headaches—stress, allergies, lack of sleep, too much caffeine, and the like.

If you feel like your marriage has become like an unbearable, unending migraine headache, don't resort too quickly to what may seem like the fastest pain-relieving solution. And don't diagnose the problem as fatal before you're sure it is. Consider the story of Mike and Jean.

If there's an opposite of soul mates, that's what Mike and Jean were. Their marriage was about as bad as a relationship can get. They had been fighting for years, but it eventually reached the point where they were actually pushing and shoving each other. This frightened them both so much that despite their mutual belief in forever marriage they decided to separate in preparation for a divorce. Shortly thereafter, Mike's company transferred him out of state. Jean decided to take the kids and move to Indiana, where she had grown up.

They had been separated for about a year when Jean phoned me. She had come back to town to visit a friend, who recommended she get some counseling for her children. They weren't doing well. They missed their father, hated their new school, and wanted to come back "home." They also showed a number of symptoms of depression. Jean was seriously concerned, but didn't know what to do.

I explained the reasons the children were having so many problems. Not enough time with their father. Too many changes all at once. An uncertainty about their family's future. I suggested to Jean that she and Mike work out some different arrangements. So Jean called Mike and asked if he would come in to see me. He agreed. It turned out he was concerned about the children as well. But like Jean, he was stymied about what to do.

When I talked with the kids, it was clear what they wanted. It was the same thing every child wants—an intact home with parents who love them and each other.

Both Mike and Jean loved their kids and wanted the best for them. They were deeply troubled by their children's distress and felt guilty about the spiritual implications of their imminent divorce. But they couldn't stand each other. And they had both met people whom they thought had future marriage potential.

Motivated by the depth of their children's pain, however, they agreed to meet to talk about working out a different arrangement. As it turned out, Mike was now free to return to the Chicago area. His company was willing to transfer him back. Jean was free to do the same. As for their new relationships, Mike's lady friend was willing to marry him and move to the Chicago area after the divorce was finalized. Jean's friend didn't have the same geographic flexibility, but she decided to move back anyway for the sake of the kids.

So they both moved back. The children returned to their old school and saw Mike much more regularly. They were less distraught but still begged their parents to get back together. Their pleas were like stilettos in their parents' hearts.

I suggested to Mike and Jean that they reconsider their decision to divorce, explaining that their problems weren't unusual—just more severe than most couples'. I explained that most of us come to marriage without many of the skills required for a long-term relationship. I pointed out basic vulnerabilities I saw in each of them, along with patterns that could explain why their marriage had deteriorated. I warned that those vulnerabilities and unhealthy patterns would undoubtedly poison any future relationships.

Jean was doubtful about getting back together but willing to give it a try. Mike, on the other hand, thought the idea was absurd. He was in love again. He had no feelings for Jean anymore. As much as he loved the children and knew that being married to their mother would be the best thing for them, he couldn't imagine ever getting back together after all the painful things that had gone on. Besides, he didn't believe in staying together "for the sake of the children." Despite his protests, however, he agreed to continue in counseling.

After several months of meeting with Mike and Jean individually, working with them to examine what had gone wrong in their marriage, I challenged them once again to try working on their relationship. "Don't *stay* in the marriage for the sake of the children," I said. "*Create* a new marriage for the sake of the children. If you fail, you have to consider where that leaves you. But don't assume failure until you've done everything you can do." This time they agreed. They didn't have any feelings for each other yet and weren't sure they ever could, but they saw a potential meaning in their marriage.

So we started through the process I've taken you through in this book. Looking at why it was they chose each other in the first place. Why they came to view each other as "wrong people." What their expectations were. We worked on changing their unhealthy thought patterns, learning basic friendship skills, and then advanced intimacy skills. We concentrated on acceptance. We labored on achieving some success in problem-solving.

And it worked. Despite all the toxic history between them, despite their mutual conviction that their marriage was impossible, Mike and Jean gradually inched their way toward becoming soul mates. Motivated by their children and their faith, they took a risk and the risk paid off.

In reality, it was Jean who took the greater risk, because she was initially more committed to the process. She exposed herself to a greater potential for pain if Mike rebuffed her. She's the one who started out carrying the cross. But it wasn't until they both took on the pain of seeking reconciliation and renewal that resurrection occurred. Having rejected the myth of self-fulfillment, having found a potential meaning in their marriage, they found that their feelings for each other gradually returned. Over time, after great pain and many tears and much bone-crushingly hard work, they bonded together as soul mates. Eventually, they celebrated their journey by renewing their vows. They wanted to acknowledge the importance of God's investment in their covenant with each other.

Is this what happens with all couples who work on their marriage? Sadly, no. But I've become convinced that most marriages could be transformed if the partners involved were able to find the meaning in their union, if they would open themselves to the possibility that God is using it to make them into the people He created them to be.

Most of us have had doubts about whether or not we married the right person. For some of us, the doubts are more serious than others. But no matter how serious the questions, the answer is always the same for each of us: Yes, I married the wrong person. So did my spouse. So did every other married person in the world. Because we're all defective. We are all weak. Despite having been made in the image of God, we are all flawed by sin. We are all wrong people one way or another. But by God's grace, two wrong people can journey toward the right marriage.

EXERCISE

Find the meaning in ministering to your spouse.

The following exercises are designed to help you and your spouse inventory your individual and joint strengths—as well as evaluate your needs and the needs around you—as a first step in the process of finding the meaning in your marriage.

(1) What emotional, intellectual, social, or spiritual needs do you see in your spouse?

(2) Are there any ways you could minister to your spouse by meeting those needs? If so, how?

Needs   How can I minister?

(3) What strengths and weaknesses do you each bring to your marriage? In what ways do these strengths and weaknesses interact so that you complement each other?

I'm strong   I'm weak

Spouse strong   Spouse weak

Ways we complement each other:

(4) What goals can each of you accomplish—either individually or together—because of your marriage that you couldn't accomplish alone? What opportunities can you respond to?

Goals   Opportunities

(5) What needs can you meet—or what problems can you overcome—
by being together?

    Needs/Problems   How to overcome them

(6) What ministry do you and your spouse have to your children? What
hopes, dreams, and goals do you have for your children that you can
work on in your marriage?

    Emotional   Intellectual

    Social   Spiritual

(7) What strengths and weaknesses do you and your spouse bring to your
marriage that affect your ministry to your children?

    I'm strong   I'm weak

    Spouse is strong   Spouse is weak

(8) What opportunities, problems, or threats related to your children can
you and your spouse respond to together? How?

Problems/opportunities/   How to respond
threats

(9) What needs exist in your church, your community, and the larger world, which you are able to do something about and want to do something about? List needs that you can better address because you are married or that you can address in partnership with your spouse.

Needs   How to address them

(10) What strengths and weaknesses do you and your spouse bring to your marriage that are relevant to your ministry to the church and the larger world?

I'm strong   I'm weak

Spouse is strong   Spouse is weak

(11) Write a mission statement for your marriage, keeping in mind the various levels of ministries discussed in this chapter.

JOURNALING

Write in your journal about how you see God working in your life to bring you to holiness and wholeness. How is God calling you to minister to your partner? Be specific about how you see God working.

SPIRITUAL DISCIPLINES

Contemplation

Meditate on Psalm 36:5–9. Speak the words written here, your own prayer, or both. Then sit in silence and let the Holy Spirit speak to you.

Thy steadfast love, O Lord, extends to the heavens, Thy faithfulness to the clouds.

As I face the stress of the present and the uncertainty of the future, help me live every hour with the confidence that You surround me with Your love.

Thy righteousness is like the mountain of God! Thy judgments are like the great deep. Man and beast Thou savest, O Lord.

As I face the stresses of the present and the uncertainty of the future, help me to be guided by what You have revealed is best for Your people.

How precious is Your steadfast love, O God! The children of men take refuge in the shadow of Thy wings.

As I face the stresses of the present and the uncertainty of the future, help me to take refuge in You when my fears threaten to overpower me.

They feast on the abundance of Thy house and Thou givest them drink from the river of Thy delights.

As I face the stresses of the present and the uncertainty of the future, teach me to draw deeply from Your strength, abundant beyond measure, so that even my weakness shall be strength.

For with You is the fountain of life. . . .

As I face the stresses of the present and the uncertainties of the future, help me realize that my first choice must be You, because You give life.

In Thy light do we see light.

As I face the stresses of the present and the uncertainties of the future, help me to trust that You will lead me out of darkness into light. Amen.